Concrete Changes

Concrete Changes

Architecture, Politics, and the Design of Boston City Hall

Brian M. Sirman

BRIGHT LEAF
AMHERST AND BOSTON
An imprint of University of Massachusetts Press

Copyright © 2018 by University of Massachusetts Press
All rights reserved
Printed in the United States of America

ISBN 978-1-62534-357-4 (paper); 356-7 (hardcover)

Designed by Sally Nichols
Set in Adobe Minion Pro
Printed and bound by Maple Press, Inc.

Cover design by Bill Boardman
Cover photo by Peter Vanderwarker, © 2017.

Library of Congress Cataloging-in-Publication Data

Names: Sirman, Brian M., author.
Title: Concrete changes : architecture, politics, and the design of Boston City Hall / Brian M. Sirman.
Description: Amherst : Bright Leaf, An Imprint of University of Massachusetts Press, 2018. | Includes bibliographical references and index. |
Identifiers: LCCN 2017050262 (print) | LCCN 2017051509 (ebook) | ISBN 9781613765982 (e-book) | ISBN 9781613765999 (e-book) | ISBN 9781625343567 (hardcover) | ISBN 9781625343574 (pbk.)
Subjects: LCSH: Boston City Hall (Boston, Mass.)—History. | Boston City Hall (Boston, Mass.)—Public opinion. | Kallmann, McKinnell & Knowles. | Brutalism (Architecture)—Massachusetts—Boston. | Architecture and society—Massachusetts—Boston—History—20th century. | Architecture—Political aspects—Massachusetts—Boston—History—20th century. | Boston (Mass.)—Buildings, structures, etc. | Boston (Mass.)—Politics and government—20th century.
Classification: LCC NA4433.B57 (ebook) | LCC NA4433.B57 S57 2018 (print) | DDC 720.9744/61—dc23
LC record available at https://lccn.loc.gov/2017050262

British Library Cataloguing-in-Publication Data
A catalog record for this book is available from the British Library.

*To Keith Morgan,
my longtime teacher,
mentor, and friend.*

Contents

Acknowledgments   ix

Introduction: The Building That Changed Boston   1

Chapter 1: Dying on the Vine   7

Chapter 2: Competition and Construction   50

Chapter 3: The New City Hall Design   94

Chapter 4: An Evolving Reputation   136

Chapter 5: Legacy and Significance   182

Conclusion: Boston City Hall at Fifty   227

Notes   245

Index   269

Acknowledgments

This book would not have been possible without the assistance, support, and encouragement of many people. Professor Keith Morgan first suggested Boston City Hall as the subject of my dissertation at Boston University, and his wisdom and guidance kept me going in the right direction. Likewise, I am indebted to Lizabeth Cohen, Bonnie Costello, Ted Landsmark, Mark Pasnik, Paolo Scrivano, and the two anonymous readers who weighed in with sage advice at different stages of this book. Similarly, I extend sincere gratitude to Lorna Condon and Jeanne Gamble of Historic New England, Gary Wolf of Wolf Architects, and the staff of the Boston Public Library's Government Documents Division for their assistance throughout my research. Michael McKinnell, Edward Knowles, and the late Gerhard Kallmann gave generously of their time and knowledge. I am also grateful to Aaron Schmidt of the Boston Public Library Print Department, Bob Collum and the family of Leslie R. Jones, Höweler + Yoon Architecture, and the Library of Congress Prints and Photographs Division for the images that enrich this biography of a building. Finally, it has been a pleasure to work with Brian Halley and Sally Nichols of University of Massachusetts Press, and with Amanda Heller, and I thank them for the enthusiasm and discernment they have brought to this project.

Concrete Changes

INTRODUCTION
The Building That Changed Boston

Few buildings in history have been as consequential or as controversial as Boston City Hall.[1] In the half century since it was constructed, it has been both praised as the sixth-greatest building in American history and scorned as the ugliest building in the world.[2] So influential and avant-garde was the building's design that it spawned imitators in cities and towns from Fall River to West Palm Beach, and from Dallas to Calgary. Yet in recent decades, many Bostonians, including the city's longest-serving mayor, have called on their municipal government to sell or demolish its once celebrated home.

The principal accolades, as well as complaints, have largely remained the same since the building was designed in 1962. Advocates point out both its architectural significance as a landmark of the Brutalist style, and the civic role it played in symbolizing and stimulating Boston's reemergence as a vital and thriving urban center in the late twentieth century. They blame current perceived deficiencies on poor upkeep, the ambivalence (at best) of public officials toward the building, and the inevitable vicissitudes of fashion and taste. Critics, meanwhile, complain that the interior is confusing, the exterior is ugly, and the exposed concrete clashes with what many regard as the "traditional" styles and materials of Boston's historic architecture.

Notwithstanding the controversy that has long surrounded the building, Boston's New City Hall embodied a revolution in the city's politics and architecture. Designed in 1962 by Gerhard Kallmann, N. Michael McKinnell, and Edward Knowles, the building boasts a distinctive aesthetic that responded to trends in European and American modernism, as well as the political and social context of 1960s Boston. By the time it was completed in 1968, the building had become an internationally recognized landmark of modern architecture and helped to resuscitate a dying city. It is not a mere reflection but rather a wellspring of political, social, economic, and architectural change during the 1960s.

Politically, New City Hall was built to serve both functional and symbolic roles. It would be both the home of Boston's municipal government and the figurative embodiment of a city steeped in history that was striving to reinvent itself. After decades of rule by largely unscrupulous or incompetent politicians, midcentury Boston was in a political and economic shambles. The downtown area experienced an exodus of residents and jobs, while federal and state development funds all but disappeared. The election of Mayor John B. Hynes in 1949, however, marked a political sea change. Hynes and his immediate successor, John F. Collins, renounced the infamous cronyism of early twentieth-century Boston politics, and both men regarded construction of a new City Hall as an opportunity to demonstrate to the world that the city's government was open, honest, and forward-thinking.

The politicians, planners, architects, and ordinary citizens involved in the City Hall project hoped it would signify and catalyze the rebirth of a city that had been plagued by decades of political disinvestment and mismanagement. To achieve this goal, New City Hall's innovatory design established an aesthetic and symbolic break with the brazen corruption and cynicism of the past and instead conveyed a sense of optimism, progress, and order. The architects hoped their unconventional design would represent a municipal government that was accessible, stable, and incorruptible. In this way, the building demonstrates a keen awareness of—and response to—the political circumstances of the era in which it was created.

Architecturally, New City Hall emerged at an important moment in the modernist movement, and it simultaneously embraced and challenged the prevailing tenets of design. The architects were inspired by the works of modernist pioneers and nonconformists such as Le Corbusier and Louis Kahn. At the same time, however, they eschewed generic principles of modernism that reduced buildings to abstract "packages," such as they saw in the works of Edward Durell Stone, Emery Roth & Sons, and many other corporate architectural firms.[3] These architects relied increasingly on universal aesthetic ideologies that applied equally to apartment houses, corporate headquarters, airports, or government buildings. Just as an envelope does not change form according to the content of the letter it contains, neither did many of these buildings take their design cues from the functions they housed.

Kallmann, McKinnell and Knowles (KMK), by contrast, sought to produce a new "Action Architecture," the hallmarks of which were, as Gerhard Kallmann explained, "violence, anti-rationality, and non-direction systematically pursued."[4] This new philosophy opposed the hyper-rationalism, abstraction, and superficial refinement that characterized much modern architecture. In addition, the reconsideration by the architectural community in the early 1960s of such controversial ideals as monumentality, historicism, and "complexity and contradiction"—which were anathema to doctrinaire modernism—would also come to bear on KMK's City Hall design.

Just as political and architectural histories converged to shape the building's design in the 1960s, so too have fluctuating ideas about politics and architecture influenced public reactions to New City Hall over the years. While it was intended both to serve as a monument to responsible government and to usher in a new era of "Action Architecture," City Hall's bold and imaginative design has met with disdain from some Bostonians who resent it as a product and symbol of the much-maligned practice of urban renewal. Moreover, changing political attitudes in the wake of the John F. Kennedy assassination, Vietnam War protests, Watergate, and the Reagan revolution have precipitated a reevaluation of the ideals of progressive government concretized in the building's design. And while the architects strove to create a timeless structure that would transcend both slavish historicism and fleeting contemporary trends, the building has suffered from years of deferred maintenance and unsympathetic alterations, thus making it seem more tired and disposable than innovative and monumental.

Despite this ironic fate, a growing number of architects and scholars now credit the building with igniting an urban renaissance in 1960s Boston and influencing the future history of architecture in America and abroad. Nascent preservation efforts and renovation proposals in the early years of the twenty-first century, counterbalancing calls for the building's demolition, suggest that Boston City Hall's future is as dependent on the inconstancy of changing artistic tastes and political mores as its history has been. Whereas in recent decades many politicians and critics have derided the building, some members of a younger generation have come to view its formal qualities and political symbolism more favorably.

Against this backdrop, the pages that follow present a detailed history of Boston City Hall, situating the building at the intersection of architecture and politics. They connect the building's genesis, design, reception, and legacy both to global architectural trends and to Boston's complex political situation in the mid-to-late twentieth century. The content is arranged thematically in (roughly) chronological order. After relating the building's design to its political and architectural contexts, I assess the critical reception of the new City Hall and the influence of changing political and architectural circumstances and attitudes since the 1960s. Finally, I discuss the local and global legacy and significance of the building, focusing on the ways in which New City Hall sparked a renaissance in Boston and served as a model for other struggling cities striving to reinvent themselves through architectural and political reforms.

In exploring these various aspects of Boston City Hall's history, this book synthesizes and expands on many excellent previous works that have focused narrowly on certain aspects of the building, treating it as but one of many components in a much larger narrative. These include Thomas H. O'Connor's *Bibles, Brahmins, and Bosses: A Short History of Boston,* which mentions New City Hall in the context of Boston's broader political and social history; Lawrence Kennedy's *Planning the City Upon a Hill: Boston since 1630,* which tells the story of efforts to guide the city's growth from the colonial era through the late twentieth century; and, more recently, Mark Pasnik, Chris Grimley, and Michael Kubo's *Heroic: Concrete Architecture and the New Boston,* a wide-ranging study of Brutalist buildings in the Boston area. What's been missing is a comprehensive history of Boston City Hall itself, and with this book I seek to fill that void by focusing exclusively on Boston City Hall, recounting its improbable story and revealing the complexities and controversies of its genesis and ongoing influence. This is, in short, a biography of a building.

While this subject has particular resonance for Bostonians, this book is more than an account of a controversial building of local interest. Rather, it exposes and dissects the inherent relationship between architecture and politics that exists in all government buildings. It is impossible to separate the daring design of Boston City Hall from the reformist politics at the local and national levels in the early 1960s. Nowhere does architecture exist in a vacuum, and never have governmental politics been divorced from the structures that not only house but also symbolize them. Readers will thus find in this story an analogue to such varied buildings as Thomas Jefferson's Virginia State Capitol, Barry and Pugin's Palace of Westminster, Albert Speer's designs for the Third Reich, Oscar Niemeyer's plans for Brasilia, and Norman Foster's reconstruction of the Reichstag. Each of these projects, like the KMK design, both reflects and advances through monumental symbolism a set of political ideals.

That said, Boston City Hall is a unique case because of both the success with which it represented and effected change in a beleaguered urban setting and the degree of controversy surrounding it. Indeed, its role as a hero in the city's history has been largely overshadowed by the debate surrounding its aesthetics; it is my hope that this book will remind people of the building's influence and importance.

Boston City Hall's remarkable story is as relevant in the twenty-first century as it was in the 1960s. Architecture—particularly for governmental purposes—has both meaning and power. The quality of public buildings can transform our lives for good or for ill. Our civic monuments affect both how others view us and how we see ourselves. Architecture has the ability to save or destroy a city (or a civilization). The lessons learned from Boston City Hall can be instructive not only to students of history but also to architects, urban planners, preservationists, politicians, and, not least of all, the general public, which has a vested interest in the buildings that define and shape us as individuals and as a society.

CHAPTER 1

Dying on the Vine

Boston's hulking concrete New City Hall emerged as a reaction to the city's political and architectural past. Indeed, it is impossible to understand how the ordinarily staid city came to choose such an unconventional building to house its municipal government without first recognizing the political, economic, and cultural challenges the city was facing in the mid-twentieth century.

Many Bostonians living in a thriving and politically stable city today find it difficult to imagine "the Hub" as ever having been rife with political corruption, economic decline, and physical decay. Likewise, at a time when Boston's rich architectural past is being celebrated and preserved, and while new buildings proliferate throughout the metropolitan area, many residents cannot conceive of their city as ever having been in an architectural and economic slump. Yet this was precisely the situation in which Boston found itself in 1960, and it was from these circumstances that Boston City Hall's distinctive design emerged.

Economic Decline

After decades of corruption and graft in municipal politics, Boston by midcentury was, in the words of one writer, a city that was "dying on the vine."[1] There were many factors contributing to the economic blight. First, the simultaneous onset of deindustrialization and accelerating suburbanization wrought unprecedented changes on the city's population and economy. Second, long-standing political corruption, as well as class and ethnic hostilities, had deleterious effects on the city's reputation and, consequently, its finances. Third, the deterioration of its antiquated transportation infrastructure and its once glorious architecture led to widespread doubts that the city could reverse its fortunes. Many people in the 1950s surely thought of "good old Boston" as the *Boston Globe* later described it: "a hopeless backwater, a tumbled-down has-been among cities."[2]

By the early 1960s, Boston's downtown was being abandoned by residents and companies alike. The city's population, which had peaked in 1950 at 801,444, had plummeted to 697,197 by 1960 as middle-class families decamped to the suburbs with the hope of finding better schools, lower property taxes, and less crime.[3] Formerly fashionable neighborhoods, such as the Back Bay and Beacon Hill, succumbed to desolation and disrepair. A 1940 editorial in the *Back Bay Ledger and Beacon Hill Times* observed, "Commonwealth Avenue is a beautiful street in many ways, but it looks like a deserted village in many block lengths, where house after house has been boarded up, and the one-time residents gone."[4] Similarly, future mayor John Collins later recalled that in 1940s and 1950s Boston, "the blight and decay was overwhelming. Seventy percent of the housing stock was substandard. The waterfront was literally falling into the Atlantic Ocean. Scollay Square had half a dozen burlesque houses, honky-tonk places, and tattoo parlors. It was just miserable—and right on the edge of downtown. Nothing new had been built for years."[5]

Moreover, Boston's job base declined from 561,854 in 1947 to 536,986 by 1963, while the number of jobs in the suburban ring increased with the establishment of many industries and electronics firms (including Raytheon, Mitre Corporation, and branches of AVCO and General

Electric) along Route 128, known by many as "America's Technology Highway."[6] The city's retail core, too, suffered from the development of suburban shopping malls: Boston's retail stores saw their sales fall by 4.6 percent between 1948 and 1958, even as prices rose.[7]

As the city's revenues fell, tax rates increased, compelling more businesses and families (who could afford to do so) to relocate. Boston's heavy reliance on property taxes was particularly injurious to its economy. A 1954 report by the National Planning Association (NPA) maintained that Boston had probably the highest property taxes in the nation, which inhibited new development at precisely the time when the city needed it most. "The need for improved taxation in the City of Boston," the report preached, "has been obvious for some time."[8]

The NPA report also criticized the state system for disbursing funds to cities and towns, noting that Massachusetts's tax revenues were not allocated on the basis of need. The earmarking of 66 percent of state tax revenues further eroded the amount that the Massachusetts General Court—that is, the state legislature—could distribute for need-based aid. The NPA report stressed the need for a change: "The revenues of a particular tax should not determine the funds available for a specific purpose. Need should be the determinant, and this determination should be made by the legislature."[9]

In many ways, Boston was not alone in facing unprecedented economic challenges in the mid-twentieth century. Cities throughout the United States were struggling to cope with thousands of families moving to the suburbs in the aftermath of World War II. Federal tax incentives for home ownership, as well as the availability of home loans for the middle class, led to a nationwide urban exodus. The postwar years also saw the proliferation of automobiles as wartime restrictions were lifted and manufacturers resumed production. The construction of new roads, such as the Interstate Highway System, further contributed to the rise of automobile culture. These factors increased mobility, allowing people to live farther from one another and their places of work. As influential urban critic Jane Jacobs noted, expressway projects, while ostensibly intended to make downtown areas more attractive to car owners, instead served to "eviscerate great cities."[10]

Meanwhile, the urban transportation infrastructure—much of which had been designed before the automobile age—was ill suited to cope with an influx of cars. This made cities seem all the more anachronistic and unsavory: city streets became increasingly congested, causing even more residents and businesses to decamp to the suburbs. Left behind were the urban poor, for whom city governments, with revenues steadily decreasing, were unequipped to provide adequate services.

As a result of this crisis, cities began experimenting with drastic large-scale measures designed to make urban life attractive again to businesses and middle-class families and to stanch the flow of taxpayers to the suburbs. In Chicago, Mayor Richard Daley launched an aggressive program to revitalize the Loop. Likewise, Pittsburgh, New Haven, Baltimore, and Albany all sponsored major projects to revitalize their downtown cores.

Perhaps the most consequential efforts were taking place in America's largest city: New York. It was there that the most prominent of all urban renewal figures in the twentieth century, Robert Moses, transformed the aging city into a modern metropolis. Moses benefited from near-autonomous development powers, as well as a keen ability to wrangle aid from Washington and Albany to finance his building projects. These were varied in purpose and scope, including Lincoln Center; public housing; the 1964 World's Fair; the United Nations Headquarters; the Triborough, Whitestone, and Verrazano bridges; pools, parks, and playgrounds; and hundreds of miles of roadways. "Moses saw New York City as a unit. His mission was to modernize the metropolis and keep it strong," Hilary Ballon and Kenneth Jackson wrote in their 2007 volume on Moses's life and work.[11] Many have likened Moses to Baron Haussmann, whose rebuilding of Paris in the nineteenth century was echoed in Moses's grand and varied projects.

Boston's situation, however, differed from New York's in several important respects. In the first place, Boston's decline was far more pronounced: the Boston area, for instance, experienced the smallest population increase (7.4 percent) between 1950 and 1960 of any of the fifteen largest metropolitan areas in the country. Also, New York City remained fixed as the key economic center of the United States, with large firms maintaining—and in some cases moving—their headquarters there. The Boston area, by contrast, was home to only one of the one hundred largest companies in 1962, and only eight of the five hundred largest companies. In fact, Lever Brothers, one of the few remaining businesses headquartered in the area, relocated from Cambridge to Manhattan in 1959. Lever Brothers had been an area staple since 1898, and its move to New York highlighted the contrasting fortunes of the two metropolises.[12]

Moreover, the opportunities that Moses took advantage of, and to some extent created, in New York City were not available in Boston. Not only did Boston not have a system in place to support a powerful visionary planner like Moses (the Boston Redevelopment Authority was not formed until 1957, and it would not be until 1960 that the city's planning and development functions were united in the BRA), but also the local political establishment was hamstrung by a reputation for graft and corruption that led banks as well as federal and state governments to withhold funding for renewal projects. Boston was furthermore hampered by inordinate state interference in municipal affairs, as well as perniciously deep-seated hostilities between class, religious, and ethnic factions. In short, Boston's challenges in the postwar years had their roots in the city's unique and calamitous political situation in the early to mid-twentieth century.

Political Prehistory

Many of Boston's economic woes arose from the city's roller-coaster politics during the early twentieth century. The political situation, in turn, was born of the changing demographic makeup of the city, as successive waves of immigrants flooded the region and the voting rolls. While Boston's business interests were still largely controlled by the "Brahmins" (the term ascribed to Boston's upper-class Protestant Yankee families by Oliver Wendell Holmes Jr.), the growing Irish Catholic population had become politically ascendant beginning with the election of Hugh O'Brien as the first Irish-born mayor of Boston in 1884. Many Irish Bostonians saw politics as a way out of poverty and social isolation.

By the early twentieth century, Irish Americans had held political office at every level in the Commonwealth of Massachusetts—from mayor to governor to United States senator. These political gains, however, exacerbated the Irish social feud with the Yankees, leading to provocative antagonism on both sides. Hostilities between the Irish and the Yankees, Catholics and Protestants, the poor and the wealthy would persist well into the 1950s. The perpetual ethnic-religious-class warfare led to deleterious political, economic, and structural effects.

One result of this animosity was that the city's Irish-dominated Democratic municipal government suffered an inordinate amount of meddling from the Yankee-controlled Republican state government. As one political analyst put it, the Yankees in the State House during the early years of the twentieth century were conducting "political guerrilla warfare on their Irish adversaries down the hill at City Hall."[13] Between 1958 and 1962, there were 1,097 bills in the legislature dealing with municipal rather than state matters, making Boston the most interfered-with city in the commonwealth. Moreover, the state rarely consulted with municipal officials when enacting legislation that concerned the city. In 1961, Mayor John Collins and his department heads submitted twenty-six bills to the legislature, yet only six of them—not even the most important ones—were passed.[14]

Moreover, as the Irish Democrats strengthened their hold on municipal politics, the Yankee Republicans in the State House further circumscribed the city government's power. The legislature set limits on the city's ability to borrow funds, prescribed a maximum for spending on public education, and refused to let Boston raise taxes or increase assessments without the express permission of the legislature. Liquor sales and operations of amusements and restaurants in Boston were regulated by a state licensing board. The Zoning Commission, too, was beholden to the state: its regulations would not take effect until twelve months after they had been filed with the clerk of the state senate. Even the power to appoint the city's police commissioner was taken away from the mayor and given to the state.

One of the most insidious encroachments on Boston's autonomy was the creation of the Finance Commission ("FinCom"), a watchdog agency, which would monitor municipal administration and investigate all matters relating to the city's finances. The Good Government Association (GGA), a reform group organized by Yankee businessmen to counter Irish control of local politics, lobbied the legislature to create the FinCom to combat fiscal mismanagement, corruption, and waste in the administration of two-term mayor John F. "Honey Fitz" Fitzgerald. Although its members—prominent business and civic leaders—were appointed by the Republican governor, the city was responsible for the FinCom's expenses.[15]

The state also had a hand in shaping the structure of Boston's municipal government. In the wake of Fitzgerald's scandal-plagued first term as mayor from 1906 to 1908, the legislature established a new city charter based on recommendations from the GGA. The charter replaced the Board of Aldermen and the Common Council with a single nine-member City Council. It also lengthened the term of mayor from two years to four years, and it stipulated that city elections be held on a nonpartisan basis. The goal of this legislation was to keep unscrupulous Irish politicians like Fitzgerald out of City Hall for good (though the ploy was unsuccessful: Fitzgerald was reelected in 1910).[16]

Ultimately, Fitzgerald was ousted from City Hall by neither the GGA nor the legislature but by another Boston Irish Democrat, James Michael Curley. Despite running on a reform platform against Fitzgerald, pledging to clean up city politics, Curley ultimately would prove to be even more of a political reprobate than his predecessor. In an effort to circumscribe Curley's power, the state again meddled in city affairs by passing a law that no mayor could succeed himself. The law, passed by the Republican-controlled legislature in 1918, was written in general terms that applied to all mayors, but it was well known that the intended target was Curley.[17]

James Michael Curley: The "Rascal King"

The antipathy of the Yankee establishment toward Curley was not entirely unprovoked. Indeed, Curley became the most infamous figure in the story of Boston's municipal political degeneration during the first half of the twentieth century, and he was both a product and a cause of the Irish-Yankee schism that would plague Boston well into the 1950s.

Curley was a ubiquitous presence in Boston politics for four decades, having served four terms as mayor between 1914 and 1950. During his four-year absences from the mayor's office as a result of the 1918 mayoral succession law, he also served a two-year term as governor of Massachusetts and three terms as a United States congressman. Curley's detractors accused him of bringing Tammany-style politics to Boston, and he had the distinction of being elected to his fourth term while under federal indictment for mail fraud.[18] Curley, however, had risen to power on the strength in numbers of Boston's ever-increasing immigrant population, and he remained in power by playing to his working-class ethnic base and portraying himself as "the people's mayor"—funneling money and services to the poor neighborhoods that were home to his supporters.

While Curley was adored as a Robin Hood figure in some quarters, he was derided as a thief and a charlatan in others. Curley's rhetoric and actions exacerbated social divisions within the city. Shortly after winning the 1913 mayoral election, for example, he proposed selling, for $10 million, the Public Garden at the intersection of the fashionable Yankee neighborhoods of the Back Bay and Beacon Hill. Half of the proceeds from the sale would be placed in the city coffers, while the other half would be used to build a new public garden in a location, as Curley put it, "more easily accessible to the general public"—meaning the Boston Irish.[19] This remark had the intended effect of delighting his loyal supporters while infuriating the Yankees.

The Public Garden proposal may have been made in jest as a deliberate attempt to antagonize his Yankee detractors, but Curley's years in office brought many more significant shenanigans. Curley virtually ignored predominantly Yankee neighborhoods while using public funds to improve the neighborhoods of his political supporters, particularly the immigrant neighborhoods of the North End, the West End, and South Boston.

Moreover, while alienating the city's Yankee bankers, he would find ways of cajoling them into lending the city money to finance his pet projects. For instance, when Philip Stockton, president of the First National Bank, balked at Curley's request for a loan to the city, the mayor reminded him that a water main's floodgates were located directly under the bank. Curley told Stockton that either he would have the money by that afternoon, or he would have the city engineer open the gates and flood the vaults. Stockton approved the loan.[20]

This confrontational relationship had disastrous results for the city, as each side went out of its way to spite the other. One historian noted that in "accepting this division of power as a political fact of life . . . Curley left the inner city to wallow in its Puritan self-righteousness while he turned his attention and his municipal favors to those in that 'other' Boston who never failed to give him their loyalty—and their votes." Meanwhile, Curley's antagonism toward the business community (which he called the "State Street wrecking crew") compelled the Yankee-controlled banks to refuse to grant mortgages in Irish-dominated Boston. "God, how the business community hated Curley!" recalled the First National Bank's Ephron Catlin.[21]

As a result of the dysfunctional relationship between City Hall and State Street, both Beacon Hill and Washington were loath to provide financial assistance to the ailing city. As outlying suburbs enjoyed new revenues from highway and real estate deals in the postwar years, state legislators from those areas saw Boston's woes as stemming from its dirty political culture. They therefore refused to support any measure that would help Boston solve its complex fiscal problems.[22]

While other cities in the United States were taking advantage of federal aid during the New Deal, Boston was left out, in large part because of the perception among federal administrators that the local political situation—particularly during the Curley years—rendered the city unable to handle large sums of money honestly, equitably, or responsibly. As Boston historian Thomas H. O'Connor writes, "Federal bureaucrats viewed the Curley administration as a big-city machine composed of corrupt political bosses and incompetent rascals who would undoubtedly waste, steal, or thoroughly mismanage whatever federal funds were put into their hands."[23] Because of this reputation, federal and state agencies were wary of sending development funds to Boston at a time when the city needed this help the most.

John B. Hynes: The "Honest Irishman"

The election of Mayor John B. Hynes in 1949 marked a political sea change. Hynes's campaign denounced the infamous cronyism of early twentieth-century Boston politics. Posters went up throughout the city encouraging voters to "Get Rid of Curley Gangsters! VOTE HYNES!"[24] Though Hynes, like Curley, was descended from Irish immigrants, Hynes had a reputation as a mild-mannered bureaucrat—the opposite of Curley, the bombastic political showman. This allowed Hynes to cast himself as a different kind of Irish politician and draw support from a wide range of backers, including those who had long opposed Curley and a new generation that was ready for change.

Future mayor John Collins later recalled: "I was just a young fellow then, fresh out of four years in the service and starting out on a political career, so I didn't know Curley very well. For that matter, I really didn't know John Hynes that well either." But Collins would end up backing Hynes in 1949, believing, as he later said, "the time had come for Boston to have new leadership. . . . I felt that Hynes had an opportunity to restore the relationship between the city and its citizens."[25] The city's business and financial community, which Curley had long delighted in antagonizing and alienating, was also, not surprisingly, eager to see change come to City Hall. Many prominent businessmen gave their support to Hynes in the hope that he would be more amenable to working with them (or at least less hostile toward them) than Curley had been.

Perhaps Hynes's chief advantage, though, was widespread dissatisfaction with the negative effects of Curley's politics. As the city sank deeper into disrepair and debt, Hynes's vision of a "New Boston"—the central theme of his campaign, which promised a reformed and reconstructed city—appealed to many voters. Hynes pledged not only to restore

Boston's good name by doing away with the arrogance, waste, and inefficiency that had long characterized Boston's municipal government, but also to fix the city's broken fiscal system and attract both private investment and public funding to make large-scale reconstruction possible.[26]

Once in office, Hynes immediately sought to make good on his campaign promises. First, he enlisted the support of the area's colleges and universities. Hynes brought in specialists from Harvard, Boston College, and MIT to devise economic studies, transportation programs, and financial and building projects. He also organized citizens' seminars at Boston College, in which experts and city residents could meet to discuss issues facing the city.[27]

More important, Hynes sought to bring together two factions that had been so hostile toward each other during the Curley years: Irish Catholic Democratic municipal officials and Protestant Yankee Republican business leaders. The process of rapprochement was not easy, though. The decades-old feud between the Irish and the Yankees could not be quelled overnight, and Hynes would have to prove himself trustworthy and capable before he could rid the city of the paralyzing enmity that had characterized the first half of the twentieth century. As banker Ephron Catlin bluntly remarked, "Nobody had ever seen an honest Irishman around here."[28]

No doubt many of Catlin's fellow Yankees felt the same. Hynes was so different from Curley in personality and conduct, though, that Bostonians gradually began to regard him as an honest and capable politician. Unlike Curley, who was prone to grandiloquent oratory, Hynes was known as "Whispering Johnny" because of his soft-spoken, reserved demeanor. Also, unlike Curley, who held grudges and delighted in antagonizing his opponents, Hynes was a man seemingly without bitterness or rancor. One of Hynes's longtime friends once asked him, "Isn't there anyone you hate?" Hynes replied, "Well, yes, there was one fellow who used to steal from the poor boxes."[29]

Hynes's actions during his first months in office improved relations between City Hall and State Street. For instance, he appointed several prominent business leaders to key city posts. Kane Simonian, whom Hynes would tap to head the Boston Redevelopment Authority, later recalled:

> Building bridges with the local business community was one area where Hynes really made a contribution to the city's future development. ... For years, Jim Curley had fought tooth and nail with the business leaders, and as a result the city had been torn apart—absolutely paralyzed. But now Hynes met with them, talked with them, and listened to them. He would form special committees composed of first-rate people like Bill Keesler of the First National Bank, Ralph Lowell of the Boston Safe Deposit and Trust Company, Bob Morgan of the Boston Five Cents Savings Bank, Tom Dignan of Boston Edison, and O. Kelley Anderson of New England Mutual Life Insurance Company to give him advice when difficult problems arose. This was a major change in the direction of city government.[30]

Some would accuse Hynes of being in the pocket of big business. But at the time, Hynes realized that without the support of the business community—those who controlled both the public and private means of providing financial support—the New Boston that he had promised would remain but a dream.

Political changes at the state level, too, led to marginal improvements in the relationship between city and state governments. In 1948, Thomas P. "Tip" O'Neill became the first Democratic speaker of the Massachusetts House of Representatives since the Civil War, and in 1959, John E. Powers became the president of the state senate. These men (both of Irish descent), and other Democrats on Beacon Hill, adopted a more conciliatory attitude toward Boston politicians, and they returned some elements of home rule while seeking to work with the Hynes administration to make the New Boston a reality.

Toward a "New Boston"

The "New Boston" was the keystone of Hynes's 1949 mayoral campaign and his ten years in office. It centered on Hynes's belief that Boston could overcome its economic challenges, as well as shed the stigma developed during the early twentieth century, only by tacking away from the Curley-era political paradigm and undertaking a series of large urban renewal projects. To that end, Hynes became a protégé of Pittsburgh mayor David Lawrence; he regarded Pittsburgh as the model of successful redevelopment, in which an active mayor and a sympathetic business community worked together to bring about urban reconstruction on a massive scale.[31]

Among Hynes's early redevelopment efforts was the establishment of an Auditorium Commission to design a modern multipurpose auditorium that would bring revenue to the city by attracting commercial, political, and entertainment groups.[32] (The Back Bay auditorium eventually bearing his name would open in 1965.) Hynes also began a series of slum clearance projects in several parts of the city. In 1951 he launched a modest rehabilitation program in Dorchester. The following year he announced a more ambitious plan: the so-called New York Streets initiative, which focused on a twenty-four-acre residential neighborhood in Boston's South End, bordered by Washington, Albany, Herald, and Dover Streets. The term "New York Streets" referred to the streets that formerly occupied the area—Seneca, Oneida, Oswego, Genesee, Rochester, and Troy—which were named to honor the connection of the Boston and Worcester Railroad line to Albany in 1842.[33]

This project called for the complete razing of a tenement district to make way for industrial development. The project was based on the theory that it would be more economically attractive to industries if the city were to demolish existing buildings and sell large vacant parcels than if the industries themselves had to buy separate small parcels, clear them, and then construct factories. Planners praised the project as proof that renewal catalyzed private industrial and commercial development, and noted that it represented a beneficial partnership of city officials and private interests who shared a common goal of improving both the city's economy and citizens' quality of life.[34]

Other projects were intended to bring Boston into the automobile age. The highway known as the Central Artery, for instance, was designed to relieve downtown traffic congestion, as well as ease suburbanites' commute into the city. The highway had been proposed as early as 1930 in the Boston City Planning Board's *Report on a Thoroughfare Plan for Boston,* but the Great Depression and subsequent wrangling with competing interests prevented construction from beginning until 1951.[35] Even then, a host of problems plagued the project: first a steel strike in 1952, then protracted court battles over disputed property rights, and even a rat infestation in the properties to be demolished, which necessitated a special rodent extermination program before construction could begin.[36] Despite these setbacks, hope sprang eternal in the breast of John Hynes. In 1956, in his third inaugural address, Hynes predicted that the new highway would prove a revitalizing force for Boston businesses by improving traffic flow into and out of the city, thus making the downtown area more attractive to businesses.[37]

To add energy and organization to these efforts, Hynes formed the Boston Redevelopment Authority (BRA) in 1957 to oversee all renewal projects in the city. This was a major step forward in Boston's midcentury urban renewal. It also was a result of improving relations between City Hall and the State House. All other Massachusetts towns and cities had long been able to maintain semiautonomous redevelopment agencies, but Boston until this time had been prevented from doing so.[38] The BRA took over redevelopment power from the Boston Housing Authority (BHA), and the BHA's redevelopment director, Kane Simonian, was named head of the new agency, taking nearly his entire BHA staff with him. The BRA's governmental structure stipulated that its five-member board would consist of four members appointed by the mayor and one by the state. The new agency also inherited the BHA's two redevelopment projects already in progress: the New York Streets initiative and a nascent slum clearance project in the city's West End.

The West End development plan, formally announced by Hynes in 1953, called for the destruction of one of the oldest neighborhoods in Boston to make way for high-rise apartment buildings designed to lure middle-class residents back into the city. Before redevelopment, the West End had been home to successive waves of immigrants: Irish, Italians, Jews, Greeks, Poles, and Russians. Conflicting visions of the neighborhood emerged in the 1950s. On the one hand, the primarily working-class residents generally regarded their neighborhood as a vibrant and healthy community, despite its congestion and reputation for squalor. They saw the redevelopment plan as a "land grab."[39] As sociologist Herbert Gans argued, the West End was a "vital urban neighborhood whose main fault, at least in official eyes, was that its population could not be called middle class."[40]

On the other hand, a younger generation of ambitious politicians and planners saw only a slum, ready for clearance. For them, the West End represented all that was wrong with the city: old buildings packed together on narrow, dirty, crowded, crooked streets. Indeed, many in Boston, including the press, the business community, and the real estate industry, thought that the solution to urban blight lay in replacing neighborhoods like the West End with luxury housing, which would, it was hoped, bring affluent residents back to the city and consequently boost its flagging economy.[41]

Although criticism would later erupt, much of the city was behind the West End project initially. The BRA deemed the area "so clearly substandard" that the only viable solution was "sweeping clearance of buildings."[42] Similarly, BRA board member Monsignor Francis Lally later recalled: "It was not an overnight local pipe dream. . . . You must remember that the project had the backing of city planners, the Mayor of the city, city officials, most newspaper dailies, and the Cardinal."[43] Mayor Hynes himself said: "This marks the start of a tremendous revitalization of the West End of Boston. . . . The development will attract and bring back to Boston hundreds of families who have left the city because of a lack of suitable and attractive urban living conditions."[44]

Despite high hopes, Hynes's urban renewal program was not entirely successful. Thomas O'Connor later characterized Hynes's efforts as "tentative, piecemeal, and clumsy."[45] A case in point is the most high profile of Hynes's redevelopment projects: the Prudential Center, a mixed-use office, residential, and shopping complex that replaced the old Boston & Albany rail yard in the Back Bay. "The Pru" was intended to be a conspicuous demonstration of corporate confidence in the city, which would be a catalyst for further development.[46] Yet the project suffered a series of major setbacks and disappointments. For instance, Hynes had enticed the Prudential Insurance Company of America with the promise of lucrative tax breaks; in December 1959, however, the Massachusetts Supreme Judicial Court struck down this arrangement as unconstitutional. The legislature was then slow to pass new legislation giving tax incentives to Prudential, which had at that point invested $6 million in foundation work.

Prudential vice president Fred Smith told the *New York Times* that unless the new tax arrangement was guaranteed posthaste, Prudential was prepared to "pack up and get out."[47] The tax problem was eventually solved, but the beleaguered center would not open for another five years.

The Prudential Center was certainly crucial to showing that a major corporation was betting big on Boston's future; when he took over the then stalled project in 1960, BRA chief Edward Logue said, "Getting Prudential Center built was essential if any of our other plans were to go forward."[48] It garnered but faint praise, though, even from some of its most prominent backers. Mayor John Collins remarked: "I never thought the Pru was a great building. . . . It was not as nice as it should have been. But it was a loss leader. We had to prove that somebody had enough confidence to put something in there."[49] Moreover, by dint of its being placed on a platform sixteen feet above street level, it failed to unite the Back Bay and South End neighborhoods, which had been divided by the railroad yard it replaced.

Likewise, a new parking garage under Boston Common, proposed in 1950, was plagued by a decade of inaction once the plans had been approved. When work finally began, it incited the ire of Beacon Hill residents, who complained about the noise and the dust.[50] Then, upon completion, rumors of graft and malfeasance abounded as the state attorney general, Edward McCormack, arranged for a Suffolk County grand jury probe into the alleged disappearance of $346,000 from the project's coffers.[51] After seventeen months, and two separate trials, five people associated with the Boston Common Garage were convicted of larceny for stealing nearly $800,000 from the construction of the garage. The story made national headlines.[52] This, of course, did not bode well for city officials who had for a decade been trying to shed Boston's reputation for municipal corruption and fiscal mismanagement.

Likewise, the slum clearance program in the New York Streets area was roundly criticized for displacing thousands of poor families. Planning historian Lawrence Kennedy recounted community activist Mel King's denunciation of the South End project, which included King's own house. King recalled that newspaper reports in the *Herald Traveler* depersonalized the slum clearance project by portraying the existing neighborhood as a Skid Row. He complained that the reports "blotted out any understanding of the impact urban renewal would have on the lives of the people," while city officials ignored the "fact that the *people* living in the area had significantly fewer options than other groups by virtue of their color, national background, and economic status."[53] Others criticized the project for being too small to have any significant effect on the city's future.[54]

But it was the West End project—at forty-five acres, three times larger in area than the fifteen-acre New York Streets initiative—that nearly brought a swift halt to Boston's nascent urban renewal program. Indeed, it was so disastrous from the beginning that it almost halted all future redevelopment projects. To begin with, no accommodations had been made for the twenty thousand working-class families who lived in the neighborhood, and the replacement structures—high-rise condominiums and upscale apartment houses, garages, and sprawling parking lots—were so aesthetically lackluster that they evoked widespread nostalgia for the neighborhood they replaced.

Residents of other neighborhoods were keenly aware of the debacle and feared that they would be displaced with the same ruthlessness as West End residents. Jane Jacobs, in her seminal *Death and Life of Great American Cities*, presented the West End project as a cautionary case study. Jacobs saw in this once "lively, stable, low-rent" neighborhood an analogue for the city's North End, which, like the West End, had been deemed a slum by planners and faced the prospect of a similar fate.[55] It became clear in the wake of these controversial projects that if urban renewal had a future in Boston, it would have to be accomplished with greater consideration for the people who would be affected, with an emphasis on high-quality architecture, and with input from a greater variety of stakeholders.[56]

John F. Collins: The Capable Leader

After ten years in office, John B. Hynes declined to run again for mayor in 1959. It would be his successor, John F. Collins, who would learn from Hynes's urban renewal mistakes and shepherd the New Boston to completion. Collins, however, was an unlikely mayor. In the first place, the popular state senate president, John E. Powers, was the odds-on favorite to succeed Hynes. Collins, considered by many to be a political lightweight, was thought to pose little competition for Powers, who had the support of several influential groups, including the labor unions and most of the local papers. But Collins cast himself as a political outsider, opposed to the mighty political machine that Powers represented. Collins's supporters portrayed him as honest, clean-cut, and wholesome, while painting Powers as a tough, arrogant machine politician. Collins's campaign posters encouraged voters to "Stop Power Politics."[57] In other words, Collins adeptly portrayed Powers as an old-time Boston politician (of the Curley ilk), while casting himself as trustworthy, responsible, and progressive, with frequent references to the "New Boston" that he would bring to fruition.

The campaign was successful: Collins defeated Powers by 24,000 votes. In this electoral upset, Bostonians declared that they were loath to return to the Curleyesque politics they had abjured with Hynes's election a decade earlier; they were ready to see the promise of the New Boston fulfilled.

While Boston had made some progress during the 1950s, Collins nevertheless inherited a city that remained in economic dire straits. There was little confidence in the city treasury, as spending and taxation were still out of control. The property tax rate in 1949 had been $56.80 per thousand; in 1959 it had nearly doubled to $101 per thousand.[58] Moreover, Moody's Investors Service in 1959 downgraded Boston's bonds from A to Baa—a lower rating than for any other major city in the United States.[59] Notwithstanding the progress of the past decade, action was still needed to halt Boston's economic decline. Once Collins was sworn in, he began taking bold steps toward turning the scarred old city into the vibrant and thriving metropolis that both he and John Hynes had promised. This included not only continuing Hynes's ambitious urban renewal program, but also working with state legislators and local businessmen to coordinate their efforts in revitalizing Boston.

Despite the progress that Hynes had made in improving City Hall's relationship with the business community and the state legislature, many challenges remained. On the state level, Collins faced particular difficulty in working with his erstwhile mayoral campaign rival, Senate president John Powers, whose wounded ego still smarted from Collins's upset victory in the 1959 election. But whereas Hynes (a mild-mannered bureaucrat who had never been involved in electoral politics before his 1949 run for mayor) had shied away from the rough-and-tumble world of state politics, Collins was a seasoned politician, ready to take on Beacon Hill. Having served in the state legislature for eight years (four years in the House and four years in the Senate), he knew well the key figures in the State House. Recognizing the danger of Powers's enmity, Collins quickly sought to bolster his relationship with House Speaker John F. Thompson. When Governor Endicott Peabody sought to oust Thompson from his powerful role, Collins came to Thompson's defense and persuaded representatives from Boston to vote on Thompson's behalf. Collins also worked to secure favor in the executive office. Although he had vexed Peabody in the Thompson affair, he built strong relationships with later governors. In a private meeting with Governor John Volpe, for instance, Collins made clear that he had no intention of running for governor, which put Volpe's mind at ease about a potential power struggle, and the two men went on to have a productive working relationship.[60]

In addition to fostering personal connections with state politicians, Collins also was more involved in the legislative planning process than Hynes had been, working closely with the men he chose as the city's lobbyists on Beacon Hill to ensure that he was seen as paying courteous attention to the needs and concerns of legislators. Moreover, Collins himself frequently made the trip up Beacon Hill to the State House to appear before legislative committees, and he had his municipal department heads do the same. This personal contact helped Collins win the respect that was needed to pass legislation for the city's benefit.

In Collins's quest to enlist support from the local business community, his most effective, albeit controversial, move to repair the State Street–City Hall relationship was to consult with the Boston Coordinating Committee. The committee, popularly known as "the Vault" since it held its regular meetings in a boardroom near the vault of the Boston Safe Deposit and Trust Company, was formed in 1959 by a group of the city's most prominent businessmen, including bankers, lawyers, developers, and executives from local companies.[61] The committee formed in secret after Moody's downgraded the city's debt, and its members were prepared to take drastic action if, as seemed certain at the time, the city should sink into bankruptcy.[62]

That event fortunately—and surprisingly—never happened; in fact, the city announced a $4 million budget surplus in 1959. But Collins recognized in the Vault a group of concerned business leaders whom he could depend on to cooperate in planning the city's redevelopment. Shortly after the 1959 election, Collins asked to meet with the Vault. He told the group that he would need its support, and he proposed that they meet every few weeks so that he could listen to their concerns and identify points of disagreement, just as he would be meeting with other groups, such as community leaders from the city's neighborhoods. The relationship that Collins forged with these business leaders—unprecedented in twentieth-century Boston—led the *Globe* to declare that the Vault was "the first durable link between the prosperous Yankee community and the tough, troublesome world of local politics."[63]

Although word of Collins's meetings with the Vault led to rumors that he was simply a puppet of powerful businessmen, Collins made clear that he was working with the business community, not for it. "Every two weeks, at four o'clock," Collins later recalled, "we would meet to set the agenda. It was I who set the agenda at these meetings, identified the problems to be discussed, and determined how they were to be dealt with."[64] Despite the rumors, Collins's positive relationship with the business community gave the city the stability needed for further progress in State Street–City Hall relations. Collins would depend on—and continue to build—these relationships throughout the planning, design, and construction of New City Hall.

Edward J. Logue: The Builder

Perhaps the most fortuitous event in Boston's urban renewal history occurred when John Collins hired planner Edward J. Logue to become development administrator of the Boston Redevelopment Authority in 1960. Logue, a graduate of Yale College and Yale Law School, had been in charge of urban renewal in New Haven since 1954. By 1959, Logue's work in that city was, as Lawrence Kennedy wrote, "already acknowledged a case study in success."[65] A *Fortune* magazine article on Logue and New Haven's mayor Richard C. Lee asserted that the two "wrote renewal history by accomplishing more with less cash than was done in almost any other U.S. city."[66]

Collins lured Logue to Boston in March 1960 with the promise of a $30,000-a-year salary ($10,000 more than the mayor himself earned) and with the attractive prospect of coordinating renewal on a grander scale in a larger city. Collins gave Logue unimpeded authority in running the BRA, yet Logue insisted that $5,000 of his salary come from the mayor's office budget so that Collins, as Logue said, "could fire me any time he wanted."[67]

Collins and Logue got along well, though, and the mayor never had occasion to dismiss his development administrator. Logue appreciated Collins's can-do approach, as well as the autonomy Collins had granted him in running the BRA. For his part, Collins had found in Logue a man who could make the New Boston a reality. As Collins later said of Logue: "He was a generalist, he knew the rules of the game, and he'd dealt with the federal people. And the chemistry was there between us." Logue also had the advantage of being an outsider, which helped him rise above the local political fray. "They start keeping score on everybody local too early," Collins explained.[68]

When Logue arrived in Boston, he inherited an agency with a poor reputation among the citizenry, as the West End debacle was fresh in the minds of Bostonians. Logue sought to change this negative public perception of the agency by altering the city's approach to urban renewal. To that end, he learned not only from the lessons of his experience in New Haven but also from the BRA's previous mistakes.

Logue quickly realized that the BRA's organizational structure impaired its ability to carry out large-scale plans. It was the prerogative of another municipal agency, the City Planning Board, to formulate long-range construction plans, while the BRA was charged with implementing discrete redevelopment projects. Logue persuaded the state legislature to abolish the City Planning Board and to consolidate planning and redevelopment powers in one office, thus giving him the authority not only to plan the city's future development but also to carry out those plans. The creation of a more powerful BRA, with its unprecedented powers (in Boston or anywhere else), has been called the true cornerstone of the New Boston.[69]

Well aware of Robert Moses's success in garnering federal aid for development in New York City, Logue set out to increase federal disbursements to Boston. Shortly after his arrival, he called on his contacts in Washington and succeeded in winning a $20 million award from the Urban Renewal Administration; under Logue's leadership, Boston went from being the seventeenth-largest to the fourth-largest recipient of federal urban renewal funds. This had the added benefit of an automatic increase in state aid, since the legislature had voted to split the cost of renewal with the city.[70]

Despite changes in the BRA's leadership, power, and focus, Collins and Logue realized that the New Boston was as yet a seemingly farfetched dream in a still ailing city. The Collins administration and the new BRA desperately needed a public relations coup to instill widespread faith in the city's ability to turn itself around. The opportunity presented itself in the form of a nascent project that had begun under John Hynes: a new government center.

Government Center

Of all the urban renewal projects during the Hynes and Collins administrations, Government Center was the most ambitious. The proposal called for new federal, state, and private office buildings—as well as a new City Hall—to replace Scollay Square (fig. 1), which the *Globe* dubbed Boston's "honkey-tonk and burlesque bastion."[71] Hynes and Collins regarded this area as a slum and an anachronism, its crooked streets reminiscent of Curley's crooked politics. In its place would rise "shining, new, modernistic buildings proclaiming the rebirth of the city and symbolizing the start of a new political era in Boston's history."[72]

While ideas for the project had been discussed informally since the early days of Hynes's mayoralty, the project began in earnest when Hynes formed the Government Center Commission in 1957 to study the feasibility of razing Scollay Square and constructing an array of government buildings in its place. The City Planning Board subsequently hired the consulting team of Adams, Howard, and Greeley to develop a blueprint for the new Government Center. The proposal was completed in 1958 and won wide approval. It called in general terms for a new governmental complex on the Scollay Square site. As redevelopment in the neighboring West End continued to garner criticism, Hynes believed that the new Government Center would not only curb disparagement of the BRA but also increase property values in the West End.[73]

Not everyone agreed that razing Scollay Square was the appropriate next step, however. Even though the area was run down, there were some who saw it as a historically important neighborhood. Many older Bostonians still referred to it as "good old Scollay Square," and they had an abiding affection for its varied (if sometimes disreputable) entertainments, from the famous "Old Howard" burlesque theater and vaudeville to tattoo parlors and striptease acts. Still others considered the idea of turning this godforsaken area into something noble a pipe dream. H. Daland Chandler, a Boston architect, wrote a rhyme poking fun at Hynes's vision:

In Scollay Square did Johnny Hynes
A stately civic group decree
Where sailors and their Valentines
Now skip it, trip it, fancy free.[74]

Many younger Bostonians, though, did not share their older neighbors' nostalgia for Scollay Square, nor were they lacking in support for Hynes's idealistic vision. To them, Scollay Square was a slum. Jerome Rappaport, a prominent developer who was a key figure in the West End project, later recalled: "Much of it seems nostalgic and colorful to people looking back at it, but in actuality it was horrendous. It was a terrible eyesore that needed to be changed."[75]

FIGURE 1. Crowded Scollay Square. The area known as "Boston's honkey-tonk and burlesque bastion" was a perfect target for urban renewal. The neighborhood was razed in the 1960s to make way for Government Center. Courtesy of the Boston Public Library, Leslie Jones Collection.

Hynes was determined to move forward with the Government Center plan, but he first needed to enlist the support of the federal government. In 1958 he traveled to Washington to meet with Franklin G. Floete, head of the General Services Administration (GSA). Floete approved of constructing a new federal office building in Boston, but the placement of this building in Scollay Square was contingent on several factors. Floete insisted, for instance, that the center include a state office building and a new City Hall. He also demanded full city participation in the project, as well as agreement on the price of the land for the federal building.[76]

After Hynes returned to Boston, Floete seemed to backtrack on Scollay Square, considering instead the benefits of a location in the Back Bay, near Copley Square, where the GSA already had purchased land.[77] This led to a backlash from the downtown business community, which objected to constructing a major office building outside the traditional business district. Planners, too, balked at locating the building away from Government Center.[78] City officials and the Massachusetts congressional delegation (including John W. McCormack, future speaker of the U.S. House of Representatives) applied political pressure. Six months of negotiations eventually led Floete to accept the Scollay Square site. Some Bostonians resented this vacillation, but they understood that the federal government's involvement in the project was essential to its material and symbolic success.

Although Government Center had been proposed under Hynes, it was Collins and Logue who got the project off the ground and made it their priority because of the "catalytic effect" it would have on future development in Boston.[79] Immediately after assuming control of the BRA, Logue made clear that his focus would be not to bring middle-class residents back to the city but rather to revitalize and create jobs in the downtown area. The Government Center project, still mired in the planning stages, served Logue's purposes well. Logue hoped to use Government Center as leverage to spur new private development nearby. Then, with more workers downtown, he hoped to persuade existing merchants to renovate the city's retail sector.[80]

In this, his first large undertaking in Boston, Logue was concerned not only with economic effects but also with aesthetics. He demanded buildings of high architectural merit—unlike the insipid towers of the West End. "Renewal and rehabilitation do not guarantee beauty," he remarked, adding: "It is the function of distinguished architecture and imaginative civic design to see that beauty is the hallmark of the renewed city. Beauty once flourished in Boston. It must again."[81] Logue formed the Design Advisory Committee, an unpaid group of internationally renowned architects living and working in the Boston area, to meet monthly and consider all projects under review by the BRA. The initial Design Advisory Committee was a pantheon of prominent Boston-based architects: Hugh Stubbins, José Luis Sert, Lawrence B. Anderson, Pietro Belluschi, and Nelson Aldrich.

The Eisenhower administration allocated funds to complete the Government Center plan in September 1960, and the state shortly thereafter enacted legislation for the construction of a new City Hall as part of the project. Logue hired I. M. Pei & Associates of New York to develop the master plan for the site. Pei had come to Boston from China in 1935 to study at MIT. After graduation, he served as director of architecture at the real estate development company Webb & Knapp. He became a naturalized U.S. citizen in 1954 and formed his own architecture firm the following year. As the venerable Boston historian Walter Muir Whitehill observed, Pei "had acquired a singular appreciation of the essential qualities of the earlier life and architecture of the city. He wished not only to preserve the significant historic buildings in the area, but to create spaces in which immense new buildings might be placed in harmonious relation to their older neighbors."[82]

Pei developed a radical plan that vastly simplified the traffic pattern in Scollay Square, eliminating sixteen streets and modifying others. While he had no hand in designing specific buildings, he ultimately had a greater effect on the look and feel of Government Center than any other individual architect, for it was Pei who established controls that limited height, bulk, and setback for each building. For Pei, the individual buildings were not as important as the relationships among them, as well as between the new structures and their historic neighbors (including Faneuil Hall, the Old State House, and the first Harrison Gray Otis House).

Pei's plan called for low, curving private office buildings to define the east and west sides of the site. The federal office building, consisting of a tower and a low block, would sit on the north side of the square, while the existing Sears Crescent and Sears Block on the southern edge were preserved. On the opposite side of Bowdoin Square, to the north of the federal building, Pei placed the state Health, Welfare and Education Service Center. Smaller private office buildings and a new parking garage at Haymarket Square rounded out the proposal.

Pei's plan also called for a private office tower to be built to the east of the Sears Crescent, on a section designated as "Parcel 8." Although placing an office tower so close to the historic Sears Crescent and Old State House raised some concerns, Pei saw the tower as essential, not only for its structural effects on the new Government Center plaza (by blocking Washington Street, thus making for a simplified traffic pattern), but also as an anchor to keep the city's businesses in the downtown financial district.[83] As the Prudential Tower rose in the Back Bay, some feared that banks and law firms would rush to follow, constructing new offices in the Back Bay and leaving the downtown financial district deserted, thwarting Government Center's intended revitalizing influence on the area. The Parcel 8 tower would defend against this mass migration of businesses to the west and also serve as an architectural segue between the existing financial district and the new Government Center.[84]

John Collins, like John Hynes before him, believed that a new Boston City Hall was an opportunity to demonstrate to the world the economic, political, and architectural transformation that was taking place in Boston. Pei, too, treated the new City Hall as the centerpiece of his Government Center plan. He set the building in a vast open space, which would emphasize its significance within the complex. Because the building would face historic Faneuil Hall, Pei mandated that its height be relatively low so as not to overwhelm the "Cradle of Liberty." It was also deliberately located near the southern boundary of the site, close to the city's existing financial center and the retail district on Washington Street, so that its presence might help to stimulate development in these areas.[85] Thus, even before the design of New City Hall had been chosen, Pei's master plan ensured that it would differ markedly from the Civil War–era building that Boston's municipal government had inhabited for nearly a century.

Old City Hall

The decision to build a new City Hall as part of the Government Center project was motivated not only by the changing political climate but also by practical and architectural concerns: to wit, Boston's burgeoning municipal bureaucracy had outgrown its nineteenth-century home on School Street and an adjacent 1912 annex. The history of what is now called "Old City Hall" (fig. 2) would in several ways influence the new building's design.

Construction on Old City Hall began in 1862, and the building opened officially in 1865. This was the first purpose-built home for Boston's municipal government since the Boston Town House burned down in 1710. Since then, city officials had occupied first Faneuil Hall, then the Old State House and a building called the County Court House (which previously occupied the School Street site of Old City Hall).[86]

In the 1860s, Boston was captivated by all things French. Paris under Napoleon III (r. 1852–1870) became, as architectural historian Douglass Shand-Tucci wrote in his history of Boston architecture, "a kind of universal architectural idol."[87] Old City Hall reflected Boston's Francophilia and was one of the earliest major American buildings in the French Second Empire style that would soon sweep the country.

The design, by the eminent Boston architectural partnership of Gridley J. Fox Bryant and Arthur Gilman, features extravagant details inspired by the Tuileries Palace and the new Louvre of 1852–1857. Architectural historian Donlyn Lyndon wrote: "The French hardly ever made it as well. To describe this building as French Second Empire is only to draw in breath before beginning."[88] Faced with white granite quarried in Concord, New Hampshire, the exterior generally follows a strict geometric principle of threes: three horizontal sections and three vertical sections of three bays each. The lowest level is also the heaviest, with massive piers expressed as a rusticated wall, pierced by round-arched windows. At the second level the windows are longer, and the piers of the ground level give way to pairs of Corinthian pilasters. The squat third level reprises the pilasters from below, which visually support pairs of ornamental brackets beneath the steep mansard roof.

A large central pavilion dominates the façade, as it is pushed forward and upward from the basic mass, breaking the rule of three with its fourth story, and further distinguished by a massive convex mansard roof. Beneath this central mansard is an attic story that features a diminutive temple front surrounding a central window. The architects carried these opulent details through the interior as well, where black-and-white marble floors greeted visitors in the entrance lobby, and grand staircases of iron and oak carried them upstairs to richly paneled offices and ceremonial spaces housing the Hall of Aldermen and the Common Council chamber.

At the dedication on September 18, 1865, Mayor Frederic Lincoln praised the building and called attention to the symbolic relationship between municipal architecture and municipal government: "May its symmetry and beautiful proportions be emblematical of the purity of life and elevated principles of those who shall occupy these seats, fill the several departments of public service, and manage the municipal affairs of this city!"[89] Despite this encomium, Old City Hall was not universally beloved, even in its infancy. Controversy erupted before the building's completion, as some regarded it as a wasteful expense at a time when the Civil War was still raging. Others objected to the heavy granite design that, as the *Globe* noted, "made the building look old before it was finished," prompting some critics to call it "a four-story dungeon."[90] It would not be long before other problems—both functional and aesthetic—would emerge.

FIGURE 2. Old City Hall; Bryant and Gilman (1865). Boston's city government quickly outgrew its Civil War–era home, which by the mid-twentieth century was widely regarded as ugly and dilapidated. Library of Congress, Prints & Photographs Division, Historic American Building Survey, HABS MASS, 13-BOST, 70-19.

By the end of the nineteenth century, Boston's population was growing rapidly, as successive waves of immigrants from Ireland, Italy, and later eastern Europe poured in. During this time, the city's physical boundaries also expanded through a series of landfill projects and annexations. The population jumped from 177,840 in 1860 to 560,892 by 1900. It would continue to rise throughout the first half of the twentieth century, peaking in 1950 at 801,644—a 450 percent increase in less than a hundred years.[91]

As the number of city residents grew, there was a corresponding increase in the size of the municipal government, which no longer fit inside the building on School Street. By 1890, the city was paying over $50,000 annually to rent office space outside City Hall. That year, the city architect's office, at the behest of Mayor Thomas N. Hart, drew up plans for a seven-story addition to the School Street building that would extend the entire length of the block to Court Street. The goal of the addition was to accommodate many of the municipal departments that had been scattered throughout the city in recent years. Prefiguring one of the eventual programmatic goals of the 1962 New City Hall, Mayor Hart proposed that all departments that naturally worked together and most frequently served the public be located on the first floor of the remodeled space to allow for ease of public access.[92]

Although Hart was unable to win support from the state legislature and City Council for this addition, further proposals for a new City Hall continued to emerge over the next sixty years. In 1900, Thomas Hart, once again mayor after a ten-year absence from office, lamented in his inaugural speech that "our city hall is antiquated" and proposed decentralizing the functions of local government to municipal buildings scattered throughout the city.[93] The following year, however, Hart suggested replacing the current City Hall with a new building on the same site.

Others, meanwhile, advocated for a new building in Park Square, near the Public Garden, on land that, at the time, was owned by the Boston & Providence Railroad. Just as a future generation, sixty years later, would use a new City Hall to boost property values and spur the revitalization of a depressed urban area, so too did city officials in 1901 expect that the new City Hall they were proposing would be a boon to property values and a revitalized Park Square neighborhood.

The debate about whether and where to build a new City Hall would captivate the political community, the public, and the press for the next decade. Whereas the *Globe* in 1902 pronounced the Park Square site to be "generally favored," there was hardly a consensus on this location.[94] Other proposals called for placing the building in Copley Square or even in the Public Garden—an idea supported by some fiscal conservatives, as it would have been cheaper to build on this city-owned property than to purchase the Park Square parcels (although the *Globe* noted that "the idea of erecting a building on this beauty spot" had "not met with general favor").[95] As late as 1909, the question of building on the School Street site, in Park Square, in Copley Square, or in the Public Garden had not been settled.

The expense of building a new City Hall was the hitch that delayed the project for half a century more, despite widespread support for (or at least fascination with) the idea. In 1912, plans for a new building were shelved indefinitely as the city instead constructed the City Hall Annex on the site of Solomon Willard's granite Greek Revival Suffolk County Courthouse, which the city had long used to house departments that would not fit within City Hall. The eleven-story Annex (fig. 3), on Court Street just behind Old City Hall, is dominated by colossal Corinthian columns, which mask the steel-framed interior loft. Donlyn Lyndon, in his book on Boston architecture, wrote that "this rather breathless piece of grandeur . . . anticipates by fifty years the scale of the new [City Hall]. . . . Entering its portals every day may have been a little too heady for the Boston Redevelopment Authority folk. The Government Center redevelopment project they spawned in here has a similar scale, uncharacteristic of Boston."[96]

Even after the Annex had temporarily relieved overcrowding at City Hall, there were still proposals for a new home for Boston's government. The Annex complicated the matter, though, in that one of the principal arguments for a new building—the cost of leasing space to house city departments outside city-owned buildings—had been mitigated. This did not stop city officials from regularly raising the issue,

FIGURE 3. Boston City Hall Annex; Edward T. P. Graham (1912). The building, intended to relieve overcrowding at City Hall, temporarily diminished the calls for a new building. Courtesy of the Boston Public Library Print Department, Leon H. Abdalian Collection.

though. In 1922 the City Council unanimously voted in favor of a resolution to construct a new City Hall. Mayor Curley vetoed the resolution because of lack of funds, even though Curley himself had long desired a new building. A *Boston Globe* article from that same year, for instance, noted that the Curley administration was eager to leave a mark on the city in the form of a new City Hall, but the Annex acted as "an anchor cast to windward" that prevented moving City Hall proper to any location far from its present site. The article continued, "Chicago is one of the several American cities where, as in Boston, indecision on a new location and want of money compels the city year after year to get along with an ugly and inadequate City Hall."[97]

Another proposal appeared in 1926, when insurance executive Fred S. Elwell advanced a plan calling for a massive Union Station underneath Boston Common and the Public Garden. The station would unite all railroad and rapid transit lines in Boston, similar to New York's Grand Central Station. The Boston station would be capped by a new City Hall, straddling Charles Street in what a *Boston Globe* article derided as "a hectic combination of commuter traffic and political activity."[98]

Proposals continued to fly even during the lean years of the Great Depression. Mayors Curley, Mansfield, and Tobin each called for a new building, with suggested sites ranging from Castle Square in the South End to a manmade island in the middle of the Charles River. All of these proposals came to naught.

With too little money spent on upkeep (despite a $20,000 1939 rehabilitation by Mayor Tobin), and with the city government continuing to expand throughout the 1940s, the old building was showing its age and inadequacy. In 1936 the *Globe* called it "antiquated and unsanitary."[99] Even the Annex turned out to be but a temporary and short-lived solution to the space problem, as, once again, the city was leasing offices in other buildings to house municipal departments.

By the mid-twentieth century, not only was Old City Hall functionally deficient, but also it had fallen stylistically out of favor as appreciation for the French Second Empire style was on the wane. In accordance with the aesthetic sensibilities of his generation, Boston poet David McCord wrote in 1948 of a (perhaps apocryphal) legend:

"A French draughtsman or associate in Bryant's office introduced the mansard roof to Boston. Bryant built the classic Charles Street jail which I greatly admire. I should admire it more if the rumored mansard-roof man had been committed to it for his sin."[100]

It is also not possible to ignore the negative symbolic associations of the building. As Lawrence Kennedy noted, "In the eyes of some Bostonians in the mid-twentieth century the structure was old and repulsive, largely because of the politicians and problems within it."[101] Indeed, the political reputation of municipal government and the architectural reputation of City Hall seemed inextricably linked. Thus the argument in favor of a new City Hall was promoted by those who saw demolition of the old building as a way to inaugurate the new civic order and repudiate old-style politics. Many subscribed to the view of Boston City Hall presented in Edwin O'Connor's roman à clef about James Michael Curley, *The Last Hurrah:*

> City Hall was a lunatic pile of a building: a great, grim, resolutely ugly dust-catcher which had been designed eighty years before . . . , and for generations it had been decried as the prime eyesore of the community. Despite this, the building had its defenders, and intermittent suggestions that it be razed had met with howls of protest from those who had worked long within it and who, with a certain rude poetic vision, saw in this inefficient, tangled warren the perfect symbol for municipal administration.[102]

Musing on the old building, John Hynes later recalled, "I have often looked out of my City Hall office (old) and noticed the sight-seeing buses stop in School st. [sic] in front of the building while the barker pointed out the hall. I could always see consternation and surprise on the faces of the visitors as they seemed to be saying, 'Is this really the City Hall of Boston?'"[103] Hynes's successor, John Collins, also recognized the inadequacy of the old building. On his first day in office, Collins was appalled by City Hall's uncleanliness, noting that the floor was pitch-black with grime, the entrance on the Annex side reeked of urine, and the bronze front doors had become black with age, neglect, and "unattended pigeon droppings."[104] Collins would not wait long, however, before he began moving forward on plans for a new building—the centerpiece of Boston's midcentury redevelopment. But questions still remained about exactly what shape the building would take. In a city rich with architectural history, the design and its relationship to existing architecture were important considerations.

Boston's Midcentury Architectural Sclerosis

In addition to the symbolic, economic, and political motives, as well as the practical rationale, for a new City Hall, the building also responded to an opportunity to usher in a new era of architectural design in Boston. The Government Center Commission stipulated that one of the project's principal objectives was to promote "aesthetic standards that will set a high mark for future developments to emulate."[105] The members of the commission, and many other Bostonians, hoped that a prominent, distinctive, modern City Hall would impart a reputation for innovative, high-quality buildings to a city steeped (some might say mired) in architectural history.

As the onetime home of such prominent figures as Charles Bulfinch, Henry Hobson Richardson, Frederick Law Olmsted, and Ralph Adams Cram, Boston had enjoyed over a century of prestige in architecture and landscape architecture from the late 1700s through the early 1900s. By the mid-twentieth century, Boston was still home to several prominent architectural firms. In addition to older, established practices, such as Shepley Bulfinch Richardson & Abbott (the successor firm to H. H. Richardson), a handful of new firms had sprouted up in the post-war years. Chief among these was The Architects Collaborative (TAC), which seven young architects formed in 1945 with German émigré Walter Gropius, and which would grow to become one of the most prominent architectural practices in the world during the next fifty years.

The Boston area also had emerged as the center of architectural education in the United States, beginning in the late nineteenth century. MIT established the nation's first school of architecture in 1865. By the mid-twentieth century, MIT, as well as Harvard's Graduate

School of Design (GSD), had become vital training grounds. These schools attracted many prominent architects as faculty members. In 1937, Gropius was appointed head of the architecture department at Harvard, and his Bauhaus colleague Marcel Breuer joined the Harvard faculty in 1938. When Gropius and GSD dean Joseph Hudnut stepped down in 1953, their roles were filled by the eminent modernists Hugh Stubbins and José Luis Sert. At MIT, meanwhile, American architect William Wurster served as dean of the School of Architecture from 1945 to 1950, and Italian-born Pietro Belluschi succeeded him, serving from 1951 to 1965. Together, Harvard and MIT produced many of the greatest masters of modern architecture, with notable alumni including Philip Johnson, I. M. Pei, Edward Larrabee Barnes, Paul Rudolph, Edward Durell Stone, Bruno Zevi, and Walter Netsch. The presence of these prominent modernists at Boston-area schools would eventually bode well for the city's architectural future. In fact, several of them—including Belluschi, Wurster, Netsch, and Lawrence Anderson (head of design at MIT in the 1940s)—would have roles in the Boston City Hall design competition. Others—Rudolph, Gropius, and Pei—would be involved in other aspects of the Government Center project.

Boston's role as a center for architectural education was summed up by *New York Times* architecture critic Ada Louise Huxtable in 1980:

> It was in the Harvard-M.I.T. crucible that several generations of architects were trained who became the leaders of the profession and the setters of the style. Nor was that style exclusively orthodox. The same sources produced the monumental corporate manner of Gordon Bunshaft, the elegant formalism of I. M. Pei, the precisely defined understatement of Edward L. Barnes, the raw, romantic concrete brutalism of Paul Rudolph, and the literate, gadfly practice and catalytic patronage of Philip Johnson. It is a long, impressive list.[106]

Even with many world-class architects studying or teaching in the Boston area, and despite the renown of architectural training programs at MIT and Harvard, there was little new building activity in Boston proper between the stock market crash of 1929 and the early 1960s.

Indeed, Boston by the early 1960s had become something of an architectural has-been. The *Globe*'s architecture critic Robert Campbell was an architecture student at Harvard in the early 1960s. Attesting to Boston's midcentury architectural sclerosis, Campbell later recalled that none of his classmates intended to remain in Boston after graduation, saying that, at the time, an architect would have to have "no ambition" to stay in the area.[107]

While Huxtable, in her 1980 article, could claim that "Boston may be known as the cradle of liberty, but it is also the cradle of modern architecture in this country," this was not yet true in 1960. None of the buildings Huxtable named as examples of Boston's modernist architectural prominence were built prior to New City Hall, and likewise, none of the prestigious architects she mentioned had a single project completed in Boston proper before 1960.[108] This conspicuous absence of modern buildings in the downtown area resulted, in part, from the city's persistent economic and political troubles in the postwar years.

Boston's architectural stagnation in the mid-twentieth century became all the more pronounced (and embarrassing) as many prominent and architecturally significant buildings began to go up in Cambridge and the suburbs. These include the Gropius House in Lincoln (1937), Alvar Aalto's Baker House dormitory at MIT (1947–1949), TAC's Graduate Center at Harvard (1948–1950), and Eero Saarinen's Kresge Auditorium (1954–1955) and chapel (1955) at MIT. But these important structures were outside Boston city limits or confined to college campuses. The significance of this latter point may not immediately be obvious, but colleges were unique among the city's institutional inhabitants. It was comparatively easy for a business to pack up its downtown offices and move to a suburban office park. In fact, several companies did just that: the venerable Boston developer Cabot, Cabot & Forbes, for instance, preferred a suburban location in the Route 128 corridor to the crowded streets of downtown Boston.[109] Rumors abounded that other businesses, including insurance giant John Hancock, were considering moving to the suburbs in the late 1950s.[110]

It would have been far more challenging, by contrast, for colleges and universities to relocate. Unlike many companies, universities would not simply be moving a few desks and filing cabinets. Both the size and the complexity of their physical plant (including spaces for classrooms, offices, laboratories, dormitories, libraries, and dining facilities) would have made relocation difficult and costly—especially given the relatively modest revenues of these nonprofit institutions. Moreover, the physical ties of many colleges to their neighborhoods were centuries old. Harvard, for instance, had inhabited its campus in Cambridge since 1634 and could hardly have easily moved its operations to, say, Lexington. Even schools such as Boston University and MIT, which had only recently constructed their purpose-built campuses along the Charles River, would have been loath to abandon them so quickly. Also, the real estate needed for expansion within Boston city limits was relatively inexpensive, given the weak local economy, and the chief impediment to private development—the city's exorbitant property taxes—was not a concern for tax-exempt colleges.

At the same time that colleges were becoming tied ever more tightly to their physical locations, they experienced overwhelming spikes in enrollment in the postwar years, leading to the construction of new buildings. College enrollment increased rapidly after World War II, first as a result of the G.I. Bill for education, and subsequently owing to the rising proportion of the population attending college. Words such as "desperate," "unprecedented," and "terrifying" were used to describe the postwar "educational explosion," which resulted in a building boom on college campuses.[111]

Because of the architecturally progressive design faculties at MIT and Harvard, the Boston area's colleges were among the first to erect modernist buildings (along with those in Chicago, where Mies van der Rohe, the last prewar director of the Bauhaus, had settled at the Illinois Institute of Technology). Whereas campus architecture as recently as the 1930s had been historicist—such as Harvard's Georgian Revival riverfront houses, designed by Coolidge, Shepley, Bulfinch & Abbott—the 1940s and 1950s saw a profusion of modern-style designs. Joseph Hudnut, dean of the Harvard Graduate School of Design, rejected the single-style master plan that had long governed Harvard's architecture, saying, "Let no building depend for its character upon its relation to another."[112]

Accordingly, Harvard in 1948 commissioned TAC to design a new Graduate Center, a modern complex next to the neoclassical Harvard Law School building. Hudnut's successor, José Luis Sert, continued to modernize Harvard's campus, not only with his own structures (including the Holyoke Center, 1958–1965; Peabody Terrace, 1962–1964; and the Science Center, 1968–1975), but also by inviting Le Corbusier to design Harvard's Carpenter Center for the Visual Arts, the renowned Swiss architect's only building in North America. In fact, Sert's early designs for the Harvard campus were regarded as so successful that Boston University in 1959 commissioned him to devise a new master plan, which resulted in the construction of four Sert buildings on that campus, introducing the Brutalist style to the opposite bank of the Charles River.

The avant-garde development taking place on college campuses did not immediately spill into the overall architecture of the city. While Boston celebrated its many historically significant buildings, it had not experienced the same kind of modernist construction boom during the first half of the twentieth century as some of the nation's other major urban centers. Thus Boston's architectural character remained firmly rooted in buildings of brick, granite, and brownstone at a time when concrete, glass, and steel were popular elsewhere.

This lack of new construction can generally be ascribed to the city's persistent economic and political problems. But even had the city not experienced such a protracted financial crisis, it is doubtful that Boston would have embraced modernism earlier. What little construction there was during the 1930s, 1940s, and early 1950s was hardly cutting-edge, even as other cities were putting up starkly modernist buildings (from Philadelphia's PSFS Building of 1932, designed by Howe & Lescaze, to New York's Seagram Building of 1958, designed by Mies van der Rohe).

The addition to the John Hancock Mutual Life Insurance Building by Cram & Ferguson in 1947, for instance, became Boston's second-tallest structure, yet its aesthetic—with a stylized mast, masonry cladding, and recessed spandrels—was almost retrograde, more akin to Raymond Hood's early office buildings from the 1920s than the modern towers that were springing up elsewhere in the late 1940s. It appeared heavy, with an emphasis on verticality, a characteristic of the Art Deco style, which had flourished and then waned in other cities two decades earlier.

Likewise, Perry, Shaw, Hepburn & Dean's design for the Jordan Marsh department store on Summer Street (1948–1951) "essayed an absurd 'Modernistic' Federal Revival style," according to Douglass Shand-Tucci, but expressed more a sense of "compromise and uncertainty . . . apology and decline, even of decay."[113] Much like the Hancock, this building contrasted with the progressive modernism that was cropping up on the area's college campuses. It would seem, then, that Boston's conservative business temperament made the city ill suited for modernism in the immediate postwar years.

By the late 1950s, modern styles had begun to creep, albeit tentatively and vapidly, into the city under John Hynes's urban renewal program. The most prominent new building to be erected in Boston in the years prior to the City Hall competition was the Prudential Tower. Although it was the tallest building in New England, the tower won scant praise for its design. The Prudential Insurance Company had rejected a widely acclaimed earlier proposal by a collaborative group called Boston Center Architects, which included TAC, Carl Koch, Hugh Stubbins, Walter Bogner, and Pietro Belluschi. The company instead opted for a design by former Lever Brothers president Charles Luckman. As architectural historian Elihu Rubin pointed out in his history of the Prudential building, Luckman was generally regarded as "an aesthetic philistine," and his design was derided by critics from Wolf Von Eckardt ("totally out of human scale" with "no relation to people and the surrounding buildings") to Ada Louise Huxtable (a "textbook example in urban character assassination"). Rubin also quotes Boston-based architect Hugh Stubbins, who asked, "Isn't it an intrusion on the public's senses to clad this huge structure in peacock blue, and remind us of its identity with the hammer blow of a sign at its top?"[114] Such reactions made clear the Prudential Tower was unlikely to enhance Boston's architectural reputation.

Before the Prudential Center was completed, the Travelers Insurance Building hinted (albeit meekly) at a resurgence of Boston's downtown business district. The $17 million sixteen-story building—the first commercial office building constructed in downtown Boston in thirty years—was designed by Kahn & Jacobs of New York, and opened in September 1959. The building had a steel skeleton, clad in white-and-blue-glazed brick and glass. A dominant center section housed the services, such as elevators, ducts, and shaftways. Two wings flanked the central tower and contained the offices.

Although the Travelers Building augured the economic resurgence of downtown Boston's business district, its economic symbolism far outshone its architectural merit. Kahn & Jacobs was a corporate architectural firm, which had collaborated with Mies van der Rohe on the Seagram Building. It continued designing Miesian office buildings that, while inoffensive, were far from the vanguard of modernism. Local architect John Ware, writing in the *Boston Globe* in 1961, admitted that the building had helped to revitalize the neighborhood, mostly by dint of its being the first new downtown construction in three decades. But Ware criticized its aesthetics, pointing out that while it broke with Boston's traditional redbrick architecture, there was nothing to distinguish it from hundreds of other tall office buildings constructed by New York firms.[115] With little fanfare, the Travelers Building was demolished in 1988. The *Boston Globe* recognized that it was a rarity when it was constructed—a modernist building in Boston—but sardonically noted that "the blue-and-white tower of bathroom tile will soon be demolished and few will mourn."[116]

Boston's architectural slumber from the 1930s through the 1950s set the stage for a dramatic reemergence of cutting-edge design in the 1960s. But as the lackluster Travelers and Prudential buildings had shown, it would take a bold design for a high-profile new building to catalyze the city's architectural renaissance. There could hardly have been a more prominent commission than New City Hall.

Toward a New City Hall

A high-profile building like the new Boston City Hall provided an unparalleled opportunity to shape the future of architecture in Boston—and beyond. This fact surely did not escape the many prominent architects and theorists involved in the Government Center project. It also was not lost on the city's Design Advisory Committee or BRA chief Edward Logue, who had promised a more concerted focus on architectural distinction in the city. To what extent, however, the new City Hall would embrace or challenge the prevailing tenets of modernism—or the new architectural philosophies and aesthetics then emerging—was, in 1960, still an unanswered question.

The cumulative effect of the economic, political, and architectural circumstances in early 1960s Boston was the resounding need for a City Hall that would function not only as a new home for Boston's municipal government but also as a catalyst for future economic progress and architectural development in the city. The opportunities for the building to effect substantive change were legion.

Functionally, it could relieve the overcrowding of the outdated City Hall on School Street. Architecturally, it might give Boston a chance to shed its staid reputation and bring international attention to a city that had not seen a major distinguished public building project in decades. Symbolically, the new building would have an opportunity to establish a clear break from the infamous corruption of Boston's political past and reassure the business community, federal and state governments, and Bostonians that the city's political future would be a far cry from the antagonism and unscrupulousness that characterized the Curley era. In short, the building could demonstrate to the world that Boston had turned the proverbial corner architecturally, economically, and politically.

The building would also be able to show that Boston was a forward-thinking, progressive city, ready to meet the challenges of the late twentieth century; it was not a place stuck in the past. To that end, it could proclaim the government's power to foster progress within the city—not to impede it. As the centerpiece of the "New Boston" envisioned by Mayors Hynes and Collins, it could atone for the urban renewal missteps of the 1950s while continuing the mission of slum clearance and redevelopment by eliminating one of the most blighted neighborhoods in the city. Moreover, it could serve both symbolically and practically (through the involvement of business leaders in selecting a design) to further the rapprochement between the Irish city politicians and the Yankee business community.

Although progress had been made on these fronts during the Hynes and early Collins years, problems still persisted. The formation of the Boston Coordinating Committee as late as 1959, in what seemed like the city's inevitable descent into bankruptcy, shows how entrenched the economic crisis really was, and it furthermore reveals continuing doubts within the business community that the municipal government had any real ability—or desire—to solve the city's problems on its own. Likewise, the faltering attempts to revitalize Boston's built environment, as demonstrated by the Prudential Center and the Travelers Building, proved that the city had a long way to go to regain its stature as one of the world's architectural showplaces.

In short, the new Boston City Hall could become yet another disappointment in a long list of failures and half starts that would further seal the city's fate as a lost cause. Or it could become the means by which Boston could at last destroy the incubus of a gloomy past and usher in a prosperous future.

CHAPTER 2

Competition and Construction

In October 1961, Mayor John Collins announced that the City of Boston would select the design for its new City Hall through an open, nationwide competition. The idea originated with local architects James Lawrence and Philip W. Bourne and was enthusiastically embraced by both Collins and Robert Morgan, chairman of the Government Center Commission.[1] The competition was not an easy sell, though, since no major civic building in the United States had been chosen by such a process in nearly fifty years.[2] Moreover, several recent competitions had proven embarrassingly problematic, which might have dissuaded the generally staid city from adopting such a risky selection process for this important building. As Boston architect Tad Stahl later recalled, "Of all the places in the world to sell a competition of this magnitude for this kind of building, Boston was the least likely."[3]

The competition found an influential early opponent in Edward J. Logue, the city's powerful development administrator, who thought the process was wasteful and did not guarantee the best result.[4] "Why a design competition for it? Every now and then, particularly for an important building, a design competition is worthwhile," Logue argued, "but that was not the reason here."[5] Similarly, Nelson Aldrich, a local architect who served on the city's Design Advisory Committee (and eventually would be chosen as one of KMK's affiliated architects for the City Hall project), opposed the competition process. "I thought that the history of competitions in the United States was pretty bad ... but I was the only one that was very vociferous about going to a single architect and got nowhere."[6]

Notwithstanding these objections, and in a show of daring uncharacteristic of Boston, the Government Center Commission moved ahead with plans for the competition. It did not take long for many initial skeptics, including Logue, to come around to supporting it too. As Logue later recalled: "Mayor Collins was convinced sooner than I that a competition was the right course. I thought we could make a good selection, but he liked the process, and I was soon persuaded."[7] Architect Frank Crimp, who served on the Government Center Commission, believed that with the "solid support" of Mayor Collins, the commission had taken on the project with zeal and was establishing "a pattern for other cities to follow which will promote the best possible design of public buildings and eliminate the subjection of good design to political patronage where public interest is not the first consideration as it should be."[8]

As Crimp's comment suggests, the decision to hold a competition, like so many other aspects of Boston City Hall's history, was motivated not only by architectural circumstances but also by political considerations. Moreover, the competition's far-reaching effects would be both architectural and political in nature. For instance, the process was intended, in part, to eliminate the appearance of favoritism by preventing the job from falling into the hands of a politically connected architect, who, in James Michael Curley's days, might have been expected to make a hefty campaign contribution in return for the commission. Also, the opportunity to include local business leaders on the jury would accelerate the rapprochement between City Hall and the business community, which the previous generation of Boston politicians had long alienated.[9] Additionally, the competition would bring to the attention of the rest of the country Boston's renaissance, being enacted by an honest, capable, and forward-looking municipal government. In that regard, Morgan predicted that the contest would "excite interest, curiosity, speculation, and hence a better understanding and acceptance among the citizens of Boston and would produce widespread favorable publicity for the city at little added expense."[10]

The open competition would also be architecturally significant. First, it set younger architects and smaller firms on a level playing field with elite national firms, opening up the possibility that the winning design would exemplify unconventional, avant-garde aesthetic philosophies from less established architects. Moreover, in the aftermath of several highly publicized competition disasters for other projects around the country, the Boston process could reinvigorate the architectural competition as a means of choosing designs for important buildings in America. In short, the bold decision by Collins and the Government Center Commission would have both immediate and long-term political, economic, and architectural effects—not only in Boston but also throughout the rest of the country.

Recent Architectural Competitions

In opting for a design competition, Boston joined a host of governments, as well as businesses, churches, and other groups, that had previously selected architects through similar processes. Indeed, the architectural competition had an illustrious history, both in America and elsewhere. Although widely varied in format, design contests had resulted, for instance, in such masterpieces as the dome of the Cathedral of Santa Maria del Fiore in Florence, the Houses of Parliament in London, and the Paris Opera House. The successes of some previous contests likely inspired the Government Center Commission, but at the same time, several competition scandals and failures might have served as cautionary tales for Bostonians who realized that this would be a make-or-break moment for a city that desperately needed a conspicuous urban renewal triumph.

When Mayor Collins announced the competition in 1961, it would have been distinguished not only by its inherent significance as a contest for an important public structure, but also by its rarity at the time: it was the first open competition for a city hall in the United States since the San Francisco City Hall competition in 1912.[11] Although separated by half a century, the Boston and San Francisco projects shared similar motivations. Whereas Boston in 1961 was in the throes of financial malaise and had endured decades of political degeneration, San Francisco in 1912 was still rebuilding from the devastating earthquake and fire of 1906. Thus, just as Boston's New City Hall was meant to herald the political and economic resurgence of a city that had suffered from half a century of economic blight, fiscal malfeasance, and political corruption, its counterpart in San Francisco was part of a new Civic Center meant to signify the city's physical recovery. Both cities hoped their competitions would serve as harbingers of municipal regeneration.

The San Francisco competition was widely regarded as a success. The winning design, announced in late June 1912, came from the firm of Bakewell & Brown. It featured a monumental Beaux-Arts building (fig. 4) with strong echoes of Jules Hardouin-Mansart's Saint-Louis des Invalides in Paris, as well as the United States Capitol in Washington, D.C., with a massive dome atop a granite façade festooned with Doric columns, pediments, gilded details, and other Classical Revival elements. Construction was completed in time for San Francisco's Panama-Pacific International Exposition in 1915, and the building served as a grand symbol of resilience in the wake of catastrophe for the millions of visitors who flocked to the city for that historic event. In 1961—nearly fifty years after it opened—the building was still in use as a well-functioning home for San Francisco's municipal government.[12]

Notwithstanding their many similarities, the Boston and San Francisco competitions differed in several respects. Overseeing the process in San Francisco were three local architects appointed by the Board of Public Works to serve as consulting architects. These men were charged not only with supervising the competition itself but also with advising the board on designing the other buildings in the Civic Center. The competition was open to any architect who maintained an office in San Francisco as of January 1, 1912. Entries were judged by a seven-member jury, which included the mayor of San Francisco,

FIGURE 4. San Francisco City Hall; Bakewell & Brown (1912). As Boston prepared for a City Hall competition in 1962, it looked to San Francisco for a model. Fifty years earlier, the California city had hosted the last open competition for a city hall. Library of Congress, Prints & Photographs Division, Historic American Building Survey, HABS CAL, 38-SANFRA, 71-.

one member of the Board of Public Works, one member of the Public Buildings Committee of the San Francisco Board of Supervisors, the three consulting architects, and one architect selected by the competitors themselves by secret ballot.[13]

In Boston, by contrast, while the new City Hall was the centerpiece of the Government Center project, its designers were subject to the restrictions of Pei's master plan for the complex (unlike in San Francisco, where the path of influence was reversed, and the consulting architects in charge of the City Hall competition had a say in the designs of the other buildings in the Civic Center). Moreover, the composition of the two juries differed markedly: in Boston the jury included no public officials, but it did include prominent local business leaders. Perhaps the most significant distinction between the two competitions was that the San Francisco contest was open only to architects who maintained an office in that city, whereas the Boston competition was open to all American-based architects. The program allowed entries from "any architect resident in the United States who during the Preliminary Stage is licensed to practice architecture in any State thereof."[14] Entries from abroad, unless in collaboration with an American firm, were not permitted.

Despite these key differences, Boston adopted some aspects of the San Francisco competition. For instance, just as the consulting architects supervised the San Francisco competition, Boston's Government Center Commission charged its professional adviser, Lawrence B. Anderson, chairman of MIT's architecture department, with overseeing its competition. Also, both city halls were to be centerpieces of grand civic center projects, necessitating collaboration between those responsible for the City Hall designs and those in charge of the larger developments—the Civic Center in San Francisco and Government Center in Boston.

As the most recent major public building in the United States selected by an open competition, San Francisco City Hall provides obvious points of comparison for Boston. Yet there had been several competitions for other public and private buildings in the intervening years that would also influence the format of the Boston contest. The Boston competition came on the heels of two international open contests: those for the Sydney Opera House (1957) and Toronto City Hall (1958). The Sydney competition garnered 233 entries from architects in thirty-two countries. The brief prescribed no restrictions on style or cost, calling broadly for two performance halls, one for opera and one for symphony concerts. The Danish architect Jørn Utzon emerged as the winner with a design that became known throughout the world as an icon of modern architecture and a visual symbol of Australia.[15] Although problems during the construction process would eventually lead to Utzon's resignation from the project in early 1966, this competition was still a viable model for Boston in the early 1960s.[16]

Likewise, architects and city officials around the globe viewed the Toronto competition as an example of a well-executed means of selecting an architect for an important public building. The city received 510 entries from forty-two countries, allowing it to boast that it had sponsored "the biggest architectural competition ever staged."[17] The jury of distinguished architects narrowed the entries to eight finalists, eventually choosing as the winner Finnish architect Viljo Revell's modernist design of two parabolic concrete office towers flanking a low, broad dome housing the City Council chamber.

The decision was reputedly influenced by juror Eero Saarinen, who arrived late to the judging and rescued Revell's entry from a list the other jurors had made of designs that could be summarily rejected. Saarinen eventually persuaded two of the four other jurors to join him in supporting Revell's design.[18] When the front page of the *Toronto Telegram* announced the winner, public reaction was remarkably favorable for such an unconventional design: the mayor, Nathan Philips, called it "breath-taking"; the international architectural press applauded it; and even disappointed fellow competitor John C. Parkin offered glowing praise.[19] Fifty years later, when concrete architecture had fallen out of style, Revell's design still ranked, in the words of *Toronto Star* critic Christopher Hume, "among the most beloved buildings in Toronto." Hume also pointed out that the competition "set the stage for acceptance of concrete as a material for use in a civic icon"—a statement that further illustrates the similarities between the Toronto and Boston competitions.[20]

Boston announced its competition within five years of those in Sydney and Toronto, but it did not simply ape these earlier contests. Each of the architects on the Boston jury, for example, was chosen for his relationship to the city, in that all had either lived, studied, or practiced in Boston. Likewise, the Boston jury included laymen (from the local business community), distinguishing it from those in Sydney and Toronto, which comprised only architects.

Recent successes in other cities did not, of course, mitigate the risk involved in the competition process. In fact, several recent competition failures might have given the Government Center Commission pause. As Sarah Bradford Landau notes, architectural competitions had been tainted by a "well-earned reputation for unfairness and exploitation" throughout the late nineteenth and early twentieth centuries. For instance, the winner of the Wyoming State Capitol competition of 1886 was found to have copied another competitor's design, and an abortive 1890s competition for New York City Hall drew protests from civic organizations, leading to a state law nullifying the contest and leaving the frustrated finalists struggling to collect their awards.[21]

Similarly, while open competitions help to break the circle of a select group of established architects getting all the big jobs, the history of architectural competitions had not always been encouraging. In fact, as a *Horizon* magazine article maintained, this history "is littered with the bones of aborted victories and justified defeats." The article continued, "The winner may get the prize but not the job or, more likely still, one of the also-rans may turn out to have had the superior design."[22] In 1891, for example, Grant LaFarge and George Lewis Heins won the competition for the Cathedral Church of St. John the Divine in New York City. In the midst of construction, though, the church's trustees fired LaFarge and turned to Ralph Adams Cram, who significantly modified LaFarge's original design, turning what began as a Romanesque Revival structure into a neo-Gothic one.[23] Likewise, in the wake of the 1922 Tribune Tower competition in Chicago, many people came to regard Howells & Hood's winning Gothic Revival design as inferior to Walter Gropius's or Eliel Saarinen's modernist ones.

Moreover, open competitions were seen as risky in that they might not produce the best results; while they were promoted by those who wanted to see new styles and building types emerge from younger firms, many clients (both public entities and private companies) favored the relative safety of invited competitions among established firms that were known to be capable of handling the task. Thus the majority of competitions held in the United States in the mid-twentieth century were contests in which only select groups of established architects were invited to participate.[24]

One problematic competition that remained controversial at the time of the Boston contest was the ill-fated Franklin Delano Roosevelt Memorial competition. From 574 entries, the jury selected a design by Pedersen, Tilney, Hoberman, Wasserman & Beer as the $50,000 first-place winner in December 1960. The design, featuring eight massive concrete stelae on which excerpts from Roosevelt's writings were to have been inscribed, incited public uproar over its scale. In February 1962, the Commission of Fine Arts (an independent federal government agency that reviews all new building designs for Washington, D.C.) formally objected to the proposal for its inharmoniousness with the nearby Lincoln, Washington, and Jefferson memorials, prompting congressional action that led to a revised design, which the commission eventually accepted in 1964. The Roosevelt family, however, spurned the new plan, and it was abandoned. The FDR Memorial Commission then invited Marcel Breuer to submit a design, which was summarily rejected by the Commission of Fine Arts. In 1978, the Memorial Commission tapped Lawrence Halprin, whose design was eventually constructed after years of funding debates, with the formal dedication taking place in 1997—nearly forty years after the initial competition.[25] Such a protracted and highly publicized debacle highlights the problems the Boston competition might have faced, but the Government Center Commission learned from the early mistakes of the FDR Memorial by producing a meticulously detailed competition brief and by involving multiple constituencies in the selection process so that the winning design would have a broad base of support.

There were, of course, many other competitions during the first half of the twentieth century that the Government Center Commission may have considered when crafting its own program, but the San Francisco, Toronto, and Sydney competitions are those most comparable to Boston's in terms of format, purpose, and legacy. That said, the decision to hold a competition in Boston was motivated not only by these previous contests but also by the specific architectural, political, and economic circumstances. For a city that was striving to reinvent itself and to emerge from under a cloud of political corruption and economic duress, the competition seemed like the city's best hope for getting local residents—and people throughout the United States—excited about the New Boston. As the politicians, architects, planners, and business leaders in charge of the Government Center project prepared for their own competition, the lessons of disaster and success from these previous contests helped to shape the model that Boston would use.

The Competition Program

With the seal of the City of Boston embossed on its cover, the official Boston City Hall competition program was released on October 16, 1961. This thirty-one-page Cerlox-bound booklet (with a thirteen-page appendix and a fold-out map of the Government Center project area), prepared by MIT professor Lawrence Anderson, spelled out the requirements for competitors. Hélène Lipstadt, in her book about architectural competitions in America, called the program "exceptionally complete" in that it not only detailed specific space requirements for the new building but also "encouraged the expression of civic values and the respect of the historic, architectural, and urban environment."[26] To that end, more than half of the program dealt with broad conceptual matters, explaining how New City Hall would fit into the existing city and its distinctive culture.

The program opened with a statement by John F. Collins, announcing that the principal motivation behind the competition was "the desire of the City to obtain the best possible design in terms of beauty, planning and harmony with other buildings in Boston's new Government Center."[27] Collins's letter also explained that the "client" of the competition was neither the City of Boston nor the Boston Redevelopment Authority but rather the Government Center Commission.

The commission, which was created by the Massachusetts General Court in 1958 to carry out legislation providing for the construction of a new City Hall, consisted of seven members. The commissioners were unpaid and represented different constituencies with stakes in the project. Three members were municipal government officials: the director of administrative services (Henry A. Scagnoli), the chairman of the City Planning Board (T. Joseph Regan), and the commissioner of public works (James W. Haley). Three other members were appointed by the mayor from candidates nominated by trade groups: vice chairman M. Murray Weiss, nominated by the Associated General Contractors of Massachusetts; architect Frank W. Crimp, nominated by the Boston Society of Architects; and John Deady, nominated by the Building Trades Council. The chairman of the commission, Robert

M. Morgan, vice president and later president of the Boston Five Cents Savings Bank, was selected at large by Mayor Hynes and continued as chairman under Mayor Collins.[28]

Following Collins's introduction, a statement from Morgan stressed that the competition would be conducted under the code of the American Institute of Architects (AIA) and that Lawrence Anderson had been appointed professional adviser to the commission to direct the conduct of the competition.[29] In this capacity, Anderson served as the liaison between the commission and the jurors, was the principal contact for the competitors, and was responsible for ensuring that the competition was run in accordance with AIA guidelines.

The bulk of the program's content fell into two broad categories: general information about Boston and specific rules of the competition. Following the foreword containing Collins's and Morgan's statements was an extensive introduction to the city, including sections on local geography, subsoil, climate, local building materials, and history. The program also summarized the main features of the Government Center redevelopment plan, including the vastly simplified street system, public transportation improvements, and new public structures and private development slated for the area. Panoramic photographs of the cityscape, regional and local maps, and images of the area to be developed augmented the text. The detailed program ensured that even architects unfamiliar with Boston would have a clear understanding of the new City Hall's role within the historic city.

To that end, these initial sections of the program forcefully emphasized Boston's rich history. They spoke to the character of the mid-century city and the considerable pride its citizens derived from its storied past. Although this brief history was not comprehensive, it nevertheless highlighted many key aspects of Boston's previous development, from the earliest days of European colonization through construction of the Central Artery in 1954. One full page, for example, contained a section of the 1722 Bonner map (the earliest complete map of Boston), which showed the downtown area as it existed in the early eighteenth century, and the accompanying text explained the city's rapid physical expansion (through both landfill projects and annexation) throughout the nineteenth and early twentieth centuries.[30]

The program also briefly recounted Boston's architectural history, with references to the contributions of several eminent Boston-based architects: Charles Bulfinch, Alexander Parris, Gridley James Fox Bryant, Arthur Gilman, and H. H. Richardson. In addition, photographs of historic buildings near the City Hall site (such as Faneuil Hall, the Old State House, the Ames Building, and the Custom House Tower) implied that New City Hall's architects would be heirs to (not at odds with) this rich architectural heritage, with their building joining these historical monuments in Boston's architectural showcase.

While some Bostonians today might regard their Brutalist City Hall as hostile to nearby historic architecture, the competition program made clear that the new building was intended to help save its crumbling neighbors. A lengthy section headed "Conservation and Rehabilitation" explained that the Government Center renewal project was expected to stimulate more intensive public use of the many historic structures in the downtown area, specifying that "as a plan where the future mingles dramatically with the historic the Project must fulfill the future's needs in a way that does honor to the past." The program urged competitors to consider the physical relationship between the new building and the important historic structures close by, noting, for instance, that "the charm of the Old State House lies in its intimacy of scale nestled in the great bulk of surrounding buildings, and this quality must not be diluted by too large a space." It also pointed out that "Faneuil Hall is backed up by the Quincy Market and in this direction the architect of City Hall will have the honor of expanding upon a theme of urban design laid out long ago by Bulfinch and Parris." Given later criticism of City Hall for not fitting in with Boston's history and clashing with the neighboring historic structures, this emphasis on the city's history and the new building's relationship to it is particularly remarkable.[31]

In addition to urging competitors to design a City Hall with a respectful relationship to the historic city, the commission also highlighted the need for a building that would both symbolize the best aspects of government and stimulate physical and economic growth.

The program stated that because City Hall would be the seat of government, "it should reflect the highest aspirations of the people served," and that "since the Project is expected to regenerate extensively a declining central business district, there is need for functional and aesthetic standards that will set a high mark for future developments to emulate." It pointed out that all available land in the downtown area had been developed by 1900, and "in our century there has been relatively little replacement and business activity has been declining." Officials hoped New City Hall would help spur development in this district at the same time that it revitalized the historic city. The program also spoke to the monumental nature of the building, drawing attention to the visual relationship of the site to the various avenues of pedestrian approach, as well as its visibility from the Central Artery, where City Hall would be "dramatically revealed to the motorist."[32]

Much of the program booklet detailed specific requirements for the design. Many of these were determined by Pei's Government Center master plan, which dictated the exact height, size, and site of the building, as well as the shape of the open space around it. For Pei, City Hall was to be the centerpiece of a larger complex, and the relationship of this building to the other elements of the civic center was of primary importance. Accordingly, the program explained how the Government Center plan was designed to create "a completely reorganized setting for City Hall." It made clear that the "extensive and detailed regulations and controls" imposed on the separate elements of the Government Center project were intended, in part, to produce "for City Hall the key position in the overall composition, because here will be housed the governmental functions of the most direct significance to the people of Boston."[33]

The relationship of the relatively low City Hall to the new federal building tower was described as "a most delicate problem in architectural harmony"; although "the main relationships of position and mass are defined in the site plan, consistency in scale will have to be developed in stages." Moreover, given the height of the federal building, as well as the private office tower anticipated for an adjacent site, the program advised architects to treat City Hall's roof as a fifth façade, since it would be visible from the nearby high-rise structures. Similarly, the program noted that the east and south façades should form effective visual closures to Dock Square and Washington Street, respectively. The north and west façades would face the plaza. Thus, the architects were given the challenge of creating five façades that related to distinct neighbors: the Washington Street financial district to the south, Dock Square and Faneuil Hall on the east, the federal building on the north, the historic Sears Crescent and City Hall Plaza on the west, and office towers that would provide views of the building from above.[34]

In addition to designing the building, the competitors were required to determine the form of the open space surrounding City Hall. Since these areas were the connective tissue between City Hall and neighboring buildings and public spaces, the program asked competitors to consider carefully the relationship of the materials to their surroundings. It noted, for instance, that the BRA intended to restore Dock Square, at the foot of City Hall, to its original granite block paving, which likely influenced the competitors' plans for the floor materials of City Hall Plaza. Competitors were to indicate on their entries detailed plans for these exterior spaces—landscape features, floors, and architectural elements—since these were "basic to the design of City Hall and to full realization of the civic design intention" of Government Center.[35]

The internal planning considerations for City Hall were based on the three general categories of Boston's municipal government: symbolically important departments, administrative departments with heavy public traffic, and other administrative departments (those not frequented by the public). The symbolically important categories included the mayor and the City Council. The program pointed out that although both are elected, the two do not have a close functional relationship, and thus they "should keep their separate identities, just as in our national government the Capitol is separated from the White House." The program also recommended that those departments dealing mainly with the public be placed on one or more levels of a "Heaviest Traffic Area" near the ground floor, with escalator connections between levels to facilitate ease of public access. Competitors could place the "other departments" in the remainder of the building, since these "need have only such elevator service as would in any case be required for movement of personnel."[36]

In addition to these general spatial needs, the program offered a meticulously detailed breakdown of requirements for each department. These included specific space needs (the reception area of the Municipal Reference Library required exactly 177 square feet, for instance), a graph indicating which departments needed to be adjacent to each other, and diagrams for individual offices showing the suggested arrangement of furniture in those spaces. Brief descriptions of departmental functions for the "Heaviest Traffic Area" category were meant to further assist the competitors in laying out the circulation through this area.

In short, the program established two primary goals for New City Hall, and it equipped the competitors with the necessary information to achieve them. First, it demanded a design that would befit a public building of this stature, one that would complement the surrounding structures and spaces, as well as relate to both Boston's past and its future. Second, the copious detail of the space requirements provided the competitors with all necessary information to design a building that met the municipal government's functional needs. This was to be neither simply a monument with an exquisite and inspiring aesthetic nor merely a utilitarian office building; rather, it was to combine the complex characteristics of both. The detailed guidelines derived from Pei's master plan were intended to help Boston avoid the debacle that had overtaken the FDR Memorial competition, where vague expectations led to a winning design that was ultimately unacceptable. As Edward Logue said, the Pei plan's guidelines were not overly restrictive, but rather they "provided a most useful discipline," and as the competition entries demonstrated, they moreover "provided an opportunity for widely varying solutions, many of them of great distinction."[37]

Finally, while the publication of such a detailed program suggests that city officials were serious about using this process to select its architect, they were nevertheless mindful of the risk involved. They therefore created an escape clause. Although the program stipulated that the competition was designed to assist in the selection of an architect for New City Hall, it was not a binding contract with the winner. Once the jury had made its decision, the Government Center Commission would then decide, within sixty days, whether to accept the final design and hire the winning architect, or whether to release the winner from any further obligation.[38] With the commission's approval, the winning entry would then be subject to review by the mayor, who had the final say in whether to build it. Not to build the winning design, though, would have been an embarrassing defeat for both the competition process and the city that had invested so much time, money, and hope in it. It was important, then, that the process be problem free and result in an incomparable design—one that would prove the effort worthwhile. The detailed program was the first key step toward this goal, ensuring that the competitors understood clearly what was expected of them. The next step—selecting the design—was in the hands of the competition jury.

The Jury

Unlike the all-architect juries of the Sydney Opera House and Toronto City Hall competitions, the Boston City Hall jury included a mix of prominent architects and laymen, appointed by the Government Center Commission. The architects—Pietro Belluschi, Walter Netsch, Ralph Rapson, and William Wurster—all had thriving professional and academic careers. Moreover, all of these men had connections to the Boston area, giving them insight into the city's culture and its architecture.

Belluschi, an Italian émigré, had built his architectural career in Portland, Oregon, gaining international renown with his 1945 design for a new headquarters for the Equitable Savings and Loan Association. The building influenced subsequent skyscraper design by pioneering such innovations as double-glazed window panels sealed in a fixed frame, and a flush curtain-wall skin of glass and aluminum.[39] Other notable buildings that Belluschi designed himself or in collaboration with others include the Federal Reserve Bank of Portland (1948); the Juilliard School and Alice Tully Hall in New York City's Lincoln Center (completed in 1969); and several brick churches throughout the country (including First Lutheran Church, Boston, designed in 1954), distinguished by their severe geometries and use of inexpensive "Glu-Lam" (laminated, glued wood) timbers. MIT chose Belluschi as dean of its School of Architecture and Planning in 1951. He relocated first to Traill Street in Cambridge and, in 1954, to Fairfield Street in Boston's Back Bay.[40] Thus, by the time he served on the Boston City Hall competition jury, he had gained a worldwide reputation as an eminent architect and educator, and he had lived and worked in the Boston area for more than a decade.

Walter Netsch was born in Chicago and studied architecture at MIT.[41] Upon graduation, he served briefly in the U.S. Army Corps of Engineers before joining the San Francisco office of Skidmore, Owings & Merrill (SOM) in 1947. He later transferred to SOM's Chicago office. Netsch's best-known designs prior to his service on the Boston City Hall jury include the campus for the U.S. Air Force Academy in Colorado Springs (1959) and the Inland Steel Building in Chicago (1957). The Air Force Academy's Cadet Chapel showcased his love of geometric complexity, with seventeen aluminum-clad spires alternating with tetrahedrons. The Inland Steel Building, meanwhile, reflected a concern for symbolism, as the building's pronounced use of shining stainless steel showcased its function as a steel company's headquarters.[42]

Ralph Rapson attended the University of Michigan and the Cranbrook Academy of Art, where he studied under Eliel Saarinen, in whose office he worked from 1940 to 1941.[43] He taught architecture at the New Bauhaus School in Chicago from 1942 to 1946 and at MIT from 1946 to 1954. The University of Minnesota then appointed him head of its architecture school. Rapson also established a successful architectural practice in Minneapolis, garnering such high-profile commissions as the United States embassies in Copenhagen and Stockholm (both 1954) and the Guthrie Theater in Minneapolis (1963). While the embassies feature a restrained modernist aesthetic of steel-framed boxes clad in limestone, the Guthrie was a geometric tour de force. An irregularly shaped seven-sided stage was thrust into the middle of the auditorium with seating nearly surrounding it, and a steep "Alpine slope" design for the seating area integrated the main floor and the balcony.[44] On the exterior, the glass-walled lobby was protected by a dramatic "cubist" screen that partially concealed and partially revealed the activity inside. (Sadly, the screen was removed in 1974 and the theater itself demolished in 2006.)

The fourth architect on the jury, who also served as the group's chairman, was the California architect William Wurster. Wurster studied architecture at the University of California, Berkeley, before opening his own office in San Francisco in 1924. He was best known for having designed hundreds of houses in the Bay Area from the 1920s to the 1940s. This residential architecture paired indigenous materials with a simple style that was well suited to the regional climate and attuned to the topography. Although some architects scoffed at his peculiar version of modernism (Frank Lloyd Wright called him "Redwood Bill" and dismissed him as a "shack architect"), others saw in his work a sensitive and straightforward regionalism. (Lewis Mumford defended Wurster's designs as a "native and humane form of modernism.")[45] Wurster began graduate studies at Harvard in the late 1930s and, before completing his graduate degree, was appointed dean of the School of Architecture and Planning at MIT in 1945. He left Cambridge in 1950 to take over as dean of architecture at the University of California, Berkeley, after having spent more than a decade in the Boston area.

The jury's laymen, prominent members of the local business community, also had distinguished backgrounds. During the competition's preliminary stage, the four architects were joined by seventy-two-year-old Harold Hodgkinson, chairman of the local department store Wm. Filene's Sons.[46] Two additional businessmen joined for the final stage of the judging: O. Kelley Anderson, president of the New England Mutual Life Insurance Company, and Sidney R. Rabb, chairman of the supermarket chain Stop & Shop. The inclusion of businessmen was meant, in part, to ensure that the jury would not choose an overly conceptual design with little practical value—a building that only an architect could love. Empowering the business community and connecting it to Boston's new municipal regime in this way also helped further the rapprochement between City Hall and State Street.

On the surface, the disparate backgrounds of the seven jurors would seem to pose a challenge, lessening the chances that they would be able to agree on a common vision for the new City Hall. Indeed, the diversity in their biographies made the unanimity of their ultimate decision all the more improbable. Hodgkinson, writing a decade after the competition, reflected on this feat: "Wonder of wonders—four professional architects, identified with four fine architectural schools in four widely separated parts of the nation, and three lay citizens produced a unanimous decision for the design of the present City Hall."[47]

Despite their varied backgrounds, the jurors did share certain key traits of philosophy and temperament. All, for instance, had a familiarity with and an abiding interest in the city of Boston: the architects had received their training at Harvard or MIT, and the laymen were all citizens of and homeowners in the city.[48] As one newspaper article claimed, the jurors "know every mood, whim of Boston," and since "all members of the jury at one time or another have lived in Boston, they felt a deep responsibility towards the rebirth of the Boston central area."[49] Moreover, these men shared a streak of bold nonconformity. The architects, for instance, while avowed modernists, rejected the doctrinaire, orthodox approach to architecture that characterized so many of their colleagues' works. Instead of mass-producing anonymous glass boxes, they were all, in their own ways, mavericks: Belluschi with his pioneering use of new technologies; Netsch and Rapson with their complex geometries; Wurster with his regionalism. As such, they were all seemingly open (if not predisposed) to choosing a cutting-edge rather than a conventional design.

Likewise, the business leaders' biographies also revealed veins of daring individualism. Hodgkinson was a self-made man who had worked his way up from basement stock boy to chairman of the company. Anderson had been active in civic affairs for some time, having been one of the earliest supporters of the New Boston and having participated in a number of Hynes's special committees and citizens' seminars. Rabb, meanwhile, had begun working at a small, financially troubled grocery store chain while studying at Harvard, and became chairman by the time he was thirty. He would introduce the concept of the modern supermarket through the radical experiment of turning the grocery store into a large self-service warehouse. This model helped the company become the biggest supermarket chain in New England.[50] The pioneering spirit of these businessmen, paired with the progressive sensibilities of the architects, virtually ensured not only that they had the ability to forge a consensus in their deliberations, but also that the winning design would be revolutionary.

The Preliminary Stage

The preliminary stage of the competition was open to all licensed architects in the United States. Unlike many other contests (such as for San Francisco City Hall), Boston allowed firms or associations to form for the special purpose of the competition, provided that at least one person in the group was a U.S. citizen and a licensed architect.[51] The winning design, in fact, came from a group formed solely for the competition.

One wonders why, coming as it did on the heels of international competitions in Sydney and Toronto, the Boston City Hall competition was not also international in scope. There is no indication in any of the archives or sources consulted for this book that the Government Center Commission ever considered this possibility, but one cannot help but indulge in speculation. An intense national pride characterized the United States during the 1950s and early 1960s. (As David Halberstam noted, during this era "few Americans doubted the essential goodness of their society.")[52] Perhaps the idea of a non-U.S. citizen designing a government building in this country was anathema to this hyperpatriotism. Moreover, during the height of the Cold War, competition planners had to be wary of the danger of embarrassment if an "enemy" should rise to victory in a cultural contest. American pianist Van Cliburn's shocking 1958 victory in the first International Tchaikovsky Competition in Moscow was still fresh in the national memory, and perhaps the Government Center Commission was loath to provide an opportunity for the Soviets to exact revenge. Had the jury unwittingly chosen a design by a Soviet architect, it would have delivered a considerable blow to the idea of American cultural superiority.

Registration closed on December 11, 1961, and entries for the preliminary stage were due the following month, on January 17, 1962. By this deadline, 256 entries had been submitted, and the Government Center Commission went to great lengths to protect their anonymity. Each entry was delivered double-wrapped, and the outer wrapping (containing postmarks, return addresses, and other identifying information) was immediately removed and destroyed by staff members unaffiliated with the jury. A sealed, removable blank envelope, containing the name of the competitor, was attached to the inner package. Receiving staff assigned corresponding numbers to the sealed envelopes and the entries. The envelopes were then secured until the jury had selected the finalists.[53]

Once the entries were numbered, they were delivered to Lawrence Anderson, who made a preliminary audit to ensure that they complied with the basic requirements of the competition. Anderson reported any instances of noncompliance to the jury, which then decided whether these warranted disqualification. Following this preliminary inspection, the jury studied all qualified entries and discussed the merits of each. As professional adviser to the Government Center Commission and overseer of the competition, Anderson participated in the jury's discussions, but he did not vote. Following these discussions, the jury selected eight finalists by majority vote. The numbers of the finalists were then given in writing to Anderson, who, in the presence of the jury, opened the numbered envelopes and announced the names of the finalists, but he did so in such a way that the name of a finalist could not be identified with any particular design, further preserving the anonymity of the entries for the final stage of judging. Anderson then notified the finalists of their selection and made the list of names known to the public.[54]

The Final Stage

After the jury announced the preliminary-stage winners on January 25, 1962, the finalists had three months to prepare their submissions for final-stage judging, with all materials, including scale models of the designs, due on April 25. Although the names of the finalists were released to the public, they were not identified with their designs until the ultimate winner was announced. Each finalist received $5,000, and the eventual winner would receive an additional $5,000, with both payments considered an advance on professional fees if the city decided to construct the winning design.

To assist the jury in determining the winner, the Government Center Commission prepared a scale model of the entire Government Center area based on Pei's master plan, with the City Hall site left empty. The jurors then were able to place City Hall models supplied by the finalists in the master model to see how they would relate to the other buildings in the complex.[55]

In addition to submitting these models, the finalists were required to provide more detailed drawings of their designs. Whereas to encourage a large participation in the preliminary stage the entries were supposed to be "simple and diagrammatic," final-stage materials were to express "fuller development of details and presentation."[56] The program detailed the specific requirements of the materials needed for each stage. Whereas the preliminary stage required only relevant notes, a site plan, floor plans of all levels, sections, all elevations, and one exterior perspective, the final stage required, in addition to all of these, interior perspectives of the City Council chamber and another major space, two exterior perspectives, a rendered detail of elevation, and a 1/32 scale model. At both stages, the jury was particularly interested in the relationship between the City Hall design and the surrounding buildings, with a special note in the program that all floor plans at the ground level, elevations, and sections should show the surrounding elements of Government Center.

Given the strict controls on height, volume, and location imposed by Pei's master plan, it is not surprising to find similarities among the entries. Seven of the eight finalists, for instance, chose rectangular patterns for their designs, with only one competitor proposing a cylindrical building. Nevertheless, there were important differences among the finalists in terms of the organization of the building's constituent functions, the relationship of City Hall to neighboring structures, and the symbolic expression of municipal government.

Five designs offered variations on a modernist office box, drawing on the conventional corporate architectural aesthetic of the time. The Chicago-based team of W. C. Wong, T. C. Chang, Gertrude Kerbis, Otto Stark, and Chan Sit, for example, proposed a square building with a central courtyard, clad in dark-tinted glass curtain walls. Eight peripteral columns raised the bulk of the building one story above ground level, creating an open approach to the ground floor, echoing Mies van der Rohe's iconic and influential Seagram Building in Manhattan, which opened in 1958. The entry by F. Frederick Bruck (an architect in Cambridge, Massachusetts) and Ervin Y. Galantay (a native of Budapest who was teaching at the Harvard GSD) took a similar approach, with a square building elevated on columns, but this design did not include a courtyard. Instead, at the center of the building was a cylindrical housing for mechanical equipment, which lent geometric distinction to a building that was otherwise a box. Moreover, rather than all-glass curtain walls, the architects opted for stone window casings. The proposal by the Appleton, Wisconsin, based team of James B. Swack, Wilbert O. Rueter, and Lloyd D. Gadau also featured a square building without a central courtyard.

Two other entries expanded the square form into a rectangle. Concord, Massachusetts, architect Joseph T. Schiffer's design resembled a rectangular figure eight, with two square courtyards. The proposal by Hsiung, Johnson, Ruffing, Waterman, Fuge & Associates of Cambridge, for its part, featured a rectangular base of two floors (housing the public areas), with a square five-story office tower rising from one end, and the roof of the cavernous City Council chamber protruding from the opposite end.

Another finalist was Progressive Design Associates, a firm formed in the 1950s and based in St. Paul, Minnesota; the principals were Thomas N. Larson, Peter Woytuk, Thomas C. Van Housen, and George E. Rafferty. The firm had previously been a finalist in the FDR Memorial and Toronto City Hall competitions. Their Boston City Hall entry resembled a giant concrete donut. The outer ring lacked fenestration, with all windows opening onto an interior courtyard. The ovoid theme extended through the landscaping, where concentric curved steps led down to a yawning entrance cut into the base of the building. Straddling this entryway was a single level of offices, concavely recessed into the bulk of the building and forming one end of a complete oval stretching into the outer layer of the curved paving on the plaza.

The Kallmann, McKinnell and Knowles entry was the most daring of the eight, and also the most expressive (fig. 5). The design's bold form challenged the suave corporate aesthetic of several of the other entries. When seeing it next to the other finalists' entries, one is struck by the KMK design's remarkable geometric complexity, created by a combination of precast and cast-in-place concrete forms atop a redbrick base. The design also featured an exterior expression of the building's internal functions. For instance, the three categories of spaces prescribed by the program were evident in the exterior massing, with the "Heaviest Traffic Area" offices conspicuously located nearest the street, with access from all four sides. The offices of the municipal bureaucracy were placed at the top of the building in a honeycomb-like structure that gradually stepped outward, like an inverted ziggurat. Between these levels are the ceremonial spaces, housing the mayor and City Council, with massive protruding concrete hoods indicating their symbolic importance. Rather than hiding these various functions within a unified skin as other entrants had done, KMK pulled them to the outside and accentuated them, in an effort to make them obvious to citizens and also to make the city visible to the public officials working within.

Of the eight finalists, Mitchell, Giurgola and Vreeland, based in Philadelphia, was the most well established firm, having been formed in 1957, and having designed the Wright Brothers National Memorial Visitor Center in Kitty Hawk, North Carolina, that same year. Their Boston City Hall design was an evocative proposal that differed from the KMK design in approach and style but shared—albeit less brashly—its overall expressiveness. Mitchell, Giurgola and Vreeland proposed three interconnected slabs for the administrative offices, attached to a smaller block housing the City Council and the mayor under a stylized lantern. The principal difference here is that the Mitchell team prefigured later principles of contextualism.[57] That is to say that the architects separated the legislative and executive functions from those of the municipal bureaucracy to better complement the surrounding environment, with the form and scale of the slabs relating to the office buildings in the nearby financial district. The attached town hall–like structure was inspired by neighboring historic buildings, particularly Faneuil Hall and the Old State House, thus symbolically and formally tying together the new seat of government with these historic shrines

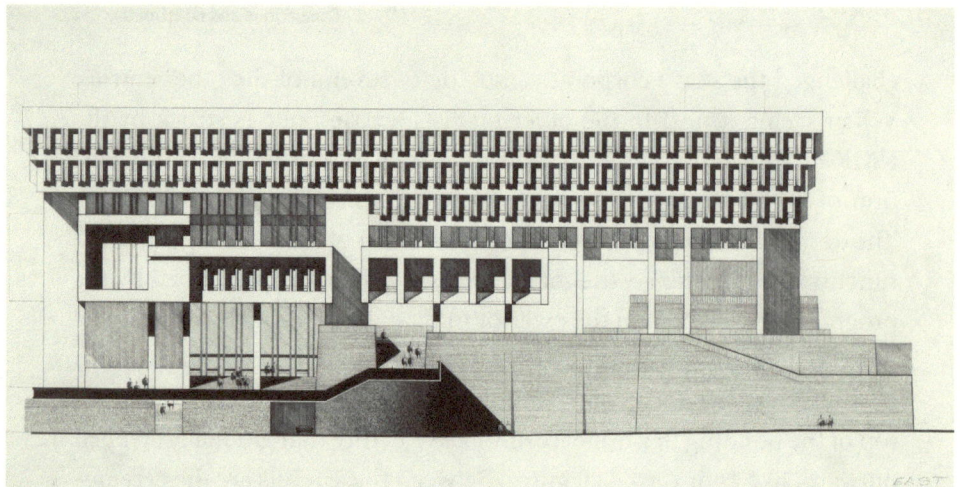

FIGURE 5. Final-stage competition drawing, Boston City Hall; Kallmann, McKinnell and Knowles (1962). Unlike the more typical glass-box modernist designs submitted by several other finalists, KMK proposed a lively geometric interplay of concrete forms atop a redbrick base. Courtesy of Historic New England.

of the American Revolution. While both the KMK and Mitchell, Giurgola and Vreeland plans abjured the abstract approach to design that was widespread in postwar architecture and evident in all of the other proposals, the firms went about doing so in philosophically different ways. Whereas the point of departure for Mitchell, Giurgola and Vreeland was the surrounding context, the KMK design, by contrast, took few cues from its historic neighbors and instead derived from the interior functions.

As architect Gary Wolf noted in an essay written for a 2008 exhibition of KMK's City Hall design drawings, "seeing the proposals of the other finalists reveals the imagination and appropriateness of Kallmann and McKinnell's design. The others tended to be bold, simplified forms, with the exception of that by Mitchell, Giurgola and Vreeland."[58] Other finalists did not challenge the prevailing tenets of modernism, as they adopted either superficially Miesian solutions or, in the case of Progressive Design Associates, a proposal reminiscent of Eero Saarinen's curvaceous aesthetic. Moreover, while many of the other finalists shared the KMK design's openness, extending the plaza to the interior spaces, they did so less compellingly. As critic Eric Larrabee sardonically pointed out, the other finalists sought to achieve this effect of openness "by trying to become a coliseum, a steel-and-glass box, or what might be the Globe Theatre."[59]

By dint of their abstract approaches to the programmatic requirements, the other finalists presented problems. The Progressive Design entry, for instance, with its lack of fenestration on the exterior of the oval, suggests insularity, as if city government were turning its back on the city—not exactly the symbolism Boston would have wanted in the aftermath of municipal political degradation during the first half of the twentieth century. The Bruck, Hsiung, Schiffer, Swack, and Wong proposals successfully adapted the aesthetic of corporate architecture to the purposes of city government, even though this did not express the various functions of the building. Instead, these entries are anonymous in composition, with rows of identical windows giving no clue to citizens outside which office belonged to the mayor and which to a stenographer. They might well have been office buildings in Anytown, USA. The Mitchell, Giurgola and Vreeland entry, which many regarded as the unofficial runner-up, generally avoids these pitfalls, but nevertheless lacks the spirited functional expressiveness of the KMK design.[60]

The jury was split on the first poll taken during the final round of judging, with the laymen and the architects coming to a "separate and independent conclusion," according to Government Center Commission chairman Robert Morgan. After further deliberation, however, the jury reached a unanimous decision, choosing the most revolutionary of the eight designs: the submission by Kallmann, McKinnell and Knowles. In their report, the jurors said that the winning design met four essential criteria: it was an "imposing symbol of city government at its best"; it handled "in a practical, efficient and flexible way the daily uses of various functions"; it related "in scale and character to the surrounding buildings and space (which will occupy Government Center)"; and it would "be within acceptable economic bounds."[61]

In addition to these functional and economic considerations, the jurors also noted that the design amply fulfilled the need for a structure that would relate to Boston's historic architecture while still heralding better days ahead. "This building is a keystone between the historic past and the brilliant future which is to come," the jurors wrote. "It takes thoughtful recognition of Faneuil Hall, Dock Square and Quincy Market, and yet is a powerful design in its own right."[62] The jury was enthusiastic in its selection, with William Wurster, at the final meeting of the jury, saying, "Mark my words, the world will beat a pathway to see this building," and another juror commenting, "It's reaching for the stars with a Boston flavor."[63] Ten years after the competition, juror Harold Hodgkinson still waxed lyrical about the building's qualities, proclaiming at a 1972 meeting of the Massachusetts Historical Society that the building was undeniably the "best civic center of our times."[64]

The winner was unveiled before an invited audience of four hundred people, including architects, city councilors, artists, public officials, and community members, at the Museum of Fine Arts at 4:00 p.m. on May 3, 1962. Before the unveiling at the MFA, Collins told the guests, "I am confident that the winning design, which neither you nor myself have seen, fulfills the requirements and will become a monument to the hundreds and thousands of Bostonians who believe in the future of their city."[65] Yet even Collins was not prepared for the radically unconventional form that lay beneath the sheet in front of him. Harold Hodgkinson later recalled that as Collins "lifted the curtain covering the mockup, surprise was evident in every line of his face, then amazement, and then executive composure. Mayor Collins said, 'It is exciting and monumental. I believe in this century it is a really historic event, a design that will live for many years.'"[66] Along similar lines, jury chairman William Wurster declared, "Because of the nature of this architectural competition, nationwide in scope, it could do for Boston, what L'Enfant did for Washington and Bulfinch did for your own city."[67] Looking back on the event several years later, Edward Logue recalled: "Finally the process ended and the announcement of the winning design was made. I shall never forget that day at the Museum of Fine Arts, when the mayor lifted the cover off the mockup. He looked at it, I looked at him, and I could almost hear him thinking to himself, 'My God, what's that?' But he didn't blink, because he believed in the process."[68]

By opting for the KMK design, the jury handed Boston the means by which to make an architectural as well as a political statement about the city government's being open, relatable, and forward-thinking. The design depicted Boston as neither beholden to the past nor trapped in the aesthetic abstraction of the present, but instead receptive to a cutting-edge building the likes of which America had never seen before, and which had the opportunity to reshape the field of architectural design. As a *Horizon* magazine headline aptly proclaimed, "Boston Chooses the Future."[69]

Citizens of Boston also recognized the unprecedented nature of the winning design and what its selection augured for the city's future. Joan Wood, who would become an architect in Boston, was a South End resident and local political activist at the time of the competition. She recalled being impressed by the distinctiveness of the KMK design: "I remember waiting for the unveiling, which was literally an unveiling—there was a sheet over the model that someone pulled off. People were really impressed. It was a *designed* building, which none of the other entries really was. And I remember being really excited about it."[70]

Similarly, attorney Herb Gleason, who later served as the City of Boston's corporation counsel under Mayor Kevin White in the 1970s, recalled at first being startled by the jury's choice. "When I saw the picture in the *Globe* of what had been chosen, I thought, my God, what is going on here," Gleason remembered. "But then I went to the exhibition of all the finalists at the MFA. Kallmann and McKinnell's was the only scheme that came even close to understanding Boston city government," in that it did not fall into "the trap of the dome." That is to say that the Hsiung team, for example, had placed the City Council in a prominently articulated space at one end of its rectangular design, and Mitchell, Giurgola and Vreeland's "town hall" council chamber separated the legislative branch from the executive and the municipal bureaucracy, which, according to Gleason, "presumed a city council grandly deliberating" in these spaces. KMK, by contrast, "realized that, in Boston, the city council was, if not peripheral, only a coordinate branch."[71]

Despite the encomiums of the jury, the mayor, and many prominent citizens, the winning design was controversial in other quarters. When it was unveiled at the MFA, newspapers reported an almost palpable sense of shock in the room, with some onlookers expressing approval while others (in the euphemistic words of the *Globe*) uttered "some remarks that were less kind."[72] The competition program stipulated that the city could opt not to build the winning design, and in fact eighteen local architects, led by William Stanley Parker, signed a petition urging the city to do exactly that. Likewise, a group organized the Citizens' Committee for a Bostonian City Hall to complain that the winning entry was "thoroughly lacking in composition, scale, and architectural feeling" and had no regard for "the background and environment in which it would exist."[73] Juror Harold Hodgkinson recalled that the controversy surrounding the jury's choice negatively affected his social life: "One highly respected architect refused to speak to me when I saw him at our club and told others that he would never speak to me again for my small part in this new City Hall."[74]

In the midst of this clamor of both praise and criticism, the Government Center Commission met to determine whether to build the winning design. As chairman of the commission, Robert Morgan took it upon himself to shepherd the design through the approval process. Hodgkinson believed that Morgan was up to this difficult task, explaining, "He had the rare quality of getting people to do what was wanted, making them enthusiastic over his leadership."[75] On June 28, 1962, the commission unanimously voted to build the KMK design. Mayor Collins signed the contract. As Ed Logue noted: "Boston then made a very important decision. The building was built as designed, and it works."[76] Edward Knowles later recalled: "We were so surprised when we won the competition, and we were flabbergasted to see that it was going to be built. There are so many competitions in which the winner never saw the light of day."[77]

Legacy of the Competition

Whereas Boston City Hall itself remains controversial, the 1962 competition is generally regarded as an unqualified success with far-reaching beneficial outcomes. Even erstwhile opponent of the competition Nelson Aldrich eventually came to praise the process, writing in the *Boston Globe*, "I feel that the competition itself was extremely successful in that it produced more than the usual number of highly successful designs."[78]

Nearly all of the finalists were relatively unknown and unproven at the time of the competition yet were quickly raised to national prominence. The most obvious benefits went to the winning architects themselves. The process took two Columbia University professors—Kallmann and McKinnell—who had never designed a building in their own names, and almost overnight turned them into practicing architects of international renown. As Ada Louise Huxtable noted: "It is as certain as politics and taxes that without the national competition that was held for this building nothing like it would have been designed or constructed. Mr. Kallmann and Mr. McKinnell were young and unknown as architects when they won. The usual route of public building commissions is through political patronage or to familiar, established names."[79]

Huxtable's reference to political patronage touches on another aspect of the competition's success. The process—unbiased, transparent, nationally open—reflected the political ideals of New Boston leaders such as Hynes and Collins and conspicuously broke with the crooked, nepotistic backroom politics of the Curley era. In this way, the competition benefited the city by achieving the goals that Collins, Logue, and Morgan had set for it. The size of the competition—with 256 entries from across the country—speaks to the national attention that the competition brought to the civic resurgence that was taking place in Boston. There was no speculation in the press about any corruption, cronyism, or mishandling of the competition process. Even those who were displeased with the result could not argue that the process had been unethical or unfair. Also, the inclusion of prominent business leaders on the jury led to greater trust between the business community and the Collins administration. The praise of these respected citizens also helped to win wide-ranging (though, admittedly, far from unanimous) public support for the winning design.

Moreover, the process helped to dispel the reputation for wastefulness and unreliability that had long plagued architectural competitions. As Hélène Lipstadt asserted, it "restored the competition process to respect as a successful means of selecting an architect."[80] After winning the design contest, Kallmann and McKinnell expressed hope that their success would encourage the use of competitions elsewhere, as well as compel more clients to follow through on constructing the winning designs.[81]

These hopes were soon realized. Half a century had passed between the San Francisco and Boston City Hall contests without an open competition for a major civic building in America, but the years after the Boston contest saw several high-profile competitions that in many cases used the Boston City Hall process as a model. These included competitions in Boston itself (such as for the Boston Architectural Center, 1963; Copley Square, 1966; and Spectacle Island, 1983), as well as across the United States (including the AIA Headquarters in Washington, D.C., 1964; the University of California, Berkeley, Arts Center, 1965; and civic centers in four neighboring cities in California: Los Gatos, 1963; Fremont, 1966; Santa Rosa, 1966; and Fairfield, 1967). Whereas Richard Upjohn, the first president of the AIA, had once claimed that competitions had brought "evil, and only evil, to the profession," the proliferation of competitions after Boston City Hall suggests that these other communities and organizations viewed the Boston model a triumph.[82]

Finally, the competition benefited the architectural profession—particularly younger architects throughout the world—by publicizing the unconventional ideas of the winning firm. KMK's revolutionary architectural philosophy would have far-reaching consequences throughout the profession. By offering newer firms a chance to test and spread their ideas, and to take on challenging problems of a scale and type they would not ordinarily encounter in their daily practice, the competition helped to give a sense of legitimacy to architectural concepts that otherwise might never have made it out of academic journals and into built form. Had the city commissioned an established firm for the project rather than relying on the open competition, it is doubtful that the changes in architecture that eventually would be wrought by the KMK design would have taken place so swiftly, if they occurred at all.

Among those seemingly converted to Brutalism by the KMK design was the competition juror Walter Netsch. Netsch had developed an architectural aesthetic he called "field theory," through which he hoped to escape "the boredom of the box" by rotating square shapes into complex geometrical assemblies radiating from a central core.[83] He demonstrated the concept in his Brutalist design for the University of Illinois, Chicago Circle Campus (1963–1968), which distinctly echoes the complex geometries cast in concrete in Boston City Hall—something not seen in Netsch's pre-1962 designs, such as the glass-and-metal box of the Inland Steel Building and the refined aluminum-clad Cadet Chapel. Netsch himself has been credited with breaking "from the boxy modernism of the 1950s and 1960s" and anticipating "the unorthodox, computer-generated shapes of such contemporary architects as Peter Eisenman of New York City and Frank Gehry of Los Angeles."[84] It is impossible to know whether he would have embraced Brutalism on his own without the Boston competition, but the general openness to the style that emerged throughout the country after the competition surely made Netsch's conversion to a concrete aesthetic more palatable to his clients.

Just as significant as the process, however, was the city's courage in following through with the construction of the winning design. Walter Muir Whitehill, the eminent Boston historian who served as director of the venerable Boston Athenaeum at the time of the competition, praised the city's decision, remarking: "Often in the past, a winning design in competition has been laid aside, unused. This one was promptly executed."[85] Similarly, a *Horizon* magazine article claimed that Boston, "a city, hitherto anything but notorious for civic incorruptibility, determined to do the right thing and, more important still, to carry through on it." Thus, the article predicted that the Boston competition "will stand for some time as a model of responsible civic conduct."[86] Elizabeth Padjen, local architect and former editor of *ArchitectureBoston*, also commented on this remarkable feat, noting in 2005: "The jurors were unanimous in their selection. The business community bought into it unanimously. And what is even more amazing, the building was built exactly as it was presented in the competition. Clearly, something was happening in the city—as we know from our own recent experience, illustrious juries and commissions don't guarantee results."[87]

Architect Tad Stahl, meanwhile, credited those in charge of the competition with this success, saying: "My sense is that things were organized quietly. With a few key civic leaders, John Collins managed to pull together a group that had influence and authority. I give Collins a lot of credit for opening up the city and making it possible for people to imagine things that couldn't be done in a really corrupt environment."[88]

While the competition in many ways could have been characterized as a triumph when the Government Center Commission unanimously voted to build the winning design, the real evaluation of its success would not be possible until the building opened. For one thing, the new City Hall was still far from a fait accompli; any number of problems might still have kept the building from completion. Moreover, a vocal segment of Boston's population was unhappy with the winning design's cutting-edge style. Could such a controversial building—even with the support of so many leading citizens and politicians—really effect the positive change that the city so desperately needed? While the competition had been successful on many levels, a comprehensive assessment of both the process and the winning design would have to wait.

Construction

Soon after winning the competition, Kallmann and McKinnell took leaves of absence from Columbia University and relocated to Boston, where they could supervise the development of working drawings and, subsequently, construction of Boston City Hall. Edward Knowles maintained his residence in New York City, but he commuted frequently to Boston.[89] The City Hall competition program stipulated that if the winning design came from an architect not licensed in Massachusetts, the winner would need to collaborate with a local architect during construction.[90] After considering several Boston-based firms, KMK chose Campbell, Aldrich & Nulty.[91] According to Nelson Aldrich, KMK came to him because he was the only local architect who had appeared in print in favor of the building. (Just after the competition, he had written an opinion piece in the *Globe* praising the KMK design.)[92] Aldrich later recalled his role in the collaboration, and his response to the invitation:

And so I said, "Sure, I'd be delighted . . . but I must have the freedom to set up the office, and if I'm going to be responsible for the building, then I must have a good deal of say about it. But I do admire the building, and I think I'm in the same spirit that you guys are about the building." And as it turned out, I didn't—the only thing I added to the design was really a subtraction inasmuch as I said—when we found out that it was a million dollars over budget when we got it designed, I said, well, the only thing to do is to knock four inches off the module. And that's what we did. And we got the million dollars back just by doing that. Absolutely the same plan, but four inches less—a module of three feet four inches.[93]

The Kallmann, McKinnell and Knowles team also formed a partnership with LeMessurier Associates as the structural engineer of New City Hall. In addition to supervising the complicated construction of precast and cast-in-place concrete forms, LeMessurier helped the team develop the combination of precast Vierendeel trusses and paired fins that allowed for the integration of structure and mechanical systems throughout the building.[94] The Vierendeel truss, developed by the Belgian engineer Arthur Vierendeel in 1896, uses rectangular rather than triangular openings. In New City Hall, mechanical, electrical, and ventilation infrastructure (such as ductwork) pass through the openings in the trusses. During the design and construction process, KMK also received many offers of assistance from local architectural students. Gerhard Kallmann remarked in a 1962 interview that it would be impossible to use all of the talent available.[95] Nevertheless, the widespread interest among architecture students speaks to the attention that a younger generation of architects was paying to one of the most consequential projects in the world at the time.

Once the team of architects and engineers for New City Hall had set up their base of operations on Boylston Street, they began drafting the construction drawings. On June 27, 1962, the Government Center Commission unanimously voted in favor of constructing the KMK design and asked John Collins to approve an $800,000 contract for the building. The commission set a timeline calling for complete preliminary drawings by December 1, 1962, with final drawings due by August 1, 1963. This initial schedule slated construction of the foundation to begin in June 1963, with construction of the superstructure to begin by October 15, 1963.[96]

In the months before the ground-breaking ceremony, KMK and their team were busy preparing final versions of the plans. When interviewed by the *Globe* in November 1962, Kallmann noted that while they had made several changes to the original design, "none can be termed major."[97] The most significant alteration was widening the north entrance facing the federal building to provide more direct access to the interior of New City Hall from that approach. In addition, Kallmann told the reporter that the City Hall team was working closely with architects of the federal building to create a more integral relationship between City Hall Plaza and the landscaping around the federal building. The team also added a large staircase on the southeast side of City Hall (descending toward Congress Street) to improve access between City Hall Plaza and Faneuil Hall. These minor alterations show the architects working to integrate City Hall and the plaza with the surrounding structures and spaces—not only the federal building and other components of the new Government Center but also Faneuil Hall and Dock Square. Additionally, at the request of Mayor Collins, a polio survivor who was confined to a wheelchair, the architects focused on making the design more accommodating to handicapped people, with all public areas of the building accessible by ramps. As a result, the building would win the AIA Bartlett Award for Handicapped-Accessible Design in 1969.

Despite the assiduous work of the architects during the winter and spring of 1963, construction hit a political snag when the City Council twice rejected the overall Government Center plan. The principal objections were not leveled at the design per se; rather, a group of five councilors accused BRA administrator Edward Logue of favoring developer Cabot, Cabot & Forbes for the office tower at Parcel 8, which would house the New England Merchants Bank, among other tenants. Logue and Collins quickly sought a way around the City Council roadblock. While under normal federal guidelines, construction on any Government Center building would have to wait until the council approved the overall plan, Collins and Logue appealed to the federal government for "early disposition" in the case of City Hall as well as the private office building at One Center Plaza. This would allow construction on these buildings to begin, even without formal City Council approval of Government Center. The City Council, to prove that its objections stemmed from perceived political favoritism in the case of Parcel 8—and not the design of City Hall—recorded itself as being in favor of early disposition for City Hall (although not for One Center Plaza). Collins flew to Washington, D.C., in August 1963 to press the case, and he was successful, allowing for construction to begin the following month.[98]

The ground-breaking ceremony for New City Hall took place on September 18, 1963, with over one thousand people in attendance—from civic dignitaries to neighborhood representatives to ordinary citizens (fig. 6). It was an auspicious occasion for the New Boston. Governor Endicott Peabody remarked that the construction of New City Hall was a dream coming true and deemed it "a pleasure and a privilege to be governor in these exciting times."[99] Mayor Collins delivered an address in which he explained that New City Hall's real significance would be as "a symbol of civic rebirth." That said, his speech did not focus solely on the future; rather, he discussed at length the new building in the context of the city's rich history. "Never let us forget," Collins exclaimed, "however enthusiastically we may speak of the New Boston, that this New Boston is firmly rooted in the three-hundred and thirty-three years that lie behind us in the Old Boston." In a rousing appeal to the many constituencies attending the ceremony, Collins declared:

> Boston is not content to sit still and dream of the day when this city was supreme in the arts, in medicine and the sciences, in education and commerce. The brave captains and seamen who set sail not so very far from this spot where we stand now to pioneer our nation's commerce with the Indies and with China will be the forerunners of today's Bostonians who by their engineering and scientific ability help guide our astronauts through the dark reaches of outer space. Great days are behind us. But even greater days are ahead. The patriots who have watered the streets of this city with their blood, the patriots who in nearby Faneuil Hall created the bright climate of independence in what is aptly called the "Cradle of Liberty," would be proud if they could know that Bostonians have not

> lost their capacity for great deeds and bold planning. And as good an example as any is perhaps this City Hall for which we are about to break ground. We have dared to hold a national competition and we have dared to choose a building of great modern design. We have dared to recreate the center of our city in a government center that has few equals in this country—or abroad—for beauty of design and breadth of concept. We have dared to say that—as Boston was once—so Boston will be again—a city prosperous, progressive, and preeminent.[100]

Following these remarks, Collins invited everyone attending the ceremony to pick up a shovel and help with the ground breaking, symbolizing that the new City Hall would belong not to the municipal government but rather to all Bostonians. Because of the number of guests, the *Globe* reported, "confusion took over" as citizens made their way forward to help. Nevertheless, many citizens did get to turn over some of the earth for the foundation of the building.[101]

After the ceremony, construction began in earnest on the foundation, with the expectation that work on the superstructure would start the following March.[102] By mid-May 1964, however, construction was not yet under way on the superstructure, and the timetable hit a further snag when the three bids for the project exceeded the Government Center Commission's budget by between $3.1 million and $5.6 million. The commission had $16.8 million left of the original $20 million bond issue from 1958, yet the lowest bid, from the J. W. Bateson Company of Dallas, came in at $19,925,000. Additionally, Vappi & Co. of Cambridge bid $20,949,000, and the Perini Corporation of Framingham bid $22,483,000.[103] The high bids reflected the rising cost of materials and the complexity and novelty of the precast and cast-in-place concrete.[104]

The commission considered three options: asking the architects to make further cuts to the building design, reopening the bidding, or asking the City Council and the state legislature for a larger appropriation. The commission, recognizing that the architects had already "pulled in" as much as possible, was reluctant to ask for further changes. It also was wary of reopening the bidding for fear that this would cause further delays and might not elicit lower bids. Thus the commission, with

FIGURE 6. Governor Peabody, Mayor Collins, and Cardinal Cushing at the ground breaking for New City Hall (1963). Courtesy of the Boston Public Library Print Department, Boston Pictorial Archive.

the blessing of Mayor Collins, requested additional funding from the legislature. Collins justified his request by pointing out that construction costs had risen yearly between 3 and 3.5 percent since the original 1958 bond issue.[105]

The following week, Government Center Commission chairman Robert Morgan announced that the mayor would send special legislation to the General Court that would approve the city's extra borrowing. Before submitting the bill, though, the mayor asked the City Council to support it. Although the mayor can submit legislation at any time, Collins wanted the added force of City Council approval to get the measure enacted before the legislature's summer recess.[106] The council eventually approved the measure, despite vocal opposition from councilors William Foley and Katherine Craven, who publicly vilified the

Government Center Commission for "wasting the taxpayers' money."[107] Following the City Council vote, the legislature approved the bill, and the Government Center Commission awarded the contract for construction to J. W. Bateson, which had earlier won the contract for constructing the federal building next door.

The new City Hall building was not the only feature of the KMK design experiencing escalating costs. In May 1965, the BRA approved plans for the plaza at $4.5 million—almost twice the original estimated cost. At this stage, the plaza design included several features that eventually, for economic reasons, would be cut: a walkway over Congress Street connecting City Hall Plaza and Faneuil Hall, as well as an outdoor skating rink in front of Faneuil Hall. Ed Logue explained that the forty-foot-by-forty-foot rink, which would have served as a reflecting pool in the summer, was intended to make the Government Center area "as lively as possible."[108]

In mid-May 1965, a year after the budget crisis, work on the superstructure finally began, after months of pile-driving and capping, as well as pouring of concrete for the foundation floors and footings. Structural steel had been placed over the Washington Street subway tunnel to support the new City Hall above it. Bateson brought in two tower cranes from France, which the company claimed were among the biggest made anywhere in the world and could handle the unusually heavy loads of concrete.[109]

Elsewhere in the Government Center area, construction of One Center Plaza (the private office building across Cambridge Street from City Hall) was proceeding ahead of schedule; work on the federal building resumed after a delay brought about by troubles fitting the precast panels; bids were being solicited for the Health, Welfare and Education Service Center; and developer Cabot, Cabot & Forbes was preparing to demolish an existing building at 10 State Street to begin construction of the office tower on Parcel 8.[110] Thus, as City Hall began to rise from a gaping hole in the ground, development of the New Boston seemed to be proceeding apace.

By February 20, 1966, the *Globe* could proclaim that construction had reached its midpoint.[111] The brick lower levels of the "mound" were completed, and the contractor was beginning work on the cast-in-place concrete of the upper levels. At this juncture, architect Joseph Eldredge offered a preliminary assessment of the design in the *Globe,* noting that the many different views from the building (of the waterfront, Washington Street, and Beacon Hill) served to "justify the original Government Center planning concept, the competition program requirement, and the premise of the winning architectural solution: that City Hall relate intimately with the fabric of the city around it." Eldredge also discussed a more practical point of construction: the detailed and sometimes complicated shaping of concrete forms. "The intricate but brilliantly organized complex of levels and spaces, not to mention the high standards of workmanship required for the pre-cast and cast-in-place concrete, would have been no small challenge to the organizational skill of any general contractor," Eldredge wrote. "The ingenious double floor system of pre-cast concrete girders and criss-cross ceiling beams took time to perfect. Those carefully formed and painstakingly poured massive concrete columns didn't just happen."[112] By the end of the year, the distinctive shape of the building's upper levels was becoming clear. In a letter to Gerhard Kallmann, Logue wrote: "The City Hall is magnificent! The workmanship is superb. It is the most exciting public building I have seen since the Red Fort [in Delhi]. Everybody connected with it is to be congratulated."[113]

The first public tour of the building was given to visiting mayors and other officials from across the country in July 1967 as the exterior was nearing completion. The response from these dignitaries was overwhelmingly positive. William Wheaton, dean of environmental design at the University of California, Berkeley, called it "the most exciting city hall built in the United States in the last 50 years." J. L. Renck, a city councilman from Riverside, California, said, "I just wonder why they didn't build it sooner." Mayor W. G. Roe, of West Plains, Missouri, praised the quality of construction, adding: "I'm a contractor and I can tell you that this is real good work. This concrete and structural steel is hard to handle and they've done a fine job with it."[114]

By December 1967, the exterior of the superstructure was nearly complete; the interior, however, was far from finished. Although the building was still unheated and unfurnished, John Collins, with only two weeks remaining before his successor was sworn in, moved into the mayor's office on December 18. Collins had intended to occupy the new building for the entire last year of his term, but persistent construction delays made this impossible.[115] Nevertheless, Collins made the most of his nine working days in the new building, hosting a "Boston Tea Party" for two thousand guests: local, state, and national dignitaries, as well as people who had worked with him to plan the New Boston during his eight years in office. This was the first time that many of these people had had an opportunity to see inside what a beaming Collins called "the most exciting public building in America," and they responded with near-unanimous praise. Governor John A. Volpe, "speaking as an old construction man," lauded the concrete work. "You don't grasp it the first time you see it," the governor told the *Globe*. "It's different, but there is no doubt it's an attraction for Boston." Likewise, former city councilor Katherine Craven—initially a vocal opponent of urban renewal—said: "It's beautiful. I hope [government officials] are as successful here as in the old one."[116]

Ed Logue, who had by this time resigned from the BRA, stated that the building would "do a lot for the public image of Boston."[117] Logue had just run unsuccessfully for mayor, losing to Kevin White. He later explained:

> My special problem, my Achilles heel, was the new City Hall itself, with its magnificent spread of B.R.A. offices on the top floor and the particularly exciting space for the mayor on the fifth floor. In 1967 I looked at it all—the city and where we were, and where we had to go, and who would be in my charge—and before the building was even occupied I attempted my leap from the top floor to the fifth floor. And that is how my seven years in Boston came to an end.[118]

Construction delays continued to push back the official opening date. In August 1967, Gerhard Kallmann declared that the major construction problems were over and predicted the building would be finished by early 1968.[119] Government Center Commission chairman Robert

Morgan told the Boston City Council that city agencies could expect to begin moving in by March 1, 1968.[120] Four months later, the completion target was pushed back to May or June 1968.[121] Actually, the first municipal departments would not begin moving until November 1968.

The frequent delays, owing both to political and budgetary hurdles as well as practical construction challenges, did nothing to diminish the eagerness among Bostonians for City Hall's opening. As the building neared completion, a *Globe* editorial noted that while New City Hall had taken five years to build, it had taken Phidias nine years to construct the Parthenon and five more to complete the decorations. "His work in Athens stands as a symbol of democracy and the apogee of classical architecture," the *Globe* proclaimed. The editorial drew particular attention to the prevalence of exposed concrete in New City Hall, noting that "apart from the brickwork, the casual viewer is struck by the use of poured concrete. It has been specially cleaned and treated, and is economical. It looks like soft, gray-tinted boards, from the lines of the wooden forms in which it was poured. In other places, it has assumed the patterns of the plywood that had rested against it. Anyway, it is intriguing and attractive."[122]

One month later, as the first city agencies were moving into the building, the new mayor, Kevin White, treated one hundred members of the press to a preview tour. White and his aides, as well as Gerhard Kallmann, showed the reporters around the building. The *Globe* reported that "the esthetic verdict was almost unanimous. It is one of New Boston's star attractions."[123] Likewise, the *Globe's* society editor, Marjorie Sherman, offered a glowing review of the new City Hall's interior, praising the views, the materials, and the clear division of services.[124]

The Government Center Commission had asked the City Council in August 1967 for $1 million to furnish the building, pushing the total price tag up to $26 million.[125] In choosing furnishings, the architects and interior designers (I.S.D., Inc., of New York) sought to keep the colors "as calm, quiet as possible," according to Michael McKinnell. "In an office you don't want background distractions from materials."[126]

Seven years after the Boston City Hall competition, the building was finally ready for its formal dedication on February 10, 1969. "It will be a party of the people, by the people, and for the people of Boston," the *Globe* proclaimed, with "everybody—from top dignitaries to school children" having been invited by "the proud host," Mayor Kevin H. White.[127] The official dedication took place before such dignitaries as Senator Edward Kennedy, Governor Francis Sargent, and Richard Cardinal Cushing, followed by a luncheon with 505 invited guests and strolling violinists. At night, there was a formal party featuring a concert by the Boston Pops under Arthur Fiedler, at which the Pops played Sir Edward Elgar's "Pomp and Circumstance."[128]

In addition to the dedication ceremony, the weeklong opening celebration brought more than forty thousand people to tour the building and watch performing groups, including the police and fire department bands, the Boston Ballet, and a bagpiper. The festivities also included art exhibits, light shows, and movies.[129] Different groups were invited to explore the building each day of the gala week. The first day was for city and county employees and their families, the second day for construction workers who helped to build the new City Hall and their families.[130] Next came an open house for the general public, complete with refreshments and a jazz band, followed by "Boston Youth Day," with fifteen hundred schoolchildren touring the building. Then the mayor welcomed the city's senior citizens for tours and music from glee clubs, bands, and a strolling accordionist. A champagne gala was the grand finale to the opening week, with two thousand Bostonians attending. The attire for the event was black tie (which, the *Globe* mentioned, "seemed to be the only appropriate dress for such an impressive building").[131]

Throughout the week, attendees marveled at the new building. "I never thought we'd have a City Hall quite like this," said one resident attending the black-tie gala, while another woman, peeking into the new city workers' quarters, remarked, "They have very nice offices, don't they."[132] These myriad events prompted the *Globe* to claim that the new City Hall was "natural as a civic center. . . . The point which was made abundantly clear by the performances during the week was that the building not only can serve extraordinary public functions but practically demands that it be put to this use."[133]

Letters of congratulation poured in to the KMK office from around the country. One of McKinnell's former students from Columbia raved, "It is truly a *Great* building."[134] Juror Walter Netsch wrote: "If it hadn't been for the snow, I would have been in Boston because I wanted to 1) see the building again on the eventful day and 2) congratulate the three of you. I was honored to serve on the Jury, and I am excited about the result!"[135] Writing from New York City, Ed Logue told Kallmann and McKinnell: "It is magnificent. It is going to do a lot for the tone of city government, and a lot for Boston's image of itself. I hope you will have many more such opportunities."[136]

Thus, after more than a decade of planning, a yearlong competition, another year of design, and five years of construction, Boston's New City Hall enjoyed an auspicious opening. Neither the construction delays and cost overruns of the past, nor the nascent controversy that would surround the building in the future, were evident as Mayor Kevin White proclaimed that New City Hall "symbolizes a fresh concern with the future of urban America, and a new beginning toward resolution of its conflicts and problems. . . . May this dedication mark a new commitment, and the strength of this City Hall be the measure of our determination to succeed."[137]

CHAPTER 3

The New City Hall Design

As soon as John Collins lifted a sheet and revealed the model of the winning Boston City Hall design, popular theories emerged about the inspiration for its unconventional form. One myth holds that the architects were influenced by the image of the Lincoln Memorial on the back of a penny, turned upside down.[1] When the building opened in 1969, a cab driver suggested to *New York Times* architecture critic Ada Louise Huxtable that it was modeled on Gothic cathedrals.[2] More recently, former Boston University president John Silber quipped that the idea for City Hall came from "a drunk Mayan architect" who built a ziggurat upside down.[3] In fact, the building responded to a host of architectural sources as seemingly disparate as Gridley James Fox Bryant's warehouse buildings along the Boston waterfront, Le Corbusier's government complex at Chandigarh, and the ancient Minoan palace at Knossos. It also embodied distinct political ideals that were popular in the early 1960s.

This is not to suggest, however, that City Hall was derivative or merely a pastiche of other buildings; on the contrary, the design grew out of the specific location, political circumstances, and functional requirements set forth in the Boston City Hall competition program. In this way, Boston City Hall reflected a distinctive and revolutionary design philosophy. By amalgamating a variety of architectural principles, KMK forged a new civic monumentality—an authentically modern building that nevertheless took into consideration both history and context—which at once represented a bold evolutionary step in modern architecture and embodied the heroic spirit of contemporary politics.

The Architects

Gerhard M. Kallmann, N. Michael McKinnell, and Edward F. Knowles might seem an unlikely trio to have won a significant national competition for a major public building. Kallmann and McKinnell were not registered architects, and neither had previously designed a building in his own name. While Knowles had formed a small architectural practice in New York City, he had never taken on a project of this magnitude and importance. Each of these men, however, brought a unique set of skills, experiences, and ideals to the project, and together they produced a design that was remarkably well suited to the needs of the Government Center Commission.

Gerhard Kallmann was born in Berlin in 1915. He began studying law at Humboldt University in 1932. After witnessing the early atrocities of the Nazis' rise to power, Kallmann decided to emigrate—first to the home of a family friend in Vienna in 1934 and subsequently to London a year later.[4] Because Kallmann's three semesters of German legal studies would be of little practical use in England, he decided to change his career path and enroll in the Architectural Association in London, where he studied from 1936 to 1941. In 1948, with the hope of better career prospects in the booming postwar American economy, he moved to the United States, where he taught at the Chicago Institute of Design, Cooper Union, Cornell, Yale, and Washington University in Saint Louis. In 1954 he joined the design faculty of the Columbia University School of Architecture. It was while at Columbia that Kallmann met Michael McKinnell.

Born in Manchester, England, in 1935, McKinnell studied architecture at Manchester University. (Significantly, one of McKinnell's teachers at Manchester was Peter Collins, an architect and architectural historian who was a proponent of modernist concrete architecture.) After graduating, McKinnell taught at Manchester for a year, then moved to the United States for graduate work at Columbia. He had traveled extensively throughout Europe and was briefly associated with three architectural firms: Percival Goodman (in the FDR Memorial competition), Carson, Lundin & Shaw, and Charles R. Colbert.[5]

McKinnell was serving as Kallmann's graduate assistant when they decided to start their own architectural firm in order to put into practice the myriad architectural ideas they had developed in their design studios at Columbia.[6] To jump-start their efforts to establish a new firm from scratch, they decided they would need to win a competition.[7] This would give them both the practical experience and the reputation necessary to garner future commissions. Fortuitously, a short time later the Boston City Hall competition was announced, and Kallmann and McKinnell began planning their entry.

Since neither Kallmann nor McKinnell was a registered architect (a requirement for entering the competition), they formed a partnership with Kallmann's friend Edward F. Knowles. As Knowles later explained, "Gerhard and Michael were teaching at Columbia, and Gerhard was an old friend of mine, and we were very close and actually had worked together on a couple of smaller projects. They decided that it was a great competition to go into and would I be interested. And I said, of course!"[8]

Knowles was born in Brooklyn in 1929 and earned a degree in architecture from the Pratt Institute in 1951. He then worked for several firms, including Philip Johnson, Edward Larrabee Barnes, and Unger & Unger. At the time of the Boston City Hall competition, Knowles was teaching at Cooper Union and Columbia University, and he had his own architectural practice in New York City. He had previously restored several old theaters, and he also was working with the New York City municipal government and parks department on smaller projects. In addition, with Ernest J. Kump Associates, Knowles had designed buildings for Pine Manor Junior College in Chestnut Hill, Massachusetts. The Boston City Hall competition would be much larger than any of these previous projects.[9]

Although all three men worked together on the competition entry, the design concept originated with Kallmann and McKinnell. "The main thrust was from Gerhard and Michael," Knowles confirmed. "My function at the earlier stages was to sit in on things and comment on things, but the thrust for the design was from Gerhard and Michael."[10] Thus the building reflects Kallmann and McKinnell's design philosophy, which they had developed during their academic careers.

Brutalism and Action Architecture

Even before winning the Boston City Hall competition, Gerhard Kallmann achieved international renown as an architectural theorist, having lectured and published widely. His writings from the 1940s and 1950s reveal the development of ideals that eventually would become manifest in physical form in Boston City Hall. For instance, soon after coming to the United States, Kallmann participated in a 1948 symposium at the Museum of Modern Art in New York City titled "What Is Happening to Modern Architecture?" In his address to the symposium, Kallmann expressed what might well be considered his nascent architectural philosophy. Even at this early juncture, fully a decade and a half before the City Hall competition, we can identify key aspects of Kallmann's approach to design: form that expresses a building's inherent functions (rather than architecture as an envelope), distinct modernism (as opposed to retrograde historicism or revivalism), and a keen regard for how people experience architecture physically and psychologically.

Kallmann praised, for example, the concern for humanism in the new design for the Municipal Hospital in Zurich as an example of a building in which the "architectural conception at all times is subordinated to the psychological requirements of the patients." This expressive, humanistic approach was at odds with the apparent trajectory of mainstream modernism, which had prioritized stylistic and aesthetic concerns (such as designing a sleek glass box for any project) over functional, programmatic, and social imperatives.[11]

The fact that MoMA hosted this symposium made clear that modern architecture was approaching a crisis of conviction. By the late 1950s, divisions among modern architects had grown more defined and more profound. In the early postwar years, European émigrés such as Walter Gropius, José Luis Sert, Marcel Breuer, and Pietro Belluschi in Boston, and Mies van der Rohe in Chicago, had brought modernism into the American mainstream. There was, however, an emerging reaction among a younger generation of architects against this orthodoxy. In particular, unease with the supposed cold rationalism of modernist approaches led some to call for a greater emphasis on humanism, expressionism, and even ideals that were anathema to modernists, such as historicism and monumentality.

In this turbulent context, the inchoate ideals that Kallmann touched on at the MoMA symposium coalesced into a singular, cogent architectural philosophy, for which he coined a new term: "Action Architecture." Kallmann saw modern architecture in 1960 at a crossroads, at a time when its pioneers—once revolutionaries—had been accepted as the mainstream. "Nothing would be easier," Kallmann wrote, "than to settle down and develop, in elegant variations, the many inventions in technology and form proliferated by the modern movement in its first unprecedented burst of creativity."[12] Indeed, this seemed to be happening already. Although he did not name any specific firms or buildings, he appeared to have in mind architects such as Emery Roth and Wallace Harrison, as well as lesser-known designers, who had adopted the glass box as their model and reproduced it as a sort of universal aesthetic—a solution to all manner of architectural problems in all locations.

In opposing this trend, Kallmann wrote that for "advanced spirits" it was essential "to move out of the shadow that falls on epigoni."[13] Kallmann railed against architects who created "vacuous decorated shells rather than buildings."[14] He also bemoaned architecture of the "premeditated image"—buildings that derived from a slavish commitment to a preconceived aesthetic rather than from their specific location and function, expressing displeasure with "large-scale flexible spaces of universal structure [that] have added new problems of expression. The impassive countenance, the uncommunicative aspect of our buildings causes a loss of individual reference to environment."[15] At the same time, however, sculpturally dramatic, purely formal architecture was not the ideal that Kallmann was seeking. Buildings should not, he wrote, be "carved or molded into some fantastic shape which the creator had in mind from the start, but rather shape is allowed to grow out of the manner of structuring, usually complex and composite."[16]

As Kallmann evaluated the state of modern architecture in the late 1950s, he saw the greatest hope for salvation in the younger generation. One movement in particular to which Kallmann drew attention in his writing was the New Brutalism. This group, Kallmann believed, was the most spontaneous in its designs and the most opposed to the premeditated image.[17]

New Brutalism (eventually the "New" would be dropped) sprang from and reacted to postwar modernism. The word itself is generally thought to have been derived from the French term *béton brut,* meaning raw—exposed—concrete. Le Corbusier, in his later years, designed a number of buildings generally regarded as proto-Brutalist, including the government complex at Chandigarh in northern India, the Unité d'Habitation housing complex in Marseille, and the monastery Sainte Marie de La Tourette near Lyon. In fact, some scholars have credited Le Corbusier with providing the impetus for the movement.[18]

Influenced by the Swiss master's later works, a group of young architects working in post–World War II Britain both codified and popularized the new aesthetic. Architects such as Peter and Alison Smithson, Ernö Goldfinger, James Stirling, and Sir Basil Spence regarded concrete as an ideal material for rebuilding the country, which had been so heavily damaged in the war. They also saw it as reflecting the toughness of the British character and symbolizing permanence, durability, and strength during the anxious years of the Cold War.

But the New Brutalism was about more than the use of concrete. Although that is the material most commonly identified with the style, it is worth noting that Brutalist principles can be applied to buildings of almost any materials, provided those materials (and the buildings' functions) are expressed *honestly*. In other words, a steel frame would not be covered up and prettified behind an anonymous glass curtain wall; instead, the structure, the method of construction, and the specific program would be revealed and even accentuated.

The Smithsons' Hunstanton School (1954), for example, which many regard as the first truly Brutalist building, appears at first blush more Miesian than Corbusian, with a steel frame and glass and brick infill. But in contrast to the Miesian philosophy of refinement in every last detail, the materials of the Smithson building are deliberately left crude. Architecture critic Reyner Banham suggested that the materials were expressed "as found," while the internal space dictated the external appearance of the building (unlike with much modern architecture, which packaged a variety of functions within a unified envelope). For Banham, this signified the emergence of a moral stance that spoke to the new style's ethical philosophy.[19] In other words, the Brutalists were making a contemporary philosophical statement. They were trying not only to convey an authenticity of materials and forms, but also (and perhaps more important) to create an architectural expression of the imperfectability of man, the human condition, and the postwar reality.

For this reason, many Brutalist architects, such as the Smithsons, admired the Art Brut of painter Jean Dubuffet, and the works of sculptor Eduardo Paolozzi and photographer Nigel Henderson—artists who were trying to capture and communicate the rough grain of modern urban life in a new art.[20] The architects saw in these works evidence of a new aesthetic blending change, coarseness, and the primitive.[21] The rational models of the International Style were anathema to them. For Kallmann, this new architecture embraced "violence, anti-rationality, and non-direction systematically pursued"—concepts that were like mother's milk to the *enfants terribles* who obstreperously opposed the rationalism of the previous generation of modern architecture.[22] As the young Peter Smithson put it, they were seeking to create an environment that would "give form to our generation's idea of order."[23]

Concrete was especially well suited to Brutalism since it could show the process of its formation and simultaneously reveal itself as the structure of the building. Its plasticity also allowed it to be molded to fit and express a seemingly infinite number of functional and spatial needs. In so doing, it would stand in contrast to the abstraction of much modern architecture, which concealed structural elements behind a sleek glass skin and packaged differing functions and spaces within mute boxes. Eventually, many people would come to label any concrete building "Brutalist" as this material became increasingly associated with the style.

As an intensely philosophical movement (not just an aesthetic one), Brutalism could be disturbing for people who were unused to this aggressive authenticity. But as Randall Ott, dean of architecture at Catholic University of America, later put it, Brutalism "was not about making buildings that looked like stuffed teddy bears that appealed to all. It was a fairly austere, fairly confrontational style."[24]

Kallmann, too, recognized even before the City Hall competition that the architecture he was advocating was inherently "difficult," in that it had the "effect of shock therapy in galvanizing architecture out of its lethargy." He acknowledged that it would "not immediately appeal to the senses," and "its maniac esthetic quality has evoked unfavorable comments, such as 'structural apoplexy,' from unsympathetic critics." Moreover, it "on the one hand refuses to be interpretative of humanist content—and therefore non-psychological—and on the other refuses to be a symbol in the classical sense. It is an architecture true only to its own manner of making and doing. In its physical concreteness and firmness of build, it strives for a confirmation of identity and existence to counter the modern fear of nothingness." Kallmann made clear that he preferred architecture that some might perceive as distasteful in its brutal honesty to one that was merely inoffensive in its banality.[25]

Shortly after Kallmann and McKinnell won the competition for Boston City Hall with their Brutalist design in 1962, they spied Philip Johnson walking toward them on a New York City street, waving his arms flamboyantly and exclaiming: "Ah! I'm so happy for you two young boys who have won this competition. Absolutely marvelous. I think it's wonderful. And it's so ugly!"[26] McKinnell later recalled that he and Kallmann thought this was great praise because that "ugliness" represented honesty; it was a critique of what McKinnell called the "decadently degenerate frippery" of much modern architecture.

The precipitating factors of change that had been evident in the 1948 MoMA symposium would reach critical mass in the early 1960s. Michael McKinnell later recalled that during this period, "definitely there was a change in the air."[27] As a case in point, McKinnell referenced BBPR's 1957 Torre Velasca in Milan. This building's top-heavy design seemingly takes its cues from medieval towers (in which the upper portion, for defensive purposes, jutted out from the body of the tower), but it also responds to different functions within. The building's lower section contains offices, while the upper floors are residential. Rather than attempting to wrap these various functions within a unified form, Ernesto Nathan Rogers and his partners allowed the apartment floors (which require more space than the offices because they contain kitchens and bathrooms) to extend beyond the office floors below. Thus, the apparent historical reference in the design derives from a candid formal expression of the spatial and functional differences between the building's upper and lower sections.[28]

In addition to the proto-postmodernist historicism expressed in the Torre Velasca, other previously taboo subjects (to many committed modernists) such as monumentality were also being reconsidered in the late 1950s and early 1960s. Whereas in 1937 Lewis Mumford had opined, "If it is a monument, it cannot be modern, and if it is modern, it cannot be a monument," a new generation of architects was seeking to reconcile the seemingly disparate ideals of monumentality and modernism.[29] Indeed, monumentality had been a source of debate for well over two decades by the time of the Boston City Hall competition.

Moreover, within two years of the Boston competition, Robert Venturi would publish his influential *Complexity and Contradiction in Architecture*—one of the seminal texts on postmodernism. Although KMK's approach to revolutionizing architecture differed markedly from Venturi's, the New City Hall design nevertheless anticipated some of the points Venturi would raise in his "gentle manifesto." The building could easily be described in such Venturian terms as "ambiguous," "allusive," "perverse," and "evoking many levels of meaning."

(That said, of course, Boston City Hall is hardly a perfect example of the Venturian paradigm, and Venturi himself does not mention it in his book.) Indeed, the building, through its symbolism of civic monumentality, and through the seriousness of its materials, would come to be regarded as too "authoritarian" by many young people (though perhaps not young architects) in the late 1960s. Nevertheless, in embodying the ideals of monumentality, historicism, complexity, and contradiction, Boston City Hall became both a symbol and a trigger of changes during this era of increasing architectural experimentation.

The New City Hall Design

If Gerhard Kallmann and Michael McKinnell entered the Boston City Hall competition hoping to create a building that embodied their architectural philosophy, by nearly all accounts they succeeded. As McKinnell later said of City Hall: "Our design philosophy has found its most complete expression in this project. It also reflects the way we work—from the specific to the general rather than the other way." Kallmann elaborated on this point, explaining that they strove to create a design that grew out of the specific characteristics of the project "in order to produce a building that exists strongly and irrevocably, rather than an uncommitted abstract structure that could be any place and, therefore, like modern man—without identity or presence."[30]

Since they opposed the constricting forces of "style," Kallmann and McKinnell acknowledged that they were not committed to any particular aesthetic or ideology, other than that the building should be "a contemporary yet enduring statement, not linked to momentary fashion."[31] They wanted to create a monument, but one that was accessible. Thus, McKinnell said that one of the key concerns was "a case of making the process of government so meaningful that it becomes monumental, involving everybody; the people going to City Hall as visitors and tourists, and those who worked there—all involved and aware. It became monumental because it was meaningful."[32] These ideas—unorthodox at the time—dictated the unconventional form of KMK's competition entry.

Additionally, the design responded to the specific needs of Boston's municipal government. Chief among these were the functional requirements of the building, as well as its symbolism. The architects also showed concern for the location—not simply New City Hall's effects on the surrounding physical environment but also its historical and social implications. An article in the *Boston Globe* recognized the relationship of the design to these circumstances. "Although most of the expressions have been used in one way or another before the City Hall design," the writer noted, "they are related in a highly specific way to a very special site. The architects do not feel that this building represents the wave of the future, or that it would answer another purpose. They do offer it as a democratic antidote to the autocratic architecture of big business and big government."[33] All of these factors—function, symbolism, and location—came to bear on the City Hall design.

Exterior

The most complete view of New City Hall is, fittingly, from Faneuil Hall, onetime home of Boston's municipal government. From this vantage point, across Congress Street, one sees City Hall's nine floors rise 138 feet in a complex arrangement of angular concrete forms suspended over an austere brick base embedded on a slope. This lively interplay of concrete and brick was modern in conception and expressed the functions of municipal government contained within.

The building's dimensions were largely determined by Pei's Government Center master plan and the competition program, which dictated space requirements as well as height and footprint limitations. There were no restrictions on style, appearance, or materials, however, and KMK's design reveals an inventiveness that took full advantage of the creative freedom afforded the architects. The preliminary-stage drawings for the competition show a departure not only from the traditional styles (such as neoclassical or, in the case of Old Boston City Hall, Second Empire) often employed by designers of government buildings, but also from the sleek modernist forms then common in corporate architecture.[34]

Instead of a unified envelope, the building is made up of three distinct sections, distinguished by differences in materials, texture, and scale. The lower section, which the architects referred to as "the mound," houses public areas and agencies that interact most with the citizenry. Much of this section is built in to the natural slope of the site, and its bulk is fully evident only from Congress Street, where its windowless redbrick walls rise like a three-tiered cliff. This stark, imposing surface met the competition program's requirement that the east façade "must form an effective visual closure to Dock Square."[35] While competition drawings show this section penetrated by a series of recessed windows at the top of each of its three tiers, the final design called for an unbroken brick façade.

Above the mound, a series of massive, irregularly spaced poured-concrete piers support the superstructure. Suspended above the fourth floor (which is the main level of entry for those approaching the building from City Hall Plaza) is a ceremonial level, housing the mayor's office, City Council offices, council chamber, and public exhibit hall. Although taking up by far the least amount of area in terms of volume, these offices are the most visually commanding on the exterior.[36] The symbolic importance of this space is reflected in the scale of poured-concrete hoods surrounding the windows on this level. These hoods project outward from the primary mass of the building, denoting the significance of the offices they frame. The eye is drawn to this section, as it is the most visually striking. The complex geometries of the hoods contrast with the regularized fenestration in the office floors above, as well as the yawning open space and the unadorned mass of the mound below.

The dominant feature of the main façade (fig. 7) is the City Council chamber. This unit projects outward above the main entrance to the south lobby and overlooks a vast plaza. The rising spectator galleries on the interior correspond to a stepping down on the exterior, like the underside of a massive staircase. At the southeast corner of the building, meanwhile, two sets of projecting hooded forms signify the mayor's office. While the architects intended this effect to accentuate the nobility of the space, Sibyl Moholy-Nagy wrote that the effect "competes rather uncomfortably" with the functionality of the office, "as if the father of the city were continuously compelled to show himself at the Appearance Window like an Egyptian Pharaoh."[37] From within, these volumes frame

FIGURE 7. Boston City Hall, main elevation, as seen from City Hall Plaza. The vast hardscaped area surrounding the building emphasizes its role as a civic monument. Library of Congress, Prints & Photographs Division, Historic American Building Survey, HABS MASS, 13-BOST, 71-1.

views of the Old State House and Washington Street (Boston's financial district) on one side, and Faneuil Hall and the waterfront beyond on the other. One critic observed that these two vistas would "bring to the attention of whoever holds the office the source of Boston's present wealth and power" with the view of State and Washington Streets, and "to remind him of Boston's past, its people, and its maritime tradition" with the view of Faneuil Hall and the waterfront.[38]

In the preliminary-stage design, the council chamber was the only space on the ceremonial level with a bold concrete frame; other offices were housed in identical, albeit prominent, pod-like structures. As the architects refined their design for the final round, the offices on the ceremonial level were unified in their expression with a massive scale and projecting concrete hoods and frames.[39]

The top three floors of the building are made of smooth precast concrete sections, which contrast with the rough cast-in-place concrete below. Paired fins separate the windows and enclose ventilation and electrical systems. Each successive floor of these upper levels is stepped out on the exterior, which corresponds to a stepping back surrounding the courtyard. This creates a protective overhang (offering shade from the harsh sun and a shelter from rain and snow) along the exterior walls, while allowing more natural light to penetrate the areas surrounding the courtyard and forming outdoor balconies. This section reflects the functions of municipal bureaucracy—resembling a honeycomb for the worker bees of city government within. It moreover closely relates to the new office buildings surrounding Government Center, which generally are large structures with identical, repetitive window units.[40] Functional considerations also influenced the design of this section: offices on these floors, KMK assumed, would not need venetian blinds, since the window casings would shield the windows from sun, rain, and snow.

One of the most significant changes to the KMK design between the preliminary and final stages of the competition was in the form and function of the fins in the building's upper levels. At first the architects envisioned these as thin separations, with a single fin marking off each window from the next (fig. 8). By the final stage, however, they had been paired, with the area between them enclosed to allow utilities to pass through them, and also to provide more visual bulk to these upper floors.[41] As McKinnell explained, "The construction was intended to give a sense of density to the outer walls, a feeling there's a zone between you and the outside of the structure, rather than a papery metallic skin."[42]

Above the bureaucratic level, the building is finished with precast fascia panels. Because many of the buildings surrounding New City Hall are taller than it, the competition program stipulated that the roof would function as a fifth façade. Here, the architects sheathed the penthouses and skylight openings in precast concrete. Thus, as one critic noted, the roof is "treated in such a way that when looked down upon it has hardly less spatial and volumetric interest than the rest of the building."[43]

The building's visual and spatial hierarchy was a deliberate and essential aspect of the design, dictated by the three functional zones (public, ceremonial, and administrative) described in the competition program. This tripartite massing also had its roots in architectural history. In fact, several critics have noted a "classical order" in the

FIGURE 8. Preliminary-stage competition drawing, Boston City Hall; Kallmann, McKinnell and Knowles (1962). Early designs show single fins separating the windows in the top section of the building. These would later be paired, providing a greater sense of density to the building's exterior. Courtesy of Historic New England.

building's three sections, which form a base, a body, and an attic.[44] The arrangement also echoes traditional European domestic architecture, in which service spaces are relegated to the first floor, principal rooms are located on the second floor (the *piano nobile,* distinguished by its grand scale, large windows, and balconies), and servants' quarters are in the attic story. The architects hoped this hierarchical articulation of function, steeped in centuries of architectural tradition, would have meaning both for those working within City Hall and for the public.[45]

Interior

The complex geometries, variety of materials, and structural honesty that distinguish City Hall's exterior are also found inside. The diversity of functions contained within the building led KMK to design an assortment of different spaces, rather than adopt a one-size-fits-all approach. "The concept was that of a megastructure, a mini-city," the architects explained.[46] (The concept of the "megastructure"—a single large building housing multiple functions that might otherwise have been located in separate, individual buildings—was popular among architects and theorists in the 1960s and 1970s.) Elected officials, municipal workers, visiting dignitaries, tourists, and the general public would all inhabit different neighborhoods in this "mini-city," yet the building was designed to accommodate all of these populations and facilitate meaningful interactions among them.

The building was designed with four entrances to promote the image of an accessible municipal government. The two principal entrances are on the north side (across from the John F. Kennedy Federal Building) and on the southwest corner (opening onto Washington Street and City Hall Plaza, across from the Government Center MBTA station). In addition, there is an entrance on Congress Street, across from Faneuil Hall, and another leading from the central courtyard.

The north lobby gives direct access to "the mound" (the lower three floors of the building), housing the agencies most frequented by the public. One of the few changes the architects made to the design between the final stage of the competition and construction was to enlarge this entrance to provide easier and more direct access to the plaza from the federal building.

The south entrance leads into a massive atrium, dominated by a grand staircase rising to the ceremonial level (fig. 9). KMK dubbed this space the "city room." It was designed to serve several functions. First, it could house the city's collection of ceremonial ornaments, such as a pair of stone lanterns (*ishidoros*) given by Kyoto, Japan—one

FIGURE 9. Boston City Hall, main lobby. The architects called this versatile space the "city room"—an area that could host functions ranging from concerts to exhibits to parties. Library of Congress, Prints & Photographs Division, Historic American Building Survey, HABS MASS, 13-BOST, 71-9.

of Boston's sister cities.[47] Moreover, the lobby's openness allows it to serve as a large gathering space, with the expansive staircase providing an indoor amphitheater that easily accommodates performances and gatherings. Kallmann and McKinnell intended for this area to function as a "city forum, a place of urban theater," which would host both celebrations and demonstrations.[48] "The amphitheater form is intended," Michael McKinnell told a journalist. "Things could happen here. We wanted the space dramatic." The sense of drama is accentuated by light shafts stretching the entire height of the building, sustaining the architects' idea that "this is a space waiting for things to happen."[49]

A series of skylit corridors links the north and south lobbies. The skylights, Charles Millard notes, "[furnish] another cue for the visitor, and [guide] him through the building with a thread of overhead daylight. If one were to proceed through the building from the north to south lobbies, the sequence of skylights would culminate in the spectacular shaft rising the full height of the building just inside of the main entrance, flooding the south lobby with diffused light."⁵⁰ Since this section is mostly built onto a slope, with the exposed side covered in a windowless brick wall, natural light enters the mound primarily through these skylights.

Passage through the four levels of the mound is made possible by a variety of escalators, ramps, and stairs. Kallmann and McKinnell pointed out that these features connected the movement patterns of the surrounding city with the building, rendering it permeable, as pedestrians were easily able to pass through while walking from Beacon Hill to Dock Square.⁵¹ The agencies nestled in this section open onto a central public space, forming what the architects called a "galleria."⁵² According to Kallmann, "the key to the lower building, and its floor plan, is that passage. A descending street through a galleria type of space—this is where the street life of the building will take place."⁵³ Later, the architects updated and Americanized their analogy, writing that the concourse running through the mound "is the analogue of a shopping mall with departmental counters facing the terraced balconies."⁵⁴

The interior spaces on the ceremonial level match the grand scale in which they are expressed on the exterior. The office suites open onto a balcony ringing the south lobby, which is connected to the south entrance via the grand staircase. At the top of the staircase is the main gallery, which was expected to host exhibits that changed monthly, enabling visitors to City Hall to combine business with culture.

Opposite the gallery is the City Council suite, comprising the council chamber, offices, and meeting rooms. The council chamber (fig. 10) was designed almost as theater-in-the round, with the audience ranged around three sides in rising galleries. "The architectural notion of the Council Chamber seeks to involve people with the legislative process," explained Michael McKinnell shortly before the building opened. "Observing the old chamber, I've always felt a sense of sheer spectacle. We'll install elaborate amplification for people who want to come down to the railing to speak their piece."⁵⁵ Veteran *Boston Globe* reporter Joseph Dinneen observed that the council chamber was one of the "highlights" of the building, as it "gives one the feeling of standing in an old Roman senate."⁵⁶ Adjacent to the council chamber is a conference

FIGURE 10. Boston City Hall, City Council chamber. Designed almost as theater-in-the-round, with public galleries rising on three sides, the space makes an architectural statement about citizen involvement in democratic government. Library of Congress, Prints & Photographs Division, Historic American Building Survey, HABS MASS, 13-BOST, 71-10.

room (ironically named in honor of James Michael Curley), followed by an anteroom, which houses the municipal reference library. The anteroom is connected to the City Council reception area, which is also accessible from the south lobby.

The mayor's suite, meanwhile, includes a variety of ceremonial-symbolic as well as functional spaces. There is a larger office for receiving guests, a smaller working office, and a private bedroom and bathroom facilities. The mayor also has a private staircase and elevator leading from the garage below City Hall to his office suite. Competition juror Harold Hodgkinson wrote admiringly of the mayor's office, noting: "His Honor's office, its entrance dominated by a superb golden eagle, bright red on the chairs, and beautiful oil paintings, lends a feeling of importance. There is an inspirational view of Faneuil Hall, a constant reminder of our fountain of liberty."[57]

The administrative section of the building, containing offices for the Boston Redevelopment Authority and agencies not frequented by the public, is in the upper levels and is reached by elevators. There are nine elevators in the building: four in the north core, three in the south core, and one passenger-freight elevator, in addition to the private elevator for the mayor. The offices in the administrative section open onto a public corridor surrounding the central courtyard. Outdoor terraces line the light court, allowing workers on these floors to enjoy the outdoors during their breaks without leaving the building.

While each distinct zone of the building is articulated on both the exterior and the interior, the sections are nevertheless interconnected. As Charles Millard describes it:

> The brick elements both push into the building and rise up against it, overlapping the concrete shapes of the second level. These, in turn, invade the space of the upper storeys in various ways. Throughout the building there are elements which interlock without joining, such as the brick stair tower and the elements of the Mayor's south office, rather in the manner of a yin-yang symbol. There is also an intricate spatial interpenetration in which interior and exterior spaces join with themselves or each other to make a flowing succession which runs uninterruptedly in three dimensions through the building, up to its roof, and out onto the plaza. This is emphasized by patterns of light and cast shadow, which break up the solid forms into an infinitely variable succession of interlocking shapes. If one could speak of a Cubist effect in architecture, this building approaches it closely—the careful locking together of numerous elements which frequently shade imperceptibly into one another.[58]

Kallmann, too, commented on these "interpenetrations," writing: "You could take one piece of the building, and in it have the sense that runs right through the whole building. This will hold together the dichotomy of the lower brick structure and the upper concrete one, which ascend and descend—they are sort of serrated into each other."[59]

As these comments make clear, the building is a cohesive unit, even as its various functions are separated visually and spatially. Thus it at once represents the multiplicity and yet the ultimate cohesiveness and singularity of purpose of municipal government.

Materials

Perhaps City Hall's most distinctive feature is the use of exposed concrete and red brick as the primary construction materials. Concrete was well suited to KMK's design philosophy, as well as the American temperament at the height of the Cold War. While Kallmann and McKinnell would use rough concrete to protest against a suave corporate modernism at midcentury, concrete was itself a principal material in many modern buildings. As Antoine Picon noted, "No material has been more closely associated with the origins and development of modern architecture than concrete," since the material "seemed to epitomize the relations between modern architecture and technology, relations that were seen as crucial by the founding fathers of the modern movement."[60] Similarly, Adrian Forty pointed out that although concrete had a long history dating back to the Romans, it is nevertheless perpetually regarded as "a material whose existence lies in the future, rather than in the present or the past."[61] As such, it was an attractive material for the early modernists in the 1920s, but equally appealing for younger architects seeking to eschew a glass box aesthetic in the 1960s.

Forty years after the completion of Boston City Hall, when asked why he and Kallmann had used this material for so many of their early works, McKinnell responded that they "were particularly interested in imbuing architecture with an authenticity. We thought concrete was the appropriate material to achieve this. When you build in concrete, what you see is what you get. The building is concrete, it is made of concrete, it is structured in concrete."[62]

McKinnell expanded on this idea, attributing the use of concrete to an inherent tendency in many young architects to "work against the system" in order to draw attention to themselves and their ideas. "At the time, there weren't many concrete buildings around," he noted. "So young architects were drawn to the material as a statement, which was perhaps largely a negative statement, that 'here I am, I'm different,

I'm opposing the architecture of Emery Roth and Edward Durrell [sic] Stone.' Concrete stood against the stream of what we considered decadently degenerate frippery and surface concerns."63 While many firms were constructing steel frames clad in limestone, travertine, marble, or glass—hiding the structure of the building behind a prettified façade—KMK used concrete to reveal the structure and the manner in which the building was made.

KMK was not the only firm embracing the iconoclastic and structural capabilities of concrete. As McKinnell remarked, during the 1960s "concrete was in the air. People were interested in the material. . . . As Peter Collins, who taught me at Manchester said: Concrete is the stone of our time." Yet while other architects, such as Eero Saarinen, Pier Luigi Nervi, and Victor Lundy, were using concrete for its "capacity to make curvilinear forms or to span with concrete shells," McKinnell continued, he and Kallmann were not interested in the material

> for its inherent structural capacities. When we designed City Hall, we really wanted to make this exemplar of an authentic architecture. The characteristic of concrete that we enjoyed most was that one material could do so much, and could be seen to do so much. It could be the structure. It could be the cladding. It could be the floors, it could be the walls. There's a kind of all-through-ness about it that I'm sure we carried to excess in City Hall. I think if we could have done it, we would have used concrete to make the light switches.[64]

The relative rarity of exposed concrete on so prominent a public building in the United States did not go unnoticed. As City Hall's construction was nearing its midpoint in 1966, Joseph Eldredge commented on the novel use of the material in Boston City Hall, writing in the *Globe:* "Architectural concrete has taken many years to come into its own. It has never been easy to convince practical construction men that it was worth making concrete with aesthetic quality that could replace conventional but more expensive stone or brick facing. Here, for the first time, on so large a job, awarded by public bidding, we are beginning to see architectural concrete worthy of the name."[65]

While the exposed concrete of the building's upper sections deliberately contrasted with the prevailing architecture of the time, the red brick of the mound established a visual connection to historic local structures and neighborhoods. Nearby landmarks such as Faneuil Hall and the Old State House were constructed of red brick. So too were many upscale residential buildings throughout the city, from the Bulfinch-era mansions on Beacon Hill to the Victorian row houses of the Back Bay and South End. It also was a common building material in poorer neighborhoods, and the architects claimed that they deliberately chose this material because it would help to connect the august new City Hall with the poorer quarters of the city, such as the tenements of the North End.[66] Thus, the use of brick linked the building to its site and the surrounding city.

On the interior, one generally finds these same materials, which reflect a conscious spatial separation of functions. In the mound, for instance, there is a preponderance of brick and quarry tile. The structure is revealed in much the same way that it is on the exterior. The columns are constructed of poured-in-place concrete, with paired precast Vierendeel trusses supporting the ceiling. Ceilings are open, revealing not only the structural trusses but also the mechanical infrastructure (such as ventilation ducts and electrical systems) that runs through them. Lighting, too, is integrated into the precast members of the ceiling, with four-foot fluorescent lights placed between the paired beams and downlights in the square voids at their intersections. Cast concrete also forms many interior fixtures, such as the window desks at city departments dealing with the public.

Woodwork in the lower levels (floors one through five) is African mahogany, while in the upper levels (floors six through nine) it is white oak. Wall coverings in the public corridors of the mayor's suite are bronze paneling. This progression of materials corresponds to an overall mounting color palette that the architects used deliberately. From the red brick, Welsh quarry tile, and dark mahogany of the lower levels, to the exposed concrete of the upper stories, one ascends from dark to light.[67]

Whereas walls in the mound and ceremonial levels are generally immovable concrete or brick, office partitions in the upper office levels are painted drywall, which can be removed. This allows for modular flexibility in office layouts as space needs constantly change. The finishes in these areas are easily serviceable, with vinyl asbestos tiles, glass walls, and painted drywall.

Plaza

The Boston City Hall competition required entrants to design not only the building but also the landscaping around it. For this area KMK proposed a brick-paved plaza with ramps and granite steps flowing down the natural slope of the site from Cambridge Street to New Congress Street and Dock Square. A planned pedestrian walkway over Congress Street (though never built) was to connect the plaza to the Faneuil Hall area. The bricks for the plaza are sand-struck and water-struck, and were chosen from many types of New England brick sources and placed at random to allow for a mottled effect.[68] A tree-lined promenade raised on a plinth fronts the federal building, with a similar promenade along Cambridge Street. Originally a fountain and sitting area occupied the corner on Cambridge Street nearest the federal building. (Because it leaked into the garage below, the fountain was closed in the 1980s and paved over in the 1990s.) KMK also designed the head house for the Government Center subway station, which took the form of a red-brick mastaba. The bricks of the plaza flowed seamlessly over the structure, with its inwardly sloping walls inversely responding to City Hall's stepped-out cornice. (The original head house was replaced with a new glass structure in 2016.)

With few exceptions, the plaza is open, providing ample space for special celebrations and for political demonstrations, but it primarily serves as a pedestrian passageway. One architecture critic praised this feature, writing that KMK "understood what a plaza in the city is all about. It is not a park, of which Boston has plenty. Greenery, so often artificially commandeered to hide mistakes of design, will be confined to a grove of hefty trees in one corner."[69]

Michael McKinnell noted that the plaza, "like a vast staircase, connects the upper and lower parts of the city. Boston has a superb park system: and now, starting at the top of Beacon Hill, we're creating a sequence of *urban* spaces, pedestrian spaces really—you don't have to cross many streets—incomparable in the United States."[70] McKinnell also pointed out that daily activity in the plaza would occur not in the center but rather around the edges as people clustered there and looked toward the center at the magnificent architectural symbol of the New Boston.[71]

The plaza flows seamlessly into City Hall through both of the principal entrances. "The bricks come in, like a street," McKinnell told the *Globe*. In both the north and south lobbies, "glass doors suggest the natural extension of sidewalks into a place where people do business."[72] Initially these glass doors had no divisions between them, to accentuate the impression of accessibility. In the interest of energy conservation, however, revolving doors were installed in 1973. Moreover, added security in public buildings, especially since 9/11, has further impeded the sense of connectedness between building and plaza.

Broad steps lead from the plaza into the building's courtyard and out the other side onto Congress Street. This courtyard (fig. 11), which the architects regarded as an extension of City Hall Plaza, allowed access, during business hours, to the city room (south lobby). The courtyard, however, was designed to remain open during all hours. The architects claimed that this area "epitomizes the concept of openness and accessibility that generated the design of the City Hall."[73] They expected that the courtyard would be filled with large flowerpots, shrubs, and civic sculpture, and they intended it as a gathering space, with the rectangular skylight housing at its center also serving as a bench. They noted that the courtyard was "originally designed as a *temenos*—a sacred enclosure—and shown in the competition drawings with a monumental Henry Moore sculpture."[74] The courtyard has been closed since the 1980s, and today is a vacant space at the center of the building.

Continual Completion

Kallmann, McKinnell and Knowles knew that their budget would allow only for design and construction—not comprehensive adornment—of City Hall. For this reason, they regarded the building not as a museum piece, to be preserved exactly as it had emerged from their drafting

FIGURE 11. Boston City Hall, central courtyard. Closed in the 1980s because of security concerns, the courtyard was intended to be always open to the public—even when the rest of the building was closed. Pathways connect the courtyard to City Hall Plaza and to Dock Square. Library of Congress, Prints & Photographs Division, Historic American Building Survey, HABS MASS, 13-BOST, 71-8.

tables, but rather as a framework that successive generations would adorn. "It isn't a finished object," McKinnell said on the eve of the building's opening in 1969. "Someday, I hope, a bequest might leave enough money to gild the ceiling of the Council Chamber. This isn't a building where the pattern is frozen, where, if you move one detail, you ruin everything."[75]

Like many aspects of the building's design, this idea of an evolving building—"continual completion"—was rooted in both architectural history and the ideals of an active and engaged democracy. As McKinnell recalled in 2010:

> Gerhard said that all public buildings in the past were never finished (maybe in the nineteenth century they were), but in the times we think of great public buildings, they were built and they were finished over great long periods of time, they were adorned, they were painted, they were decorated with tapestries, they were changed by the people. And what he was very interested in was the idea that architecture was the only art that bears the imprint of time. . . . Public buildings should be a palimpsest.[76]

In this way, the building is a physical manifestation of American democracy and an analogue for the United States Constitution. In this document, the nation's founding fathers established a strong framework for government, yet they also left room for future changes, through amendments and reinterpretations. So too did the KMK design create a durable home and symbol of the city's government that could be altered and embellished to meet the needs of and remain relevant to future generations. "The process of democratic government is the meaning of City Hall," said McKinnell. "It should never be finished."[77]

In reflecting on this idea of "continual completion," local architect Gary Wolf pointed out that embellishment could include new signage, graphics, furnishings, tapestries, plantings—"signs of active and proud occupancy"—as well as physical improvements that had not even been considered in the 1960s (such as double glazing, green roofs, solar energy systems, geothermal mechanical systems, high-efficiency heating and cooling, and so on).[78] By the early twenty-first century, the architects recognized that the "continual completion" they had hoped for had not occurred. Yet Kallmann and McKinnell remained optimistic, conceding that the adornment of City Hall, "to our great regret, has not happened and perhaps we were naïve. But we are naïve still, and there is still time."[79]

Architectural Influences

Nearly everyone who has written about Boston City Hall seemingly has come up with a different set of antecedents for the building. Some have claimed that KMK amalgamated principles from a variety of architects and styles. For instance, Sibyl Moholy-Nagy bafflingly described the function of the sculptural hoods on the ceremonial level as "a frank homage to the constructivist heritage from Rietveldt to Le Corbusier and Kahn, brought into the contemporary fold by Venturi's canonization of complexity and contradiction."[80] A *Globe* article, meanwhile, traced elements of the building's design to European ecclesial architecture, pointing out that "there is, on the lower levels, the blending of poured concrete and red brick, and the awesome use of light and space that somehow seems a disparate and yet logical descendant of the Romanesque at Mont St. Michel and the Gothic at Chartres."[81] Gary Wolf, by contrast, observed that the openness of the mound relates not only to nearby Faneuil Hall—designed with an open marketplace on the ground floor—but also to municipal buildings of Europe, which often contained government offices in the upper stories with arcades and markets below.[82] Paul Heyer, meanwhile, found "an almost Auguste Perret–like classical sense of structure in the building."[83] And according to Charles Jencks, there was even an inspiration from modern music and Mannerist architecture:

> Here we find a steady beat of top windows (a, b, a, b, etc.) while it both continues (on two levels) and is interrupted (on one). This interrupted rhythm and fugal counterpoint were inspired by Stravinsky's music, among other sources. The clash of opposing themes, in all its sculptural

weight, is reminiscent of Michelangelo. There are even Mannerist inversions at certain points: a stair hangs out over space instead of resting on supports, and a concrete fascia makes two right-angled turns to end up as an oversized balcony.[84]

The architects themselves have added to this potpourri of interpretations. Kallmann and McKinnell pointed out that the siting of the building within the open plaza "evokes ancient structures—an acropolis, a temple, a palazzo, city ramparts." They also said that the courtyard was conceived as an open space, connected to the city, much like the Cortile of the Palazzo Ducale in Venice. Indeed, the mysteriousness of New City Hall's antecedents was deliberate: "To retain its attraction during changing times and tastes, we believed that the imagery had to be complex, evocative, and perhaps enigmatic. We thought it should be many-layered, alluding to subtexts of cultural memory, history, and myth." Accordingly, they were delighted that Robert Campbell had ascribed to the building "a narrative of an ancient castle which has endured and survived the ravages of time," while others compared it to the Minoan palace at Knossos, or the works of Le Corbusier, along with a wide variety of other interpretations.[85]

Kallmann and McKinnell—both born and educated in Europe—invariably brought with them a familiarity with the architectural heritage of the cities in which they had lived and studied. The architects have admitted as much. When asked about the use of exposed concrete in New City Hall, for example, McKinnell replied: "Gerhard and I were basically Europeans.... So we were carrying our European legacy with us, and concrete was the material of choice in Europe. Steel was somewhat exotic." Also, when the architects received the detailed competition program, which outlined specific space requirements, Kallmann thought, "There is something missing: where is the beer hall?"[86] (He then tried—unsuccessfully—to persuade the city government to include a Rathskeller, such as was present in many German town halls, in the basement of City Hall.)

There were several architects whose work KMK seemed, to varying degrees, to have responded to—either positively or negatively—while designing Boston City Hall. Perhaps chief among these was Le Corbusier, a pioneer of modern architecture whom McKinnell called "our master."[87] Kallmann likewise acknowledged a debt to Le Corbusier, whose "genius" he had earlier praised in his article on Action Architecture.[88] Kallmann appreciated that Le Corbusier approached each project without a preconceived aesthetic in mind—an important factor in Kallmann's own design philosophy.

Several aspects of the Swiss architect's buildings are reflected in Boston City Hall. For instance, the exposed concrete protrusions and perforations that make up the variegated façade of Le Corbusier's Secretariat building in Chandigarh (1953) appear in amplified form on Boston City Hall's exterior (particularly on the ceremonial level). In both buildings, the architects varied the rhythm and shape of the fenestration to indicate differences in internal spaces and functions.

Le Corbusier's influence on Kallmann, McKinnell and Knowles becomes most evident in a comparison between Boston City Hall and the monastery of Sainte Marie de La Tourette (1960). Le Corbusier designed the rectangular monastery around an open courtyard. The projecting upper stories are supported by slender columns, creating a cavernous open space on the ground level, into which the surrounding landscape flows without interruption. Above this, the congregational areas, including the refectory, classrooms, and chapel, are denoted by window walls punctuated by concrete panels. The top of the building is crowned by two protruding rows of honeycomb-like balconies of the monks' individual cells. In a nod to the asceticism of monastic life, Le Corbusier used exposed concrete on the building's interior and exterior.

Even a cursory comparison between this building and Boston City Hall reveals similarities in massing, geometry, and materials. Just as the grass-covered landscape surrounding La Tourette flows into the courtyard through an open ground level, so too in Boston does the brick-paved plaza continue into the public levels of the building and the courtyard. Above this, both buildings include a *piano nobile*, signified by accentuated fenestration. Finally, New City Hall is crowned with three rows of trabeated window casings for the municipal bureaucratic offices, reminiscent of the cells at La Tourette. Within both buildings, one finds the same copious use of exposed concrete walls, ceilings, and furnishings.

Many scholars and critics, as well as the architects themselves, have noted Le Corbusier's influence. Michael McKinnell, for example, said that one of the reasons for the exposed concrete in City Hall was that "our master, Le Corbusier, built in concrete."[89] Charles Millard remarked that La Tourette was Boston City Hall's "nearest relative."[90] Also, on the building's opening in 1969, Sibyl Moholy-Nagy pointed out that "Le Corbusier contributed, as he does to all true architecture of this century, scale and modulation held together by the visible ligaments of structure."[91] And Renato De Fusco, in his *Storia dell'Architettura Contemporanea*, discussed at length the Corbusian influence in Boston.[92]

These similarities may seem to indicate that Boston City Hall was merely derivative of Le Corbusier; there are also profound differences, however, which reveal that Kallmann, McKinnell and Knowles were not simply aping him. One of the principal distinctions is that the KMK design incorporates Boston's unique political circumstances. When asked if Le Corbusier had been an influence on the City Hall design, Edward Knowles replied:

> Oh yeah. Definitely. We had the Corbu books and things and were looking into a lot of Corbu's solutions, but this of course was a new approach to that whole aesthetic. There's an additional overlay of, I would say, civic responsibility and so the look of the building is definitely a result of the philosophy of the building having to educate what was happening on the inside of it in terms of the government. Corbu's buildings didn't do that. They were great sculptures, but I don't know of a Corbu building that did what Boston City Hall does.[93]

Several scholars and critics, too, have seen KMK as doing more than simply copying Le Corbusier. Charles Millard wrote that "if Kallmann and McKinnell fall short of Le Corbusier's absolute greatness as an innovator, they are far too good to be merely imitators."[94] Likewise, Paul Heyer noted that while KMK "clearly found strength in Le Corbusier's example, their design is more than a mere Le Corbusier aperitif. Nor is it vastly apart from the spirit of many younger American architects, as a look at the efforts in a few architectural schools—certainly those on the East Coast—will show."[95] Indeed, Heyer's emphasis on KMK's similarities to younger architects rather than the old "master" aligns with Kallmann's reverence for the work of young practitioners expressed in his writings. Perhaps the fact that Kallmann and McKinnell came not from an established firm but rather from the academy, where they were constantly in touch with new ideas about architecture, compelled them to incorporate novelty into their own design philosophy.

Another European source of inspiration for Boston City Hall is BBPR's Torre Velasca in Milan (1954–1958). In 1958, Gerhard Kallmann wrote a defense of the controversial building in the *Architectural Forum,* describing it as a "valiant essay in the neglected art of fitting modern architecture into a historic continuity of building" and a successful effort to integrate "construction and ornament, new technology and ancient forms."[96] As David Dillon wrote in his monograph on Kallmann and McKinnell, his words could very well be "a blurb for Boston City Hall."[97] In the Milan building, BBPR looked to medieval towers, where upper portions, which were bracketed out, contained portholes in the overhang that could be opened to allow boiling oil to be dropped on attackers below.[98]

Likewise, in their own efforts to break with the modernist doctrine of abjuring historical sources, Kallmann, McKinnell and Knowles considered the past when designing Boston City Hall. This audacious return to historicism at the height of the modernist epoch was at once allusive and potent: allusive in that New City Hall's historical references are suggestive rather than explicit (there are no marble columns, gilded domes, or other "pompous pratfalls to the Classical past," as Ada Louise Huxtable noted), yet potent in that scholars and critics who have studied the building have observed the historical influences.[99] Sibyl Moholy-Nagy, for instance, discussed the building in terms of "binding the past to the future." She pointed out that the "ancient harmonious canon of base, body, and attic" is reflected in the tripartite massing of the building. She also mentioned City Hall Plaza's connection with the "directed centralized movement of Mediterranean city plazas," such as the fan-shaped Piazza del Campo in Siena.[100] Indeed, Kallmann and McKinnell recognized this historical reference when they claimed that their plaza was "more medieval than Renaissance in character."[101]

One possible additional source of historical inspiration for Boston City Hall is the Minoan palace at Knossos. Gerhard Kallmann said that when designing Boston City Hall, he was constantly thinking of this ancient complex.[102] Remarkably few references to the connection between the two buildings appear in the literature on City Hall, although Peter Collins's 1962 review of the design does fleetingly liken the building's complexity to that of the Minoan palace.[103]

Whatever connections exist between the palace and City Hall are certainly more subtle and suggestive than pronounced and literal. Indeed, some might argue that these connections are tenuous at best. Nevertheless, Kallmann's earnest assertion warrants consideration, and what follows are connections that the architect may have seen between his own building and the ancient palace. To begin with, the monumental scale of both buildings was counterbalanced by their meaningfulness. That is to say that not only were these monuments to the civilizations and the rulers who built them, but also they served prosaic purposes in the daily lives of citizens. At Knossos, for example, farmers and merchants would come to the palace to sell their goods, in addition to going there for purposes related to civic administration and religious ritual. Likewise, KMK anticipated that citizens would use Boston City Hall as a passageway from Scollay Square to Dock Square, and they expected that pushcart vendors would populate the plaza.

One further similarity is the idea of "continual completion." Just as the palace at Knossos was constructed over the course of three hundred years (1750–1490 BC), with each successive generation adding to and embellishing the complex, Boston City Hall's architects expected that their building would not be finished when the construction crews left. Rather, they hoped that the building would be continually updated and amended to meet the changing needs of the city and its citizens. As Kallmann and McKinnell wrote in 2005: "When we designed the City Hall, we envisioned not only a fragment of the city, but also a fragment in time. That is to say, we regard the construction of the building to be the start of a process that would engage successive generations of the citizenry in the embellishment, decoration, and adornment of the robust armature that we had designed."[104]

KMK had affinities not only for European architects and historical sites but for American designers as well. Michael McKinnell said that in the sad state of American architecture in the late 1950s and early 1960s, one of the few architects he and his partners respected was Louis Kahn.[105] Charles Jencks recognized KMK's connection to Kahn, writing: "What Kallmann is doing then is close to the work process of Louis Kahn: starting with a conclusion and then working back towards a beginning. It is the exact reverse of the process which Gropius and others had preached of washing one's mind of all preconception and starting from scratch with a clean slate."[106] Just as Kahn famously asked when beginning a project, "What does the building want to be?" so too did KMK imbue this building with a form derived from the specific functional, symbolic, and contextual imperatives of the project.

The architects also admired Frank Lloyd Wright. Edward Knowles admits to being deeply influenced by Wright, and credits Wright with inspiring him to become an architect.[107] Moreover, observed Sibyl Moholy-Nagy, "Wright's kaleidoscopic light and shadow modulations of a building designed quadrilaterally, and his mastery to adjust building and site to each other can be felt [in Boston City Hall]."[108] Alex Krieger, meanwhile, offered a more thorough explication of the relationship between KMK's architecture and that of Wright. "Though they may have spoken of Wright less often than of Kahn or Corbusier," Krieger suggested, "the debt they owe to his work is perhaps greater. A similar cause conservative—of finding new insights among ancient sources—motivates the work of Kallmann and McKinnell." By way of explanation, Krieger continued:

> Like Wright's, the architecture of Kallmann and McKinnell is conservative in a more profound way. The architecture aims to support the purposes for which it is commissioned. It reinforces the values of the sponsoring institutions, indeed strives to enhance their civic status. . . . As it

was for Frank Lloyd Wright before them, the basic role of the architect is believed to be that of a *constructor;* in McKinnell's terms, "reinforcing a feeling of stability in a world that is shabbily made."[109]

Edward Knowles, who had previously worked for Philip Johnson and Mies van der Rohe, believed that several of the skills—though not the ideals—he acquired in those offices came to bear on the Boston City Hall design to some extent. "I was very good in terms of solving architectural problems—how to build things and building processes," Knowles recalled. "This is something which I contributed in the Johnson office, and I think I brought a lot of those ideas to the Boston City Hall. If you go back and look at the drawings, the way things fit together and the integration of lighting with structure and air conditioning and how the partitions would work with the structure, these are things which I was able to bring to the group."[110]

In addition to the variety of architects and buildings worldwide that inspired Kallmann, McKinnell and Knowles, there are also myriad buildings that Boston City Hall reacted against. KMK, for instance, opposed the tenets of dogmatic modernism that characterized much of American architecture in the postwar years. The functional abstraction of such buildings was anathema to architects who wanted a more responsive, dynamic architecture. As Michael McKinnell put it:

> We were surrounded by a depressing era, particularly in New York, of commercial buildings that were built in steel. There were third-removed Miesian firms like Harrison & Abramovitz, who were not bad architects, but who were producing buildings for commercial clients which we were in revolt against. Nothing that we looked at in such work was actually authentic. It had a steel structure, clad in travertine or limestone or marble. Hung ceilings erased all the mechanicals from view. It was a type of cosmetic architecture. For ideological reasons—and in Gerhard's case for philosophical and aesthetic reasons—we were in revolt against this architecture.[111]

The use of concrete in New City Hall, McKinnell said, "was an act of resistance against the likes of Emery Roth architecture."[112] Similarly,

Knowles maintained, "we were all very critical of Emery Roth and [Edward Durell] Stone. Stone did some interesting buildings, but in any event there wasn't a philosophical commitment to the purpose of the building on their part. It was a matter of exercising an aesthetic. I wouldn't even say that Emery Roth exercised an aesthetic, but in any event he was a commercial architect."[113] New City Hall signified a clean break from the corporate architecture of the 1950s and sought to establish a new architectural paradigm that synthesized the revolutionary spirit of the early modernists and the time-honored principles of architectural history.

Despite the strength and variety of Boston City Hall's associations with buildings throughout America and abroad, the design was not merely an amalgamation of references to non-local architecture without any link to its immediate surroundings. Local influences on the building abound, revealing a structure with deep ties not only to global architecture but also to its hometown. As Charles Millard wrote, "In the Boston City Hall they have produced a building of great quality that is wholly engaged both with its particular program and with the nature and requirements of the city around it."[114] Similarly, Gary Wolf observed that the new City Hall "forges essential, often overlooked connections with historic Boston."[115]

Thus, the building responds to the historic fabric of the surrounding city. For example, one can find references in New City Hall to Alexander Parris's Quincy Market. As Wolf noted, the "rhythm and scale of City Hall's upper levels establish a visual connection to that of the trabeated upper level of Alexander Parris' main market building a few hundred yards away, with its hefty Greek Revival granite frames."[116]

David Ellis, writing in the *Globe,* picked up on the relationship between the new building and previous city halls in Boston, remarking that while "the new City Hall should outlive all its predecessors," it nevertheless "combines the features of most of them." For instance, Ellis quotes a historical source which explains that the first town hall built in Boston, which stood from 1657 to 1710 (when it was destroyed by fire), was built on pillars "so that the open room between the pillars may serve for Merchants, Masters of Shippes and Strangers, as well as the Towne, to meete in." The openness of this meeting space corresponded to that of New City Hall's south lobby—also raised on pillars and allowing for large meetings. Ellis goes on to write that "in the [1860s] what is referred to as old City Hall was built on School street. Contemporary critics said it was an eyesore, was too expensive and took too long to build. That all sounds familiar to anyone who has listened to criticism of the new City Hall."[117]

Gerhard Kallmann remarked that the building is in "dialogue" with the rest of the city, adding that "the building was described as a miniature city, as it has the building materials of the rest of the city."[118] The concrete of the upper sections, for instance, follows in the Boston tradition of "emphatic, forceful" architecture, as exemplified in Solomon Willard's Bunker Hill Monument, the rugged granite buildings of Gridley James Fox Bryant, the brawny designs of H. H. Richardson, and the thick masonry structure of Shepley, Rutan and Coolidge's nearby Ames Building.[119] The muscularity of these buildings, demonstrated in their heavy massing and large, often rough-hewn stone blocks, contrasts with the delicate, genteel redbrick architecture of the Back Bay and Beacon Hill residential districts. Yet even these are referenced in City Hall, in the redbrick plaza that flows into and through the public areas of the building. Similarly, there are references to the historic city in the brick base along Congress Street (which echoes the brick massing of the eighteenth-century Blackstone Block across Congress Street).[120] Thus the red brick, representing the old city, serves literally and symbolically as the foundation on which the New Boston is built, establishing a visual connection between the building and its neighbors.

The competition program called for saving the nearby Sears Crescent, Old State House, and Faneuil Hall. For this reason, the new City Hall does not tower menacingly over these older neighbors, as a skyscraper might; rather, it respectfully distances itself from them while maintaining a sympathetic horizontal scale. Moreover, the building's placement on its site shows that the architects were mindful of its location in the city's historic center. That is, KMK offset the building slightly on the site that Pei's master plan had established for it, thus allowing the large staircase beside the south entrance to align with Faneuil Hall—a deferential nod toward the 1742 building. The perfectly framed views of Faneuil Hall from within the building, both in the south lobby and in the mayor's suite, accentuate this relationship. These gestures reveal the same respectful attitude that Alexander Parris showed in the 1820s when he aligned his Quincy Market buildings with the older Faneuil Hall. "Thus," Wolf wrote, "two of Boston's grandest undertakings of their day created a new grouping of important civic structures embracing 220 years of Boston history—an ensemble that lies at the heart of the multifarious city."[121]

The relationship between New City Hall and its surroundings notwithstanding, there was a concerted effort among the architects and politicians to make a bold, modern statement that in many ways eschewed the Old Boston. To that end, New City Hall distinctly departs from the Beaux-Arts symmetry of the Second Empire Old City Hall and from the historic character of Scollay Square, which it replaced. One of the principal purposes of the building, after all, was to symbolize a new direction for the city, and the New Boston required a novel architectural statement for its new City Hall.

Political Influences

City Hall's design also responded to the local and national political environment of the early 1960s. One can recognize the local political situation reflected in the KMK design, in that the stylistic differences between New City Hall and its predecessor signified a break from the political corruption and consequent economic decline of the past. The building demonstrated that the people who worked within it were committed to progressive ideals. For instance, the use of exposed concrete, according to Michael McKinnell, corresponded to a need for a definitive statement about Boston's political future. After an earlier generation of politicians had all but run the city into the ground, the new building was intended to symbolize a new political era. "Boston was in a cataclysmic economic and social decline," McKinnell recalled.

> There were serious racial problems and poverty, a precipitous decline in public services, and a lack of faith in the city from the financial com-

munity. City Planner Ed Logue told Mayor Collins that Boston had to make a powerful statement of faith in the city. And that statement was Government Center. Simply put, Government Center is what turned Boston around. Very soon after its completion, the commercial market revived. Now, interestingly enough, most of the buildings built in the complex were in concrete.

City Hall's concrete thus served a politically symbolic purpose. As McKinnell said, it "symbolized a faith in the future—that the building was going to last."[122]

Moreover, the building's expressive massing further broke with tradition in order to make a political statement. Rather than hide the functions of government on the inside of the building, buffered by corridors and passageways, KMK pointed to them on the outside, proudly displaying the locations of the mayor's office, City Council chamber, and councilors' offices through distinctive exterior elements. In turn, from these locations elected officials could not help but see and hear the people of the city passing or gathering outside their windows. Susan and Michael Southworth, in their *AIA Guide to Boston,* recognized this functional lucidity, pointing out that the building's diverse exterior forms (from the "pigeonholes" in the crown to the dramatic thrust of the mayor's office) communicate the variety of governmental functions taking place within.[123]

Boston City Hall, however, expressed a more enduring and widespread political sentiment than simply localized hope for Boston's political future. Several critics, as well as the architects themselves, have ascribed the boldness of the building's design to the optimistic view of government that characterized the Kennedy years—City Hall's monumentality symbolizing a renewed faith in government. As McKinnell later put it, "We always thought that our design for the City Hall should make a 'political statement'—it should be overtly testifying to our beliefs or thoughts about democracy."[124] To that end, McKinnell said, the use of concrete—a serious material—was spurred, in part, by the "euphoria with Kennedy as a heroic figure."[125]

Similarly, Gerhard Kallmann recollected in 1991, "It was the Kennedy era, and we thought of government as more open, which is why we incorporated four entrances into the design."[126] This openness was intended to make the building a meaningful civic center for Bostonians, not only by providing an accessible structure in which to conduct official business, but also by luring pedestrians into and through the building as part of their daily routines, exposing them to the workings of the government around them and reminding city officials who it is that they are serving—essential elements of democracy.

This accessibility stemmed from a heroic conception of government. The architects wrote: "The deliberate openness of the building invites and encourages entrance and passage by people into and through their City Hall. The manipulation of the public spaces seeks to make memorable and significant all aspects of public contact with city agencies. The design of the New Boston City Hall seeks to have built form respond to a new kind of inter-action between people and their government."[127] Perhaps nowhere is this ideal represented more clearly than in the walkway from the upper plaza, passing through the courtyard, and exiting on Congress Street. The courtyard—designed to remain open even when the rest of the building was closed—allowed citizens to observe the workings of their government not only from the exterior (along the street and the plaza), but also from the very center of the building. The *Globe* may very well have had this feature in mind when it described the building as "exciting municipal theater in the round."[128]

Despite the building's progressive aesthetic, Michael McKinnell noted that he and Kallmann always thought this "would be the most conservative building that we had ever designed." By way of explanation, Kallmann said:

> There is good reason for this: government is a very conserving activity, and we felt the building needed staying power. It cannot be iconoclastic if it is concerned with these particular values. There is a certain vigor of government that we wanted to express. Maybe this was influenced by the Kennedy Administration at the time, when there was more optimism about the usefulness of government. In retrospect we may not have thought of this consciously, but it seems to have half come through.

We had to make these elements of government exist with a very strong but not authoritarian presence. This was more important to us than the precise plastic form that they would be, and is sensed in the way we lead stairs and levels up close to them. They have the intimacy from this closeness which is necessary in a democratic government, as well as the dignity necessary to allow the people who govern to be dignified.[129]

Unlike some of the other competition entries, which revealed their designers' preoccupation with formal concerns as they wrapped the multifarious functions of government in a uniformly sleek skin, KMK's was more concerned with functional expression, symbolism, and the spatial and aesthetic relationships among different parts of government. The forms derived not from a "premeditated image" but rather from a visual conception of democratic government.

The resulting complexity of the scheme speaks not just to the architectural debates raging at midcentury but to the nature of the government it houses. McKinnell noted that when looking at paintings of old city halls, one could easily recognize the variety of activities taking place there, "from assignations to buying and selling. A City Hall should be robust enough to withstand the good, terrible, funny and even vulgar events that happen" there.[130] In a similar vein, Charles Millard wrote, New City Hall "embodies classical order and modernist irregularity, traditional and contemporary materials, rugged massiveness and an almost playful spatial continuity, deep shadow and intense highlight, in what is probably the most successful architectural expression yet conceived of the contradictory nature of present-day government, with its conflicting bureaucratic and symbolic functions."[131]

This is not to suggest, however, that Kallmann and McKinnell were both beholden to partisan political ideology. While McKinnell readily admits to being swept up in the optimism and passion of the Kennedy years, Kallmann was more concerned with a timeless and nonideological expression of democracy. As McKinnell put it: "There are these interpretations and transformations of Classical architecture, and for Kallmann the idea that Classical architecture is related to the roots of civilization and democracy. So the politics were important."[132]

Thus, just as Charles Bulfinch used neoclassicism in the Massachusetts State House to establish a direct visual connection between the new American democracy and its antecedents in ancient Greece and Rome, KMK's sense of democratic associations with classical architecture were modernized and manifested in New City Hall.

CHAPTER 4

An Evolving Reputation

It was the best of designs, it was the worst of designs. One critic praised it as "a triumph in architecture"; another derided it as "the blight that is about to visit itself upon the City of Boston." It was at once hailed as a building "as stunning and vast as any Piranesi conceived" and denounced for looking like "the maw of some devouring beast from which you might never emerge alive." Indeed, even a cursory examination of the vast trove of published opinions about Boston's New City Hall over the years reveals that, as in the famous Dickens portrayal of 1790s Europe, "some of its noisiest authorities insisted on its being received, for good or for evil, in the superlative degree of comparison only."[1]

This clamor of criticism erupted as soon as Mayor John Collins revealed the winning design at the Museum of Fine Arts on May 3, 1962. There was an almost palpable sense of astonishment at the unveiling, which led to a variety of reactions from politicians, architects, the media, and ordinary citizens. The *Boston Globe*'s front-page headline announcing the jury's selection presciently read, "And Here's New City

Hall, Apt to Stir Controversy."² More than fifty years later, the controversy shows no sign of abating.

Scholars, architects, journalists, and even politicians have made many attempts over the years to characterize this controversy in Manichaean terms. Conventional wisdom holds that architects love it while everyone else hates it. Others have framed the debate either as a generational split or as a divide between traditionalists and modernists. In tracing the critical reception of Boston City Hall from the 1960s through the early years of the twenty-first century, though, one finds that the building's reputation is much more complex than these simplistic dichotomies suggest. Some of the most vitriolic criticism, for instance, came from established architects (and modernists at that!) such as Edward Durell Stone and J. J. P. Oud, while the building's ardent defenders included some of the city's staunchest cultural conservatives (such as historian Walter Muir Whitehill) and those with no formal training in architectural design (such as Mayor Kevin White). Perhaps the only common characteristic among these many reactions is that there are seemingly no neutral attitudes. Nor is there agreement as to what, exactly, makes New City Hall so wonderful or so awful. Aspects of the design that some people praise (say, its departure from Boston's "traditional" architectural aesthetic) are objects of opprobrium for others.

How, then, is one to make sense of this cacophony of criticism? An exploration of the building's reputation over the past fifty-plus years reveals that both positive and negative reactions tend to address five general characteristics of the design: its aesthetics (how the building looks), its relationship to physical and cultural contexts (how it "fits in"), its functionality (how it works), its symbolism (what it means), and the plaza (which is sometimes discussed concurrently with the building and sometimes evaluated independently).

Published opinions about the building reveal that reactions to it stem not only from architectural tastes but also from political mores. Vicissitudes in political as well as architectural circumstances and sensibilities have led to changes in the building's reputation. Thus the critical reception of the building, and the story of its evolving reputation, are important to Boston City Hall's history—not only for what they say about the building's design and the government it houses, but also for what they reveal about shifting perceptions of both architecture and politics in Boston and throughout the United States.

Aesthetics

Boston City Hall's appearance has long excited both praise and derision. The building's bold and expressive form, molded mostly in exposed concrete on both the interior and the exterior, introduced a novel aesthetic to Boston's downtown area and also largely contrasted with contemporaneous building designs elsewhere throughout the country. Such a progressive style was bound to elicit strong opinions from both admirers and detractors.

Initial reactions in the local press were generally positive. A *Boston Globe* article printed the day after Mayor Collins unveiled the jury's choice was full of praise, predicting that this new building would put Boston in the forefront of architectural innovation. While recognizing that the style was not to everyone's liking, the reporter brushed off negative criticism as little more than the fleeting visceral reaction of traditionalists opposed to a progressive aesthetic. "Like much that is new in art," he noted, "it shocks some at first glance, or even second. To embrace the new always requires an intellectual effort that is not easy." Novelty was, in his view, the design's best attribute. Whereas the old City Hall was "too imitative to excite controversy," the new building was an "imaginative conception" that "imitates no other, but could set a fashion in a decade that badly needs one."[3]

Several national publications praised this unconventionality as well. *Horizon,* for instance, featured the building in an article by the design critic Eric Larrabee admiringly titled "Boston Chooses the Future." Larrabee lauded the "rhythm of changing patterns and volumes that will emerge as one walks the halls and climbs the stairs," thus making City Hall an aesthetically "interesting building to move around in, which is perhaps the most generous gift an architect can bestow." Larrabee also claimed that by opening up the interior, with the public area at ground level flowing seamlessly into the ceremonial spaces above, KMK had achieved "a quality suitable to civic ceremonial, both imposing and inviting."[4]

Reactions within the architectural community, meanwhile, were split mostly along traditionalist-modernist lines, with some notable exceptions. One outspoken critic was the curmudgeonly local architect William Stanley Parker. In a scathing review, he wrote that the winning design lacked all of the "various qualities that appeal such as simplicity, orderliness, composition of the exterior, a principal focus of interest on the main entrance to a structure, the relation of openings to solid structure, etc."[5] Similar criticism came from ninety-one-year-old Edward T. P. Graham, whom the *Globe* in 1962 dubbed the "dean of Boston architects." Graham, who had designed the imposing 1912 City Hall Annex on Court Street, objected to New City Hall's lack of "stateliness" and "timeless appeal." He also claimed that it was stylistically "too far ahead" of the period and the people of Boston.[6] When a *Globe* reporter inquired about his antipathy toward the building, Graham retrieved from his files a twenty-five-year-old design that he had produced for a new City Hall, which would essentially have been an expansion of his 1912 Annex, featuring a limestone-clad one-hundred-foot façade on School Street adorned with a massive colonnade. This design speaks to Graham's traditionalist stylistic sensibilities, and since Graham had been awarded the lucrative Annex contract by Mayor John F. Fitzgerald, it is also possible that he had political objections to KMK's symbol of the New Boston. In any event, Graham's staunchly historicist vision for a new building could scarcely have contrasted more with the KMK design's avant-garde aesthetic.

While the antipathy of older traditionalists such as Parker and Graham was to be expected, there were some modernists and younger architects who objected to the winning design as well. Edward Durell Stone, for instance, remarked that the building looked like "the crate that Faneuil Hall came in."[7] Similarly, Dutch modernist J. J. P. Oud reportedly criticized it for being a "super-academic" invention of paper architects.[8] Still others chided the design for being too derivative. For instance, in *Perspecta 9/10*, the 1965 issue of the Yale architectural journal, editor Robert A. M. Stern, then a graduate student in architecture who would later champion postmodernism, included fifteen pages of plans and drawings of New City Hall. These appear without commentary, except for a one-paragraph blurb in the table of contents, in which Stern noted that the KMK design "began as a somewhat stilted evocation of Corbusian form with an admixture of shapes derived from the work of Aalto by way of England." Subsequently, Stern relented a bit, pointing out that the building "has, under the pressures of actual construction, evolved into a rich, demanding, and in many ways, highly original building."[9] Very little in the design had changed between its unveiling in 1962 and the time when construction was well under way in 1965 (and, for that matter, in 1969, when the building opened), so this comment suggests more a change of heart on the part of the editor himself than a change in the structure.

The distaste of these men notwithstanding, many modernists came out in support of the design, including the most prominent architect working in the Boston area at the time: Walter Gropius. "I'm very much impressed and honestly think it has a beautiful scheme," Gropius remarked shortly after the jury announced its decision. The architects, he said, had produced a design "of human scale, a large simple body subdivided in small parts with real richness and detail—a very fortunate scheme."[10] Gropius was not alone in this assessment. Many younger or iconoclastic architects, in particular, celebrated the building's break with aesthetic tradition and its forceful challenge to the dogma of orthodox modernism.

Even Philip Johnson, who had long been a champion of mainstream modernism, congratulated Kallmann and McKinnell after they won the competition. While Johnson would eventually move from modernism to postmodernism in his own designs, he had yet to make this leap in the early 1960s. The Boston City Hall competition took place only five years after Johnson had worked with Mies to design the Seagram Building. While Johnson's own designs from the early 1960s—including the Amon Carter Museum in Fort Worth and the New York State Theater at Lincoln Center—show that he had advanced beyond the stripped-down Miesian aesthetic of the Seagram Building and his own "Glass House," they are nevertheless straightforwardly modernist in their composition. Although the KMK design differed from Johnson's own aesthetic philosophy at the time, he nevertheless graciously appreciated the proposed building on its own terms.[11]

Accolades also came from at least one of the "also-rans" in the competition. Local architect Robert Sturgis wrote that he was "tremendously pleased with the winning design," and he predicted that for the people of Boston, the "new City Hall will be a pleasure to visit. It will belong to us." Sturgis recognized that "the overall form is unfamiliar to most Bostonians, but perhaps only one who has grappled with the problem can appreciate how difficult it was to make this vast building something which can be understood by the man on the street." Acknowledging condemnation from some quarters, Sturgis suggested that once the building opened, the experience of it would win converts in a way that viewing a model could not.[12]

Debate over the design was not limited to architects and scholars; ordinary citizens weighed in with their assessments as well. The *Globe* described the response among those who viewed the KMK model on display at the MFA in the wake of the jury's announcement: "Some of the kibitzers looked annoyed, some pleased, and some puzzled."[13] A flood of letters to the editor revealed similar reactions, ranging from ire to delight to bafflement. Among opponents, few minced words. One citizen wrote trenchantly of "the blight that is about to visit itself upon the City of Boston in the form of your new City Hall," saying that the "orgy of self-expression" from the architects would conjure up "the horrors of war in perpetuity."[14] Even letter writers expressing admiration recognized that there was a great deal of controversy about it. As one writer asserted, "The exciting design will frighten the cautious; but in a project of this importance, Boston has a great opportunity to achieve a kind of stardom among the cities for a bold exciting and certainly new City Hall."[15]

While some reveled in the mysteriousness of the design's stylistic antecedents, delighting in conjecturing about the apparent references to Gothic, Egyptian, Minoan, or Asian architecture, others balked at such complexity. "Even its approvers find it difficult to trace its origin:

Is it Grecian? Is it Oriental? A mixture of both?" complained one letter writer.[16] Much of this early criticism can be attributed to the novelty of the aesthetic. Michael McKinnell, in recognizing this, believed that "the more this model is explained to the people, the more people should like it."[17]

By the time City Hall was approaching completion in early 1969, the initial shock had worn off, and many reviews complimented the building's appearance. A February 1969 *Globe* editorial dubbed it the "Jewel of the New Boston," noting that the architects "have given Boston a civic monument worthy of her highest political and artistic aspirations." As it had done seven years earlier, the editorial board dismissed criticism, claiming: "The mere passage of time, we predict, will render the building acceptable to many of the traditionalists who now condemn it. Meanwhile, this sturdy, dignified, welcoming edifice of brick and concrete offers myriad perceptual delights to all who are not intellectually or emotionally wedded to the architectural norms of the past."[18]

Praise for the building at this juncture was no less vigorous in the national press. *Time* magazine noted that on City Hall's exterior, "visitors see soaring public spaces as stunning and vast as any Piranesi conceived in his 18th century etchings."[19] Likewise, the *Washington Post*'s Wolf Von Eckardt wrote, "In the chaos of construction work, it is clear that the Kallmann—McKinnell—Knowles City Hall provides precisely what was needed to make Boston's government center the greatest triumph of urban design since New York's Rockefeller Center was built in the 1930's."[20]

The building also found an early and indefatigable admirer in Ada Louise Huxtable, architecture critic for the *New York Times,* and perhaps the most prominent arbiter of architectural taste in the popular press at the time. Writing on the occasion of the building's inauguration in February 1969, Huxtable praised the aesthetic boldness, finding virtue in the building's roughness and expressiveness. "The result," she wrote, "is a tough and complex building for a tough and complex age, a structure of dignity, humanism, and power. It mixes strengths with subtleties. It will outlast the last hurrah." Moreover, she commended the architects for not producing a building that was merely an abstract package—"space as container," in Huxtable's words. Instead, this was "space molded to function, form, and expressive purpose," in which the irregular shapes on the building's surface revealed the mechanical services and functions that were taking place within.[21]

Huxtable also offers a potential clue as to the origins of the myth that architects love the building while everybody else hates it. The article begins with an anecdote about a Boston cabbie:

> "Whatever it is, it's not beautiful," said the Boston cabdriver taking the visitor to the new City Hall. "What would you call it, Gothic?" asked another. Which about sums up the architectural gap, or abyss, as it exists between those who design and those who use twentieth-century buildings. . . . Not only cabdrivers are puzzled by the unconventional structure. Cultural and community leaders who are also society's decision makers and a public with more and higher education than at any time in history also draw a blank. Too bad about that architecture gap.[22]

Huxtable may not have been the first to propose such an "architecture gap." Nevertheless, her stature as the preeminent American architecture critic would certainly have lent credibility to a notion that is proved specious by even a cursory glance at the many letters of approbation from community leaders and the public.

The early aesthetic controversy among architects seemed to dissolve into nearly unanimous praise when the building opened in 1969. Robert Sturgis, the also-ran local architect who had admired the KMK design in 1962, again chimed in with accolades, noting: "The new city hall has received unanimous praise from the most hard-bitten of professional critics, even from normally-critical students. Earlier critics are given pause and are discovering new things."[23] When the American Institute of Architects met in Boston in 1970, its members from across the country were virtually of one mind regarding the benefits of the design. Architects from places as disparate as Florida, Oklahoma, Connecticut, and Washington, D.C., heaped praise on the building. One architect from Kansas told a reporter, "I'm very impressed with

City Hall. It's a great bit of architecture," while another from Los Angeles added: "I like City Hall. A couple of young men had the courage to break away from tradition. It makes great use of space and good arrangement of brick and concrete.... As time goes on, your City Hall will live."[24]

The adulation among architects at this moment would seem to suggest that the idealistic vision of a New Boston, symbolized in a grand modern home for its municipal government, had finally come to pass. But the young building was still not without its critics—even within the architectural profession. In a June 1970 article in *Architectural Review,* Columbia University architecture professor and preservationist James Marston Fitch criticized the building's many overhangs for needlessly creating spaces with "no life-support capacity."[25] Fitch was an ardent preservationist and a foe of urban renewal projects in general, so it is not surprising that he would have opposed this design.

Similarly, the eminent British architectural historian Nikolaus Pevsner wrote that "aggressive and overpowering" are "the dominant, the domineering qualities of the new Boston City Hall," which he called "wildly arbitrary in its motifs, oppressively top-heavy and forbidding rather than inviting. It is a *tour de force,* and one marvels at the courage of the City authorities in accepting it."[26] Pevsner, who had penned several volumes about modern architecture—focusing on its early practitioners—likely objected to the unorthodox modernism of the KMK design.

Negative criticism in the popular press at this point was more wistful and subdued. By the time the building opened, many opponents had come to accept it, ruefully, as a fait accompli, which no amount of ex post facto complaining could undo. For instance, *Globe* columnist Anne Ford wrote in 1970: "The new City Hall may be an architect's delight, but it will take many years before the average citizen can shout huzzah. It's like an elderly lady putting on a mini-skirt. Takes a while to get used to her foible. Meanwhile, one is tolerant, a bit embarrassed for her, but hopes to get used to it."[27]

The opinions of one group warrant special attention: the politicians and officials who worked in City Hall. Soon after the unveiling, Mayor

Collins dubbed it "exciting" and "monumental," adding, "It's not a routine piece of architecture, but it's not supposed to be."[28] Governor Volpe echoed Collins's sentiments, calling it "exciting, bold, imaginative, and economical."[29] Senator Edward Kennedy praised the building when he participated in the opening celebrations, characterizing it as "historic, impressive and controversial," with the controversy (in Kennedy's estimation) being a product of its greatness. "Every important building is controversial," he said.[30] BRA chief Edward Logue even credited the new City Hall with influencing his decision to run for mayor in 1967. In a brief note to Kallmann and McKinnell, Logue wrote, "I spent an hour in the new mayor's office, and I decided I couldn't bear not to occupy it!"[31]

Collins's successor, Kevin White, was initially ambivalent about the building and at first found it difficult to adapt to his new home. "We automatically think of temple façades and classical gingerbread when we think of a City Hall," White told *Newsweek* in 1969. "It's hard to give that up for a way-out building like this. It was a traumatic shock at first." But he soon became an admirer as he found the style analogous to his political philosophy. "Now," he said, "I have a great pride of residency and find the building functions remarkably well. Perhaps a progressive architecture can prompt a more progressive politics."[32]

Not everyone who worked in the building was pleased, though. City Councilor Patrick F. McDonough quipped, "The only thing missing is the gas pumps."[33] Another municipal employee (identified in a 1969 newspaper article only as "an old timer") said on the eve of his impending move to his new office: "The old place was comfortable—an old shoe—but this one is cold. It's like working in the Under Common garage."[34] In 2005, an *ArchitectureBoston* article included reflections from three current and former city employees. Ted Landsmark, who worked in the office of the mayor from 1988 to 1997, focused on what he perceived to be the "cold and businesslike" feel imparted by the concrete. "I always found that full frontal view to be rather intimidating," he recalled some years later. "The dental-like nature of the front façade makes you feel as through you're stepping into the maw of some devouring beast from which you might never emerge alive."[35] Similarly,

Carter Wilkie, who worked for Mayor Thomas Menino from 1997 to 2000, complained that City Hall "is probably the most cheerless building I've ever worked in, in my career." He too objected principally to the material, saying, "All of the dark, gloomy, bleak concrete, wall after wall of it, is oppressive as you walk through."[36]

Ellen Lipsey, executive director of the Boston Landmarks Commission, who began working in City Hall in 1980, took a different view. Looking back, she praised the building as a "landmark visually, and in terms of international architecture. . . . It fits into the tradition of grand civic architecture, although it's not traditional. I think it is particularly important now [in the early twenty-first century], because Boston has become known, in a pejorative sense, for red-brick contemporary buildings, and for being timid and very conservative about architecture."[37] Thus for Lipsey, the novel aesthetic, and the concrete that Landsmark and Wilkie disdained, were benefits.

As the years passed, criticism of the building's appearance persisted among politicians, yet even the most strident denunciations met with equally ardent defenses of the design. In 2004, for instance, Councilors John Tobin and Paul Scapicchio proposed demolishing City Hall, which prompted an editorial in the *Globe* reproving them for their youthful rashness. According to the editorial board, these councilors were "too young to remember the era in which Boston City Hall was conceived and built. . . . The bold modernism of the design showed that city government was ready to engage the culture of the mid-20th century. Boston has transformed itself in the intervening four decades, and City Hall, rather than being torn down as the councilors suggest, should be recognized and buffed up to reflect its importance to the city's history."[38]

Thomas Menino, mayor from 1993 through 2013, twice proposed abandoning the building in favor of a new structure. In an editorial response to Menino's first call for the city to tear the building down, a *Globe* editorial maintained that even with its flaws, the Government Center complex "still enhances Boston's reputation as a center of government. . . . City Hall, to be sure, is not a perfect building. Henry Wood, a partner in the firm that designed it, acknowledges that the concrete has not weathered as well as had been anticipated. But the deft use of this material with brick, combined with the particular arrangement of angles, compels attention even after 30 years."[39]

Thus, controversy over New City Hall's aesthetics is as complex as the geometry of the building's exterior. From day one it has been the subject of both praise and criticism, with no agreement among (or even within) the various groups weighing in on the debate. As Huxtable wrote in the *Wall Street Journal* in 2009, "Boston detests its City Hall. Attacks on the beleaguered building include calls for its demolition by a mayor determined to get rid of it and a public persistently unconverted to modernism and particularly hostile to the Brutalist aesthetic."[40] Thus, on the whole, the general perception of the building's aesthetic reputation is that Bostonians have not—despite the hopeful predictions of some early defenders—come to admire its appearance. That said, the ardor of the building's admirers has not diminished over time, and perhaps when the pendulum of aesthetic tastes swings back in favor of concrete architecture, the building may yet gain the widespread appreciation it deserves.

Context

While Boston City Hall's appearance elicited both criticism and praise, so too did the building's relationship with its physical surroundings and with the city's history and culture. Most people agree that the KMK design has little in common stylistically with Boston's traditional architecture. The point of contention, then, has been whether these inherent differences are good or bad, and whether such a novel building can ever coexist peacefully with its historic neighbors.

Even those who admire the building have noted its peculiarity in the context of downtown Boston. Peter Collins, who had been Michael McKinnell's teacher at the University of Manchester, pointed out the building's stronger aesthetic and philosophical connection to Europe than to its hometown. "Certainly the ideas [the architects] have incorporated into it seem more related to avant-garde ideas in Europe than to those current [in America]," Collins wrote in *The Guardian*.[41] Similarly, architectural historian Sibyl Moholy-Nagy deemed City Hall more European than American because of the contradiction in the architects' desire to create a building that was at once monumental and populist—a clash of ideals that Moholy-Nagy believed Americans were incapable of reconciling. "Perhaps it is permissible for a fellow European to point out to the architects the contradiction between involving everybody and monumentality," Moholy-Nagy wrote. "The dignity and aloofness of public office and its paradigmatic quality are Old World traditions that have fallen short of an architectural solution in Boston because they are meaningless in the U.S."[42]

Not surprisingly, traditionalists objected to this divergence from Boston's existing architecture. William Stanley Parker acidly remarked: "The winning design ... suggests rather that it might be a design for a City Hall in Cairo or Venice or some other city in the Near or Far East. It just doesn't look to me like a City Hall for Boston. That doesn't mean that it should look as if it had been designed by H. H. Richardson or be a copy enlarged of the old State House, but it should somehow 'look like Boston.'"[43]

Both Parker and fellow traditionalist Edward T. P. Graham were among eighteen architects who formed the Citizens' Committee for a Bostonian City Hall, which submitted a petition shortly after the announcement of the winning design, urging the city not to construct it. (Nelson Aldrich, whose firm served as KMK's collaborating architects, later said of this committee: "The people who criticized were not very formidable as influential architects. But it was splashed all over the papers, you know, how the papers would react to that kind of thing.")[44] The committee listed many perceived deficiencies, but perhaps the most important of these (as the name of the group suggests) was that the proposed building was incompatible with Boston's culture and historical architecture. As the petition stated:

> The winning design is thoroughly lacking in composition, scale, and architectural feeling; and has no regard for the background and environment in which it must, perforce, be a major and dominant edifice.
>
> The criticisms of the design, noted above, we believe are valid and we believe that they indicate why the design fails so significantly to do that honor to the past that the commission desired.[45]

Other local architects and scholars, meanwhile, embraced the design's exoticism. MIT architectural historian Albert Bush-Brown, for instance, praised the building for precisely the reason that the Citizens' Committee criticized it. "No bows to the Georgian," Bush-Brown wrote. "No weak-kneed copying of the State House Dome. Or the Faneuil Hall roof. Nothing but a whole-hearted affirmation of a new time, new social needs and the new technology and new aesthetics to declare our faith in the civic instrument of government." Other Bostonians, Bush-Brown predicted, would in time come to admire this novelty too. "Overall," he averred, "the form is compelling, a unique image whose dignified bearing and sensible arrangement will impress themselves upon Boston's citizens."[46]

Local architect Hugh Stubbins, who served as chairman of the BRA's architectural advisory committee, also praised the avant-garde style, noting that life in mid-twentieth-century Boston was different from that in previous ages, "and therefore our physical environment will be different in each successive era." Stubbins accordingly dismissed criticism from traditionalists and argued that architects "can no longer imitate"; instead there "has to be a new style for Boston which will and must express our own times . . . needs, economic way of life."[47]

In addition to considering the broad physical and historical context of the new City Hall, observers also considered the building's relationship to its immediate neighbors in the Government Center area. I. M. Pei complimented the design for its harmonious contributions to his master plan, saying that it succeeded in "bringing back to downtown Boston the urban space which we don't have."[48] Walter Gropius found that City Hall "fits in very well with the Federal Building," which Gropius's firm, TAC, had designed.[49] Stubbins agreed with Gropius's assessment, saying that City Hall would dominate the space, while the smooth federal building exterior would serve as an effective and agreeable contrast to the rugged City Hall.[50]

As was the case in the debate over aesthetics, many citizens also weighed in with their opinions on the winning design's relationship to the historic city. One Bostonian lamented that it "suggests nothing of the origins of Boston and its history," and that it "has nothing to do with Boston—it is an anonymous, unrelated structure belonging everywhere and nowhere."[51] Another wrote, "When it has ceased to be new, and its challenge has worn out and other newer forms have captured our attention, who shall say whether it will have become endeared to us or, on the other hand the butt of our ridicule?"[52]

Other Bostonians, meanwhile, applauded the building for not slavishly aping the redbrick or gray granite architecture that had long dominated the city. One resident recalled the words of the German architect Karl Friedrich Schinkel: "Every great age had its style of building, why shouldn't we have ours?" This novelty "comes at a time when this city needs to reevaluate and revamp herself. . . . Indeed we should be proud that the chosen design does not sing by the present day melody of Beacon Hill and Boston, as one letter writer whimpered. The melody I hear around here today is a rather dissonant and declining one, not to mention scandalous."[53]

The debate found its way into the news pages of the press as well. *Globe* critic Robert Taylor wrote:

> There are a number of obvious reasons why the layman might venture subjective opinion. New City Hall preserves the scale of the surrounding area: despite the size required, the building proper looks like a place human beings may comfortably inhabit (the slabs and overhangs of the simple facade won't numb; on the contrary, the average office skyscraper, which one often can't tell is connected to the ground, inspires far greater uneasiness); and finally, new City Hall links together sections of the Government Center appearing, till now, planeless.[54]

In the *Quincy Patriot Ledger*, veteran Boston City Hall correspondent Ian Menzies praised the building's use of concrete, noting that by contrasting with its historical neighbors, City Hall demonstrated that Boston's government was strong and forward-looking—not beholden to its history, nor (as in many other cities) relegated to a purely utilitarian office tower.[55]

On the eve of the official opening, the *Globe* downplayed differences between the new building and the historic city. The paper argued: "The new City Hall is as much a product of the environment of Boston as the Old State House. The two can live cheek by jowl and not betray the centuries which separate them." A later *Globe* article also lauded City Hall's relationship to Boston: "It is more than an architectural monument, it is a testament that Boston for all her faults has always done things with a grace and touch of boldness that is lacking elsewhere."[56]

Globe writer Anthony Yudis recognized that the building contrasted with its surroundings in 1969, but he foresaw it eventually fitting in, as the novelty was sure to be a catalyst for other bold changes throughout the city. Writing on the occasion of the building's opening, Yudis invited his readers to take a mental leap in time and view the city of 1979 from the windows of City Hall. From this vantage point, one would see a skyline that had been reinvigorated by this building. He predicted that within a decade, Boston's historic architectural monuments would gain much-needed energy and liveliness from their new neighbors. "Even the restoration of the old historic Boston adjacent to us is somewhat of a startling change," Yudis wrote, "for Boston could not enjoy its old architectural treasures ten years ago as it does now in this new setting."[57]

Even sportswriter Bud Collins weighed in, writing that City Hall, "a wild political bunker, with all that concrete and those thousands of bricks inside and out may seem cold, but it is undeniably exciting, too." Collins saw the revolutionary spirit as fitting in perfectly with the city's storied past. "Samuel Adams," Collins wrote, "standing in bronze across the street, does not appear perturbed by the encroachment of the exotic hulk taking some of his sun. Sam, one of the ancient Scollay warriors, was, after all, a revolutionary."[58]

Like the press, Boston's politicians, too, have disagreed about the building's relationship to the surrounding city. Raymond Flynn and Thomas Menino routinely lambasted what they regarded as an un-Bostonian design. Flynn's predecessor, Kevin White, however, lauded it, both during his term in office and afterwards. In 1991, in response to criticism that the building did not look like other Boston architecture, White observed:

> I was in Australia for a conference of architects that was stimulated by Prince Charles' complaint that London's new buildings looked horrible next to cathedrals. I argued that you don't want buildings to look alike.... Each period has to express its own vitality. I don't want to sound like a broken-down arts major from Williams College, but Bulfinch didn't have half the credentials Kallmann has. Half the time, Bulfinch was a developer, and his State House is a copy of St. Paul's Cathedral in London, in a way.[59]

For White, as for Stubbins, Yudis, Bush-Brown, and many others, the stylistic variety that the modernist New City Hall introduced to downtown Boston was a virtue. They saw in the design a bold statement that Boston's cultural, political, and architectural histories had not ended in the age of Bulfinch, Bryant, or Richardson. Rather, the city would continue to be enriched by new forms serving as epochal monuments within a dynamic metropolis.

Functionality

Even before construction began on New City Hall, critics were admiring its purported functionality. It seemed both suitable for municipal government workers and accessible to the public. A writer for *Horizon* magazine, for instance, commended the jury for choosing a design that "had 'solved' the problem—that is to say, it had reconciled and fulfilled the requirements of the program both spatially and structurally."[60] Similarly, Peter Collins wrote in *The Guardian*, "Architecture asserts itself, and it is clear, even from the plans and the model, that the civic dignitaries here will enjoy such a labyrinthine sequence of spaces, and such a breath-taking variety of levels and ceiling heights, as has not been seen since the collapse of King Minos's palace at Knossos." Whereas later critics would use the term "labyrinthine" pejoratively, Collins saw it as a benefit, writing, "The practical and aesthetic virtues of this kind of compositional planning are undeniable."[61]

Another encomium came from MIT architecture professor Henry Millon. What Collins regarded as a virtuous labyrinth, Millon saw as a simple and accessible building. To that end, Millon asked his readers to make an imaginary trip to the (as yet unbuilt) New City Hall. "Note how easy it is to find your destination on the public levels," he wrote. "The route has been clear and easy to apprehend. Your path has been simple and direct." Millon also predicted that the building would provide a welcome respite from the elements in extreme weather. "The lower floors, deep in shadow, will suggest inviting coolness on a hot Summer day and, at the same time, on a short gray Winter day, the illuminated lower floor will invite you in as it suggests warm enclosure."[62]

Incidentally, the anticipated accessibility that Millon praised would eventually be challenged by other observers once the building opened. For instance, Millon failed to recognize that the vast plaza would expose passersby to the blazing summer sun and the frigid winter winds. Also, the simplicity (as Millon judged it) of the route on paper contrasted with the complexity of the space in reality (as Bostonians paying a visit to the completed building would later make clear). Millon's comments reveal that functionality, more than any other feature of the building, was difficult to assess from drawings and models. As Sibyl Moholy-Nagy pointed out, "prenatal word-fencing"—commentaries on a design rather than on the completed building—is of little use. "Architecture is pure pragma, the thing done," Moholy-Nagy asserted. "It is the salvation and sometimes the tragedy of the architect that the accomplished fact obliterates the fictitious image that preceded it. The only justification of any building is its impact on the user."[63]

Once New City Hall opened, analyses of its functionality became more specific and more justifiable. This is not to say that all praise was replaced by criticism. An adulatory review appeared in the February 21, 1969, issue of *Time*, claiming the completed building had actually proven its early detractors wrong. "Those who expected to find the building's interior gloomy and intimidating have been surprised by its airy openness," the article pointed out. "It is bathed in natural light, which pours down a central courtyard and through wide light shafts rising the full height of the nine story building." The review also lauded the "magnificent ceremonial flight of stairs" and the "two tremendous lobbies," and claimed that the building was "extraordinarily accessible" by dint of its central location in the city and the concourse running through the fourth floor.[64]

This issue of accessibility was particularly contentious. For instance, architectural theorist David Monteyne wrote that one of the dominant objections to the building was "a lack of function in the political process hosted in the space, especially the Council Chamber."[65] Many Bostonians, however, praised the new chamber as being far more accessible than the top-floor council chamber in Old City Hall. One letter to the editor noted, "To attend meetings of the City Council, we will no longer have to ascend five floors in a tiny elevator but may reach it directly in its prominent location on the second floor."[66]

Some of the most vocal critics of the building's functionality have been those who work within it. Early antipathy came from city councilors who felt that they were being downgraded in the transition from the old building because their offices and the council chamber were still not complete when nearly all the other departments had moved into the new building.[67] Also, a controversy about substandard furnishings (such as a cracked conference table for the City Council) further incited ire. Yet ever-contentious municipal politics was more to blame for these conflicts than the building's design. Councilors who were fighting over the new furniture refused to allocate $24,000 for a room-size horseshoe-shaped installation of desks that would have completed the new council chamber. Ada Louise Huxtable scoffed that as the building opened, Councilors John L. Saltonstall and Joseph Timilty were working "side by side at old desks moved from the old City Hall that suggest the old politics.... Tradition dies hard in Boston."[68]

In 1988, Councilor David Scondras, calling the building "truly an albatross," proposed selling City Hall and replacing it with an office tower to house city government. Scondras's complaints were chiefly about functionality: a leaky roof, high heating bills, and a confusing layout.[69] Three years later, councilor Albert "Dapper" O'Neil echoed Scondras's complaints and claimed that the building's functional problems were beyond hope: "We've already spent a fortune on City Hall, and the goddamn place is still a disgrace."[70] In response to calls to sell the building, though, *Globe* architecture critic Robert Campbell penned a vehement defense of the design, arguing that it "remains a memorable and powerful image" and urging that the city needed to start treating the building with pride rather than with neglect.[71] Similarly, a *Globe* editorial pointed out that "while officials complain about the layout inside, it is far more friendly to infrequent visitors than the State House a few blocks away."[72]

Some politicians also defended the building's functionality. For instance, Kevin White maintained that City Hall "functions remarkably well." Even after having been out of office for nearly a decade, White still insisted: "The design is brilliant. I've walked the hallways a million times—I'm not sure I wanted to know what was going on inside the offices—but I'll tell you, I was never bored. The Mayor's office? Magnificent. George McGovern stopped by and said he didn't know where I was going politically, but in terms of an office, it would all be downhill" (fig. 12). White claimed that he preferred City Hall to the State House, saying of the latter, "Sure, it says something about Boston that no one wants to take away, but the governor's office is small, the building's expensive to heat and it's dark in the middle." When Ray Flynn complained that City Hall, too, was difficult to heat, White responded, "I worked at City Hall, and if Ray Flynn needs a portable heater, somebody's putting paper in his pipes or else it's his thin Irish blood, because, you know, he comes from the south of Ireland, Kerry."[73]

As these comments make clear, seemingly everyone who has worked in City Hall has had something to say about it. This is not a recent phenomenon. A *Globe* article from February 1969 claimed that as two thousand workers were moving in, two thousand opinions were emerging. The article found the battle lines drawn between "old-timers" who were "creatures of habit, [and] had been looking out the same windows for a collective total of three centuries," and younger employees, who saw the move as "an exciting experience."[74] Perhaps the biggest gripe among employees had nothing to do with the design itself but rather with the lack of a cafeteria in the building, while compliments frequently dealt with the cleanliness and improved amenities (more restrooms, better air conditioning, and reliable elevators).

FIGURE 12. Boston City Hall, Eagle Room. Part of the mayor's suite, this room was initially intended to be the municipal library. Ed Logue claimed that after spending time in the mayor's office, he couldn't bear not to occupy it, and he announced his candidacy for office. Library of Congress, Prints & Photographs Division, Historic American Building Survey, HABS MASS, 13-BOST, 71-12.

On the whole, employees early on seemed excited by the new building. As local architect Joan Wood recalled, "I remember the pride people took in it—the secretaries, the people at the front desk, all got dressed up for work, which they never did in the old City Hall."[75] Herb Gleason, who served in Kevin White's administration from 1968 to 1979, praised the building for being "very workable, remarkably flexible."[76] Indeed, as a 1969 article indicated, the objections of a few "old-timers" and the odd disgruntled city councilor notwithstanding, "the combination of newness of the surroundings and the obvious comparison with the dingy old city hall and annex make most city employees glad of their new temple."[77]

As the building has aged, younger generations have assessed the building's functionality less favorably. Some have complained that the interior layout is too confusing. Others have lambasted the outmoded

HVAC infrastructure and what they regard as excessive heating and cooling costs for the building's vast atria. And as interest in environmentally friendly architecture has increased in recent years, some critics have claimed that City Hall is woefully inefficient and not "green."

Thirty-five years after City Hall opened, a *Globe* reporter asked Gerhard Kallmann about some of these perceived functional problems. In response to claims that the building is difficult to heat, Kallmann blamed maintenance deficiencies and pointed out that because of the engineering that left ductwork exposed through open trusses, the process of updating the infrastructure would be relatively easy.[78] Regarding the confusing floor plan, Kallmann explained, "The building is sited on a hillside, which makes it complex and exciting." Years earlier, Kallmann had conceded:

> Well, it's not the easiest building to find your way around in, but we believe it's not impossibly difficult. Any significant building makes demands so that it cannot be taken for granted. It should be a challenge. As with the environment, you need gritty inner space to make you feel you exist, a certain pressure. I'm fascinated by labyrinths as a metaphor for life. You can make things too easy so that there's nothing to resist you. The marvelous thing in life is to find a slight bend, as the torrent in the mountain that has to make a detour. When the way is clear, we enjoy the eddy. Without it, life is banal and obvious.[79]

To the implication that efficiency and functionality had been sacrificed on the altar of complex aesthetics, Kallmann shot back: "A civic building is an opportunity for artistic expression, and the iconic aspect becomes more important, but you pay for the beauty in some way. We are interested in images of complexity and stability that can hold our interest over a long time, and architecture that is not iconoclastic but a celebration of contemporary life and its institutions."[80]

Kallmann's comments remind us not only of his noble goals for New City Hall, which the Government Center Commission, the Collins administration, and many Bostonians embraced in the early 1960s, but also of the nature of architecture as one of mankind's greatest cultural achievements. "A bicycle shed is a building," wrote Nikolaus Pevsner. "Lincoln Cathedral is a piece of architecture."[81] Some there are who would prefer a purely utilitarian City Hall. But Kallmann, McKinnell and Knowles understood that New City Hall must do more than simply enclose space; it must combine functional imperatives with aesthetic appeal and sensuous effect. For this reason, they designed not a bicycle shed but a cathedral for Boston's municipal government.

Symbolism

All parties involved in the New City Hall project—the architects who designed it, the jurors who selected it, the government that built it—knew that the building would serve more than a purely functional role. It was also a symbol of the New Boston. That being the case, it is not surprising to find among the many published opinions about the building a host of comments concerning its symbolic successes and shortcomings.

Anthony Yudis, who had covered the design and construction in a series of articles for the *Globe*, wrote in 1969, "New City Hall . . . symbolizes not only architectural attainment linking Old Boston with the New Boston, but serves significantly as well as a 'centerpiece' symbol and prototype for the wider architectural and planning drama that surrounds it." Yudis predicted that the painful memories of Boston's sordid recent past would quickly be swept away with the new architectural and political tide. "With the New City Hall," Yudis concluded, "the early years of the 20th Century's 'last hurrah' have all but been forgotten."[82] For Yudis, then, this was a smashing symbolic success. The building represented not only a new and prosperous era in the administration of the city, but also a progressive architectural aesthetic effectively related to both the city's illustrious history and its promising future, in which the political divisiveness and ethnic tensions of the past would be but distant memories.

In the national press, Ada Louise Huxtable lauded the building's symbolic achievements in much the same terms. She averred, for example, that it successfully represented the best qualities of the municipal government under Hynes and Collins. "It confers, in a kind of architectural status transferral," she wrote, "an instant image of progressive excellence on a city government traditionally known for something less than creativity and quality. That is an old trick of architecture called symbolism." She furthermore praised the building's physical and symbolic openness at the ground level, its concrete and brick construction (which was "meant to be impervious to the vicissitudes of changing tastes and administrations"), as well as its refreshingly modernist take on monumentality.[83]

Wolf Von Eckardt also lauded the building for the message it conveyed about municipal government. He praised the vast atrium of the south lobby as "a gathering place, all open and public with magnificent stairs, balconies and terraces, a great agora, a place that proclaims the majesty of government, by the people."[84] Similarly, art historian Charles W. Millard, writing in the *Hudson Review* in 1970, called it "the most successful architectural expression yet conceived of the contradictory nature of present-day government, with its conflicting bureaucratic and symbolic functions."[85]

There were, however, many who disagreed with these positive interpretations of the building's symbolism. In response to Von Eckardt's glowing review, one Bostonian wrote that the building was "distant, oppressive, hulking—the perfect home for some remote mechanized bureaucracy. Is this the visible form we want our supposedly democratic system to take?" The writer acknowledged that the building was "the work of a highly gifted and intelligent artist," but he called it "tragic" that the design "should exemplify, consciously or not, precisely those forces in modern life which depress and repel so many; the massive, uncaring impersonality of our present-day institutions."[86]

Symbolism would become even more of a contentious issue as New City Hall aged. As MIT architecture professor William Mitchell observed, "Any symbolism, especially in something like a city hall, is a crystallization of the cultural attitudes prevailing at the moment when it was conceived."[87] For that reason, the powerful metaphors of 1960s government that the architects were deliberate (and, it would seem, successful) in incorporating into their design rendered attitudes about the building vulnerable to changing political mores. As ideas about politics evolved, so too did opinions about the architecture. For instance, *Globe* columnist Tom Keane remarked in 2007:

> To me, what the building says about government is not a welcome message today. The building tends to stand alone, moat-like. It is an authoritarian presentation of faceless bureaucrats. The building, and especially the concrete, signals that government is not a grand thing, but an ordinary thing. The problem is that a lot of people ... think those are the wrong themes for today. We don't want government to be removed from the people. We want it to be accessible to the people. We don't want to think of government as something that's anonymous and bureaucratic but as something that's very human-scaled. And at the same time we want government to communicate a sense of aspiration rather than a mere obligation.[88]

In response to Keane, Gary Wolf said, "I think that is about as profound a misinterpretation of this building as is possible." Wolf claimed that much of what Keane criticized—the symbolism of inaccessibility, for instance—was a product of use rather than the design (since two of the four original entrances are now closed, and the remaining ones have been fortified with armed guards and metal detectors). He noted that offices frequented by the public remain conveniently located on the lower level, and that the concrete, at the time of its construction, was "a bold, modern material," not ordinary and banal. "This is intended to be a monumental building in the good sense of the term," Wolf argued, "suggesting that government represents the aspiration of the people, and that the building belongs to the people, who can come and go and participate in government as well as in special activities and events."[89]

In 1972, a student term paper about Boston City Hall touched on these political associations. The author recounted a conversation with an unnamed employee in the architects' office:

> One draftsman in the office of Kallmann and McKinnell told me that the City Hall is really a dated building. The days of the monumental public building are over, he said. Now, the buildings are quiet and unobtrusive; they just blend unnoticed into their surroundings. Perhaps

this is a result of the changing image of government: The Kennedy era is no more; Nixon is president. An anonymous building is an appropriate environment for faceless technocrats—unless the architect is trying to use his subtle influence to give those technocrats faces and a personal responsibility for government. The building is an expression of standards which exert a pressure upon the official to live up to them.[90]

Not only this unnamed draftsman but many others as well have recognized that the local and national political climate changed dramatically after the Boston City Hall competition, and these changes necessarily affected attitudes about the building's political symbolism. As violent political protests shook the nation in the late 1960s, Michael McKinnell observed that "many adverse reactions to the Hall are the product of political preconceptions about present-day government."[91] In a similar vein, Sibyl Moholy-Nagy wrote in 1969, "This is a society notorious for its contempt for government and its inclination toward violence."[92] Decades later, this assessment still held true. "You have to remember," said Herb Gleason in 2005, "that we've had at least 16 years of a national government which preaches against government and against the public sector, and that makes a difference."[93]

As Boston's economy thrived with the approach of the new millennium, many Bostonians seemed to have forgotten how essential this symbol of a strong government was to the city's resurgence during the mid-twentieth century. This was the argument of Ed Logue, who, in response to Mayor Menino's 1998 proposal to tear down or sell City Hall, wrote that Boston should remember what the building represented and what it accomplished in terms of Boston's midcentury rejuvenation. "The New City Hall is a monument to the New Boston," Logue wrote. "People have short memories. In the prosperous, booming Boston of today, with its thriving neighborhoods, it is hard to remember how low Boston had sunk only 40 years ago."[94]

Not everyone, though, has found this symbolism a relic of the distant past, without current relevance. David Eisen, architecture critic for the *Boston Herald,* called the building "a sculptural evocation of a democratic government's enduring strength," recognizing that "the structure of democracy is so clearly articulated—it's architecture as civics lesson, out there for all to see. The architects . . . gave us a Greek temple for our complex post-industrial culture."[95]

Similarly, Ian Menzies, the *Quincy Patriot Ledger*'s correspondent in Boston City Hall for sixteen years, admitted that although he had been ambivalent about the building at first, he had come to accept it as a great monument to the city. "To me," Menzies recalled, "and most others of my era, Boston's new city hall signified the birth of the New Boston." Moreover, he wrote, "Boston City Hall is a symbol; a symbol that marks the city's renaissance from a gray, dowdy, spiritless capital (a leftover from the Great Depression), to an upbeat, renewed and competitive world city with a surging sense of new-found pride."[96]

A 1996 *Globe* editorial urged, "City Hall deserves to remain the prime building for city business as an unforgettable symbol of the time when Boston shook off its reputation as a dowdy city of the past."[97] Two years later, another *Globe* editorial situated the KMK design alongside other architectural landmarks in the city: "Just as Faneuil Hall shows the vigor of Colonial Boston, the State House reflects the confidence of the Federalist period, and Trinity Church typifies the elegance of the emerging Back Bay, City Hall represents a decade in which the city reinvented itself as a thriving urban center."[98]

Local author William Landay took a different view, maintaining that City Hall is important precisely because it stands for aspects of Boston's culture that some people either do not understand or would rather not think about, as it represents city government in the metonymical sense:

> The poet Robert Lowell wrote that the [Robert Gould] Shaw memorial [on Boston Common] "sticks like a fishbone / in the city's throat." City Hall sticks in the city's throat, too. Boston politics—"City Hall" in the abstract—has always been a little "brutalist." The building sits atop a bulldozed neighborhood. And on those "Original Boston City Hall Pavers," Ted Landsmark was gored with a flagpole, our own Iwo Jima image. True Boston: complex, inaccessible, chilly, even fierce. Is it possible to love such a place and such a building? To find them beautiful *because* they are difficult? I do. But then, I'm from Boston.[99]

The symbolism of grittiness, complexity, and durability that Landay identified in City Hall in 2007 has lost none of its power or relevance. In the aftermath of tragedies in Boston (such as the 2013 Boston Marathon bombings) or elsewhere in the world (such as the 1989 Tiananmen Square protests), people flock to Government Center for vigils because no building better represents Boston's enduring strength in the face of adversity than its City Hall.

The Plaza

Anthony Yudis, in 1969, foresaw future generations referring to City Hall Plaza "as one of the great public spaces, rivaling even those famed plazas and squares of Europe."[100] Similarly, Albert Bush-Brown wrote, "I predict the Boston public will be proud to stand in [this] plaza,

FIGURE 13. Boston City Hall and plaza. Over the years, the hardscaped area surrounding City Hall has been one of the most criticized aspects of the KMK design. Courtesy of the Boston Public Library Print Department, Boston Pictorial Archive.

paved in red brick and step down to their city hall."[101] At the same time, an article by John Morris Dixon recognized that final judgment would not be possible until the Government Center project was completed in its entirety and the plaza put to full use. "The attraction of these spaces as gathering places and their effectiveness as circulation routes," Dixon wrote, "will be the real test of the Government Center and their success will determine to some extent the future of the large-scale plaza in United States cities."[102] Three decades later, the Project for Public Spaces gave the plaza a place of infamy in its "Hall of Shame."[103] As these comments reveal, the vast plaza (fig. 13) has become just as contentious as the building at its center.

Those who admire the area tend to point out that it replicated in Boston the great urban plazas of Europe. To that end, Thomas Boylston Adams, while praising the building, reserved his greatest plaudits for the plaza surrounding it:

> The plaza that has now come into being is something unique in America. Like Boston's common it will be copied and repeated in old cities seeking new life and in new cities rising. There is nothing like it in America, nothing half so good. . . . Boston is now unique among American cities. It has recaptured its past in the very nick of time. It had created a great plaza in many felicitous levels that rivals Venice and Rome, suitable to its climate and to the use of single individuals or great concourses of people. There is a unity of art and utility. When it is achieved, and it is achieved but rarely—in Athens, or Venice, or Chartres, or Rome—there time stops. Ages unborn will hold it in remembrance.[104]

The rarity of vast hardscape spaces in America was a common theme among commentaries about the plaza. John Morris Dixon wrote, "There has never been anything else in the United States like Government Center's 16 acres of interconnected brick-paved spaces."[105] In the *Washington Post,* meanwhile, Wolf Von Eckardt commended KMK for not creating yet another park ("of which Boston has plenty"). Instead, Von Eckardt regarded the plaza as a space "as hard and tough as the city itself," calling it "essentially a place of passage, of congregation and of celebration."[106]

Those who criticize the plaza, by contrast, call attention to its barrenness and its lack of social infrastructure. Moreover, they too find the vast hardscape an anomaly in the United States, but unlike Von Eckardt and Dixon, they do not deem it successful. James Marston Fitch, for instance, sardonically wondered in 1970 "exactly what sort of ceremonies are we to imagine transpiring here . . . perhaps a presidential assassination?"[107] Again, Fitch's preservationist sensibilities are likely the reason he found the plaza—which replaced a historic neighborhood—so distasteful.

Thirty years later, in its "Hall of Shame" citation, the Project for Public Spaces catalogued a host of deficiencies, pointing out that

> everything about City Hall Plaza and the surrounding Government Center is all wrong. Bleak, expansive, and shapeless, it has an exceedingly poor image in a city where image should be paramount. It conveys nothing in the way of information about Boston, its history, or its sense of place. The buildings around it are uninteresting and devoid of activity and the streets around it, too wide; all of this contributes to a lack of access (despite the fact that five subway stops are in the area). The layout and changes in grade deny the natural paths that people want to take. There are no vistas here, and natural connections—such as the one to Faneuil Hall across the street—are actually discouraged. When it comes to activities and uses, you'd be hard-pressed to find a worse place. This barren, alienating place has little if any activity—let alone a simple place to sit. Sociability is minimal at best.[108]

Of course, KMK's initial design called for connecting the plaza with Faneuil Hall via a pedestrian bridge over New Congress Street—a feature that eventually was abandoned. Many of the criticisms relating to the lack of connections would have been mitigated had this element of the original design been realized.

Even some who defend City Hall have found fault with the plaza. Robert Campbell, for instance, in an otherwise ardent defense of the KMK design, described the plaza as too big and too ill defined.[109] (In an earlier article, Campbell was even more strident in his criticism, writing, "Although City Hall plaza is to pedestrianization what gonorrhea is to friendship, at least it's better than a parking lot.")[110] Likewise, Ian Menzies—another admirer of the building—complained about the "bare, brick, windswept barrenness of its mostly treeless plaza."[111] In response to criticism, Gerhard Kallmann pointed out that the three subway lines running underneath make it difficult to plant trees in the area. Also, he explained that he and his partners wanted a hard-surfaced area that would stand in contrast to the green of Boston's large park system, including the Common, Public Garden, and Emerald Necklace.[112]

Gary Wolf, writing in 2008, explained how the plaza's perceived deficiencies stem not from any inherent design flaws but rather from a lack of imaginative use:

> The Plaza is at its best hosting ice cream and chowder fests, political protests, concerts and sports celebrations. It accommodates tens of thousands, drawn from throughout the region for gatherings that number among the country's most memorable urban events.
>
> It is at the everyday level that the Plaza falls short. Critics observe its inadequate response to the climate, the absence of mid-scale structures and spaces, too little nature, and an overall lack of activity. While design improvements can address such faults, city and federal policies must be supportive and coordinated, which has not always been the case. For instance, KMW's proposed rathskellar was rejected. The subway station was kept in a distant corner. Commercial vendors were banned; a new hotel, nixed. The recessed fountain was shut off, then covered over. Maintenance has been insufficiently funded. A City Hall designed to welcome the public is now barricaded for security.[113]

As Wolf's remarks suggest, the plaza suffers not from poor design but rather from the same malign neglect that has long afflicted New City Hall. Happily, as of this writing, the city was in the midst of repaving the plaza. Crumbling brick pavers from the 1960s were being replaced, new granite benches were rising naturally out of the hardscape in the area surrounding the MBTA station, and public art installations broke up the monotony of the hardscape. These investments, along with creative use of the space, should go a long way toward creating a vibrant urban space in what has for decades been little more than a desert.

Vicissitudes of Taste

Thomas Boylston Adams, writing in the *Globe* nearly a year after New City Hall opened, hailed the building and its plaza as "a triumph in architecture." He saw it as "a unique achievement in America. It may well prove to be the landmark achievement of twentieth century architecture and planning. It is so good that the world must beat a path to Boston's door."[114] Likewise, an article in *Interiors* magazine declared that Boston City Hall was "the best public building of our time."[115] Forty years later, however, freelance architecture critic Walt Lockley would write: "This is one of those buildings that regular people hate. Everybody hates it. They don't like looking at it, they fantasize about its sudden disappearance."[116]

These comments would appear to confirm the conventional wisdom that Boston City Hall's popularity has waned during the past half century. If this is true, we might justifiably ask why it has plunged so far, so quickly. Certainly, concrete architecture is at its reputational nadir today. There are, however, many other elements weighing on the building's reputation. Careful analysis reveals that the city government (particularly the mayor), the press, and herd mentality bear as much responsibility for this phenomenon as changing architectural tastes.

Proponents of the building in the 1960s, while quick to recognize the controversy surrounding it, could hope in those early years that Bostonians eventually would grow to love the building. As Robert Taylor wrote in the *Globe* in 1969, "The structure, part of democracy, provokes healthy debate." But he remained optimistic, as did so many of his fellow citizens, about the building's future, predicting, "In the long run I think it will come to be recognized as a model—the very prototype of what a City Hall ought to be—combining beauty, function and character."[117]

One letter to the editor, published six months after the building opened, admitted to just such a change of heart. The writer began: "I just couldn't stand it, and tons of people agreed with me. Boston City Hall was atrocious!" She had originally objected to the intrusion of the concrete behemoth so close to the "most traditional, sophisticated, and historical part of the city"—Beacon Hill. After experiencing so much "history and quaintness," the writer continued, "it now seemed as if I were approaching a man-made dragonfly, perched on a square of brick blocks." But after reading an article about the building having won the AIA Honor Award, she decided to spend a day exploring it with an open mind. "So, anyway," the writer concluded, "I have now become adjusted to the new character of Boston City Hall. I acquainted myself with it (as I hope others will do) the best way I knew how—by immersing myself in its environment. And somehow I have come to respect the building for what it is, and for what Kevin White has helped it to become for the City of Boston."[118]

As this letter suggests, during the late 1960s, Mayor White made sure thousands of citizens had the opportunity to experience the building in person, beginning with an opening week gala, followed by a variety of special events throughout his tenure as mayor. After the opening ceremonies, the *Globe* expressed hope that the south lobby would host concerts, school drama performances, sculpture and artwork shows.[119] Initially, the city used the space for just such events, and it served these purposes well. In May 1969, for instance, White announced a new project that would bring exhibitions—of paintings, sculptures, graphics, and other works that emphasized Boston's history and culture—to be displayed in City Hall on a rotating basis. To that end, White formed an Art Advisory Committee to select works worthy of being exhibited in the new building.[120] These included portraits by Gilbert Stuart, lent by the Museum of Fine Arts, as well as a large oil painting, *Laying of the Cornerstone of the Beacon Hill Reservoir,* lent by the Bostonian Society. In July and August 1969, an exhibit of NASA's Apollo space program brought more than four thousand visitors to the new City Hall each day.[121] In November of that year, the spirit of the dedication week was revived as "the biggest and poshest party in years" took place in City Hall, drawing thousands of Boston's high society to an event sponsored by the Institute of Contemporary Art.[122]

Throughout the next decade, the building continued to enjoy generally positive attention. In 1972, in a speech to the Massachusetts Historical Society titled "Miracle in Boston," Harold Hodgkinson praised the design he had chosen a decade earlier, noting, "The world is already beating a pathway to this building." He pointed out that he was not alone in regarding the building highly, and he recalled hearing a "prominent Bostonian" say:

> I am very sure that the new City Hall in the Government Center is the most important building that has been built in the United States since Louis Sullivan put up his first skyscraper. It is the only public building, or for that matter private building, that I know of built during this century that has provided an interior space expressive of real feeling. In former times, people expressed in churches their desire for mystery and hope. Probably no public building in this country has done this until Boston City Hall was conceived. For a public building of equal importance, I am inclined to believe you have to go all the way back to the Doge's Palace in Venice. The real value of this sort of thing can only be determined after the lapse of hundreds of years, but I have enough informed critics on my side to make the belief in the excellence of Boston City Hall at least a good bet for the future.[123]

Hodgkinson's unnamed Bostonian touched on many of the same points architects had long emphasized. But coming from a non-architect, the remarks revealed the public's high hopes for the building. Four years after Hodgkinson's speech, in the AIA's Bicentennial list, "Highlights of American Architecture, 1776–1976," a survey of scholars and architects had Boston City Hall tied with H. H. Richardson's Trinity Church as the sixth-greatest building in the history of American architecture.[124]

As is the case with any building, the novelty and initial renown of Boston City Hall faded over time. Even some who had favored the design at first seemingly had second thoughts as the building approached middle age. In 1991, nearly thirty years after he served on the jury that unanimously chose the KMK design for City Hall, businessman O. Kelley Anderson admitted to a reporter: "I hate to say it, but I rode by the other day, and thought, gee, it's just another building, not nearly as attractive as I thought. Maybe it's poorly laid out, and heating empty spaces—well, that's a damn good criticism, something we never thought about.

Maybe we made the wrong choice, although we had a damn good committee and spent a lot of time on it."[125]

Byron Rushing, a Massachusetts state representative who had been a community organizer in the 1960s, pointed out that although the new City Hall was controversial from the beginning, the tone of the controversy had changed over the years. When it first opened, it was "not so controversial that there was a call for it to be changed or undone," Rushing said. "Even the people who said they didn't like it, didn't actively hate it. No one wanted to get rid of it."[126] One reason for this decline in popularity was that the stylistic tastes of the city had changed. Joan Wood suggested that "there's an anti-arts, anti-intellectual aura—and also a lack of humor—that has settled over city government."[127] Henry Lee agreed, noting, "We had this sudden burst of Modernism that allowed us to build City Hall in the '60s, but we are still an awfully conservative city when it comes to the arts."[128]

Some have blamed the slump in popularity on pernicious neglect of the building during the Flynn and Menino administrations. Robert Campbell wrote, for instance:

> What Boston City Hall really needs is what it has never received from the city councilors or anyone else. It needs imaginative inhabiting. Buildings aren't finished when they're finished. They have to be loved and nurtured, like a private home or a garden. They have to be maintained. I feel sure that nobody has ever scrubbed the walls around the elevator doors since City Hall was built. They're filthy. Furniture is ancient. Junk is stored anywhere. Lights go out and are never replaced. Wall clocks tell the wrong time. The atmosphere, everywhere in the building, is one of depressing neglect—as is usually the case in Massachusetts government buildings. When people criticize City Hall, they're reacting as much to its sad state of upkeep as to its architecture. We might feel different about City Hall if it were maintained with the zealous care shown by the Rouse Company at Faneuil Hall Marketplace.[129]

Ada Louise Huxtable agreed with Campbell's assessment. In a 2009 *Wall Street Journal* article, she juxtaposed the unfortunate fate of Boston City Hall with another Brutalist icon, the newly renovated Art and

Architecture Building at Yale. "The current City Hall," Huxtable wrote, "is being systematically and willfully destroyed by abusive neglect, aggravated malfunction, and spreading bureaucratic blight." She went on to discuss in detail Yale's recent renovation: "In conspicuous contrast, Yale's building has been sympathetically and beautifully restored and updated for use by the architecture school. . . . The trip from Boston to New Haven might as well be measured in light years as in miles; Boston remains obdurately clueless."[130]

Likewise, Gary Wolf observed that attitudes toward the building changed following Kevin White's administration. "At times this reevaluation may have been abrupt, as when a new administration establishes its priorities and finds that maintaining a grand civic symbol is low on the list. The consequential impact may be gradual, as a lack of attention slowly affects day-to-day occupants and users of the building."[131] In other words, perceived deficiencies could be remedied, at least in part, if the city were to make a deliberate and sustained investment in upkeep. Yet continued deferred maintenance would surely cause the building's already low reputation to sink further.

Architect Henry Moss also blamed the city for damaging the building's reputation. Moss, though, took issue not with maintenance but with usage, saying: "I always find it absolutely demeaning to have to use the Congress Street entrance after hours. Remember, that entrance was designed pre–Quincy Market and was never intended as a main entrance. But anyone whose primary experience of the building is after-hour meetings knows the feeling of being forced through that narrow little corridor. In terms of symbolism, the city doesn't really care how I feel about the building."[132]

The five men who have inhabited the mayor's office from 1967 through this writing have had a substantial influence on public perception of the building—not only through their control of maintenance and usage, but also through public pronouncements of their own opinions. The building enjoyed a generally positive reputation during the Collins and White administrations, in large part because those mayors celebrated the building conspicuously. "Then in later years," as Herb Gleason recalled, "it became fashionable to denounce the place as unworkable and inconvenient, because people pick up on the signals from the leadership."[133]

John Collins was the building's first great champion. Although visibly surprised by the competition jury's choice of winner (and although under the terms of the competition the city could have opted not to construct the winning design), Collins saw the project through, and the city constructed the building almost exactly as the architects had designed it. Collins sang the building's praises throughout his tenure.

Collins's successor, Kevin White, was equally effusive in his admiration for New City Hall. In an introductory letter in the City Hall employee guide published in December 1968, White wrote, "You and I are both fortunate to be among the first occupants of this magnificent new City Hall—a building which is surely destined to be one of the greatest edifices of modern times."[134] White's actions—like Collins's—buttressed his praise of the building. During sixteen years in office, White succeeded in turning City Hall into a showpiece, with school group performances, concerts, art exhibitions, and even a gala luncheon for Queen Elizabeth II. White's conspicuous esteem for the building and his creative use of its public spaces for a variety of events raised the building's reputation in those early years.

In a roundtable discussion in 2005, a group of former and current government officials, civic leaders, and architects reflected on a mayor's role in affecting City Hall's reputation. "Kevin White had his inauguration in the Great Hall" of the new building, recalled Gleason. "He loved the building. . . . There were lots of gatherings, lots of parties, lots of community meetings. . . . And that is what really contributed greatly to the building's original good looks and to its positive feeling of hospitality."[135] In other words, if people visit the building only to conduct business with the municipal bureaucracy, this surely colors their perceptions of it. Celebratory public events (of the kind Kevin White hosted) alter the social context in which people use the building. These everyday experiences can shape attitudes: if people routinely go to City Hall to enjoy concerts or black-tie parties, reception of the building will almost certainly be different than if they go there only to pay parking tickets.

Following the White administration, Boston's subsequent mayors have not been so well disposed toward the building. Ray Flynn, first elected in 1983, said that he would rather be in Old City Hall—"one of Boston's most beautiful buildings... sitting where Curley sat."[136] When Flynn made these remarks in 1991, of course, the new City Hall was more than twenty years old, and Old City Hall had been successfully repurposed for use as private offices and an upscale French restaurant. Flynn's comments reflect Bostonian nostalgia for the old building yet also show Boston's short memory (neglecting the fact that the old building was considered "a dirty hulk," and that most city workers were delighted to give it up in favor of the new building).

Beginning with Flynn's mayoralty, New City Hall's upkeep noticeably diminished. "One of the practical problems," explained Boston resident and president of the Friends of the Public Garden Henry Lee, "is that any suggestions for improving the interiors were usually shot down by [Mayors Flynn and Menino] partly, I suspect, because they didn't want to appear to be spending public money on 'frills.'... I think Ray Flynn in particular was afraid of losing some populist support."[137]

Thomas Menino, who assumed office in 1993 when Flynn was appointed U.S. ambassador to the Vatican, twice proposed abandoning City Hall for a new home, claiming that the building was too small and did not adequately represent the city or its history. Menino's antipathy toward the building was widely recognized. Tom Keane, who served as a Boston city councilor in the 1990s, recalled: "When Menino was a city councilor back in the '80s, he couldn't stand City Hall. He hated working there. When he became mayor, one of the first things he said was that he wanted to do something with the building, because he was so unhappy with it."[138] In 1998, Menino proposed dedicating $250,000 toward studying the possibility of selling City Hall—then only thirty years old—and moving municipal government to a new building.

The proposal met with surprising resistance in the local press, which had long reveled in exploiting controversy surrounding the building. A *Boston Globe* editorial panned Menino's proposal, chiding, "As the mayor's preservationist instincts ought to tell him, this is a building worth keeping."[139] The editorial page of the *Herald* was less enthusiastic about the building but nevertheless asserted that such a move should be low on the city's list of priorities. "We wouldn't like to see City Hall torn down, ugly as it is," wrote the *Herald* editorial board. "Its very ugliness gives it distinction."[140]

In addition to the *Globe* and the *Herald*, City Hall's longtime admirers also came to its defense. Ed Logue wrote an op-ed piece in which he, like many others, attributed the late-1990s antipathy toward the building principally to "mayoral neglect." Logue pointed out, for instance, that recent mayors had used the Parkman mansion on Beacon Hill—instead of City Hall—to entertain prestigious guests. "At the beginning of his long tenure, Kevin White put Kathy Kane in charge of City Hall," Logue wrote. "It sparkled then, and it could again—if someone were in charge. Our City Hall needs a housekeeper who will make it sparkle and a master of ceremonies to keep it lively." Logue proposed that the city decorate the building with "lots of flags, inside and out, and lots of flowers. The city's garden clubs could help."[141]

Local architecture critics also balked at Menino's proposal. Robert Campbell accused the mayor of "succumbing to occupational megalomania." Menino's "lust for new quarters is a depressing manifestation of a throwaway society," Campbell wrote. "Let's tell the mayor to fix [City Hall], not forsake it. Let's remind him that he once had a pretty good reputation as a preservationist."[142] Similarly, David Eisen, writing in the *Herald*, derided Menino's plan ("One can only imagine what the mayor is looking for. A New England town meeting house, blown up to big-city proportions?") and also joined the chorus that blamed the building's perceived deficiencies on deferred maintenance and lack of imaginative use. Eisen suggested that rather than selling the building, the city should dress it up with tapestries and plants, as well as a café and other public uses. "Spaces could be reorganized, efficiency increased. It's time, with citizen participation, for the architects to rethink how the building is used."[143] The *Quincy Patriot Ledger* also weighed in, maintaining that the money Menino had budgeted to study a new building would be better spent on renovating the interior of the existing structure.[144]

In 2006, Menino renewed his proposal to sell the building and move municipal government to a new city hall on the South Boston waterfront—an area that Menino had striven to develop. Again, a small but vocal group of citizens, architects, and scholars objected. The *Globe* wrote compellingly that "great buildings should be preserved and restored, as Yale University plans to do with its Art and Architecture center, not demolished and replaced, as Mayor Menino envisions for Boston City Hall."[145] Similarly, Donlyn Lyndon, former head of the architecture department at MIT, declared that "to lay waste to a great building that is positioned so effectively and created with such vigor and skill is a foolhardy proposition."[146] A *Boston Phoenix* article panned the mayor's proposal and gave a backhanded compliment to Boston City Hall by saying that it "may not be easy on the eyes, but it's hardly the ugliest building in town."[147] The *Phoenix* also highlighted the growing opposition to the plan from local architects, preservationists, and even some city councilors. Nevertheless, City Council opposition may have been motivated more by politics than by love of architecture. According to the *Phoenix* article, Councilor Michael Flaherty, who opposed Menino's proposal (and who would run for mayor against Menino, unsuccessfully, in 2009), made it clear that he had little love for City Hall, but he saw Menino as too brash and his plan as under-studied.

At the same time, there were those who seemingly were open to the idea of a new City Hall. Thomas H. O'Connor, the dean of Boston's local historians, asserted that if the building no longer worked, then a new one should be built—but in the same central location.[148] David Kruh, author of two books on Scollay Square, took the view that Menino's proposal for a twenty-first-century City Hall was as timely as Collins's 1960s plan.[149] Even some architects supported Menino, including Frano Violich, the head of the Boston Society of Architects' design committee, which suggested building a new City Hall but not destroying the old one, and David Dixon, who said he would be open to demolishing the current building if it meant a new City Hall with "more vigor."[150]

It was at this juncture that the building's admirers stepped up their advocacy. A group of architects, scholars, and ordinary citizens petitioned the Boston Landmarks Commission to grant landmark status to the building. The petition highlighted the building's importance in terms of the city-sponsored design competition, urban planning, local architectural significance, significance for local tourism, national architectural significance, and significance as the first work of a major, internationally acclaimed architectural firm.[151]

In some ways, Menino's proposal harkened back to the kind of underhanded politics that City Hall originally was built to overcome. Gary Wolf, a local architect who has led the preservation effort, noted that some of his colleagues felt uncomfortable signing the petition against the mayor's proposal because of the possible political ramifications. "I've heard that it was suggested to architects, in personal conversations with people in City Hall, that it would not be to their advantage to speak out against the demolition or removal of City Hall," Wolf revealed. "Whether those were innocent conversations or politics in its worst form, there definitely are rumors, which I believe on the basis of the people I heard them from. People tell me they didn't feel comfortable signing the landmarks petition or writing letters of support because they felt it could hurt their business. They simply said, 'The mayor's all powerful. That's the way the city works.'"[152]

In addition to mayoral neglect, City Hall's reputation has suffered as a result of its being not only a product but also a symbol of midcentury top-down urban renewal. Despite the earnest, if naïve, intentions of politicians and planners to use large-scale urban renewal projects to instill both a new functional meaning and heroic monumentality in the city center, future generations have looked back with contempt on this high-handed approach to development. Thus, while the building symbolized a break from Curley's politics that favored individual aid at the expense of the greater good of the city, critics today see the building as a symbol of government programs that swung the pendulum too far, ignoring the needs of individuals to focus on large-scale projects.

Some citizens have developed nostalgia for what had been destroyed by the Government Center project (fig. 14). In one letter to the editor in 1998, a citizen pined for the Scollay Square of old: "Gone was the Old Howard [burlesque theater]. . . . Gone was the Crawford House Hotel. . . . Gone was the true Boston, with its relaxed blend of past

FIGURE 14. Cornhill and Scollay Square (ca. 1901). The Sears Block and Sears Crescent (center foreground) were eventually preserved, while the area to the left would be razed. The cupola of Faneuil Hall is visible in the center, with Quincy Market and the waterfront beyond. Courtesy of the Boston Public Library Print Department, Boston Pictorial Archive.

and present. Destroyed was the city's intriguing labyrinth of streets and eclectic mix of uses. What we got was . . . the dullest, dreariest project west of Bucharest."[153]

Such postmortem nostalgia has led to widespread delusions about a neighborhood that was, by nearly all accounts in the 1950s and 1960s, a slum. Thomas Boylston Adams, scion of two Brahmin families, wrote that by the 1950s, "Scollay Square became a disaster area, hardly pleasing even to a drunken sailor with his arm 'round the waist of an Old Howard girl."[154] Similarly, a *Globe* article embraced the urban renewal project, declaring, "Out of the tumble-down red brick destruction of Scollay Square has risen Boston's phoenix—the new City Hall."[155]

As City Hall's reputation suffered, its architects occasionally responded to the negative criticism. Gerhard Kallmann remarked in

2004: "I've never been upset by criticism. I understand that people feel critical when they confront something with which they're not familiar. But I suggest they not judge City Hall from the outside, but go inside, and also look at the building from the marketplace, from the southwest, the best corner."[156] In 1988 Kallmann told the City Council that he agreed with some complaints but also pointed out that some aspects of the original design were never carried out or were eliminated.[157] "We designed a cafe on the plaza and a Rathskellar in the basement, but the city provided none of it," he reminded a reporter.[158] And when asked about the interior "gloominess," he replied: "If it's gloomy, that's a problem of adornment. We always thought there would be art work and sculptures and tapestries and great flags and flowers, like potted geraniums."[159]

This unfulfilled process of "continual completion"—the idea that successive generations would adorn and modify the building to keep it relevant to their own times—is an issue that others have noted as well. Gary Wolf, for instance, suggested that "if deferred maintenance and changing [architectural] tastes are two factors affecting the perceptions and treatment of City Hall, a third is the simple fact that, in many eyes, the building was never finished! Signage and graphics, furnishings, tapestries, plantings, good lighting: such 'embellishment' of the building's 'robust armature'—signs of active and proud occupancy—are missing. The continual process of 'completion' of City Hall that Kallmann and McKinnell envisioned did not occur."[160]

One further problem for the building's reputation is herd mentality: it has become fashionable to denounce Boston City Hall. The extent to which the perceived mindset or actions of a group can affect individual ideas and behavior has been much studied by psychologists, sociologists, and historians. The details of these various studies and theories need not concern us here, but suffice it to say that the so-called bandwagon effect, in which people have been observed to conform with what others do or think without considering the rational basis of their own actions, has been well documented. Just as peer pressure influences the clothes we wear, the movies we see, the books we read, and the stocks we buy, so too does high-profile disparagement go a long way toward shaping our perception of architecture. In other words, if someone perceives that nearly everyone disapproves of a particular building, his or her own opinion will likely conform to the group's.

Group mentality also can be influenced by certain powerful individuals, such as political leaders. Freud, for instance, wrote that the group is "an obedient herd, which could never live without a master." This master "possesses a strong and imposing will, which the group, which has no will of its own, can accept from him."[161] This explains why Boston's mayors have held sway over popular opinion about Boston City Hall. So too have architecture critics. People often look to a critic, as an "expert," to explain concepts that most know little about, and those who do not study architecture professionally rely on learned commentaries to help them understand a building.

While this public scrutiny is useful in many ways, it comes at a cost: the subjective media spotlight shines on real and perceived deficiencies of a few buildings, even as many others (sometimes equally bad or worse) benefit from remaining so shrouded in obscurity as to escape attention. Brutalist buildings, which were purposely designed to stand out against the backdrop of monotonous corporate modernism, are by dint of their aesthetic and philosophical aspirations particularly prone to attract this critical focus.

Moreover, recent changes in the field of architectural criticism have not been propitious for the reputation of Brutalism in general and Boston City Hall in particular. An increasing number of newspapers and popular magazines employed experts as professional architecture critics throughout the late twentieth century, with nearly forty critics writing on a regular basis by the 1990s.[162] These men and women could interpret a complex building like Boston City Hall and explain its architectural virtues to the public. For the first few decades after the Boston City Hall competition, writers such as the *New York Times*'s Ada Louise Huxtable, the *Washington Post*'s Wolf Von Eckardt, and the *Boston Globe*'s Robert Campbell stood between the building and the masses, patiently proffering thoughtful, informed analyses and educating the public on the merits of Brutalism's difficult aesthetic qualities.

In recent years, however, many publications have been trimming staff as their print circulation and advertising revenues dwindled in the Internet age. The architecture critic is often regarded as the second-most-expendable employee (after the classical music critic). As a *New York Times* blogger observed, "You can almost count the number of architectural critics at major newspapers on one hand, and while there's been an explosion of opinion design and architecture blogs in recent years, they tend to preach to the converted or veer, with few exceptions, toward noncritical celebration or gleeful snark."[163]

As this comment suggests, the tone of nonprofessional criticism proliferating on the Internet differs markedly from that of the experts. While professional critics had specialized expertise and training in architectural history (Ada Louise Huxtable) or architectural practice (Robert Campbell) and could bring that knowledge to bear on their reviews, there is no guarantee that their successors in the blogosphere have this same pedigree. Moreover, professional criticism was subject to editorial scrutiny and high standards of journalism, while design blogs are posted on the Internet with no such assurance of accuracy or quality. Whereas the previous generation of critics were trustworthy and serious arbiters of architectural taste, leading an uninitiated public to a more informed perspective on the built environment, the Internet has allowed the architectural blind to lead the blind. In any event, it has become increasingly difficult to separate the architectural-critical wheat from the attention-grabbing chaff.

The upshot of these developments is that the popular reception of architecture is now likely to be shaped more by hyperbolic, scandal-mongering blog posts than by informed, dispassionate analyses. As Mario Vargas Llosa observed: "In the days of our grandfathers and great-grandfathers, criticism played a central role in the world of culture because it helped guide citizens in the difficult task of judging what they heard, saw and read. Now critics are a dying breed, to whom nobody pays attention unless they also turn themselves into a form of entertainment and spectacle."[164] One way of achieving this level of spectacle is to sacrifice intellectual analysis in favor of attention-seeking hype. The result is an increasing number of "Worst Buildings," "Ugliest Buildings," and "Most-Hated Buildings" lists compiled by sources ranging from Prince Charles to *Esquire*. As a conspicuously controversial building, Boston City Hall often appears on (and even tops) such lists, which offer not the thoughtful, reasoned criticism of Huxtable, but rather incendiary commentaries notable more for their shock value than for their intellectual quality.

In a way, the clamor of criticism that has surrounded Boston City Hall since its inception reveals that the architects were successful in creating a new "Action Architecture." Instead of an easily ignorable abstract form, City Hall is a building that elicits strong reactions. It purposely fails to escape notice, and its admirers continue to hold out hope that future generations will yet appreciate it. As Huxtable wrote in response to persistent criticism of the building: "Déjà vu, anyone? Its predecessor, Boston's Victorian City Hall, was similarly detested and eventually saved and successfully recycled. Tastes change as surely as the seasons, only it takes a little longer."[165] Near the end of his life, Gerhard Kallmann said that he too was hopeful about the future of the building. "I get a sense I may live to see City Hall come back into fashion," Kallmann told an interviewer. "People come up to me in Cambridge, where I live, and they tell me they like City Hall. Of course, people who don't like it may just not talk to me."[166]

Kallmann passed away in June 2012, aged ninety-seven. While it would be an overstatement to say that City Hall had "come back into fashion," Kallmann could take comfort in knowing that the praises of many longtime admirers of the building (such as Ada Louise Huxtable and Herb Gleason) had not faded. Moreover, a younger generation of architects, scholars, and citizens had come to appreciate Boston City Hall as an architectural triumph.

CHAPTER 5
Legacy and Significance

Despite vicissitudes in its reputation over the years, Boston City Hall has had far-reaching and long-lasting effects on both architecture and politics. The building was born at a time of political change (if not upheaval) in America, as well as at a turning point in architecture. The design not only reflects this turbulent epoch but also catalyzed further change by dint of its local prominence and international reputation. While this legacy understandably has been strongly felt in Boston, it also stretches beyond the Hub.

It's difficult, in some ways, to distinguish between the legacy of Boston City Hall and that of the larger Government Center project. I hope to show, however, that the new City Hall was by all accounts the centerpiece of both Government Center and the New Boston in terms of not only planning and intent but also reputation and influence. Wolf Von Eckardt referred to the building as Government Center's "keystone," while the *Boston Globe* editorial page dubbed it the "crown jewel" of the the city's redevelopment efforts.[1] Likewise, Mayor John Collins, in his remarks at the building's ground-breaking ceremony, proclaimed that the building "will be the dominant feature of this new Government Center."[2] Thus the legacy of both Government Center and the New Boston largely resulted from the impact of Boston City Hall.

The Firm

One of the most conspicuous aspects of Boston City Hall's legacy is the effect it had on its young architects. Kallmann, McKinnell and Knowles—a firm created for the express purpose of entering the Boston City Hall competition—did not remain intact following the building's construction. While Michael McKinnell and Gerhard Kallmann relocated to Boston, Edward Knowles chose to remain in New York City with his family and his established practice. Knowles's subsequent projects differed markedly from those of Kallmann and McKinnell. After Boston City Hall, Knowles went on to design, with John Mac-Fadyen, the Filene Center for the Performing Arts at Wolf Trap, as well as residential projects throughout the United States and Puerto Rico. Several of these projects have been featured in newspaper, magazine, and journal articles, as well as books and television programs.

Kallmann and McKinnell, meanwhile, moved to Boston after winning the City Hall competition and eventually created a new architectural firm with Henry Wood. This firm, Kallmann McKinnell & Wood (KMW), became one of the most prominent firms in Boston. Without their initial success in the Boston City Hall competition, however, it is unlikely that two untried architects would so quickly have garnered the stream of high-profile commissions that came after the City Hall project. Gary Wolf, in recognizing Boston City Hall's catalytic effect, wrote: "Boston City Hall is not only the building that symbolized the creation of the 'new Boston'; it is the building that launched the career of its architects. The young office followed its competition-winning achievement in Boston with such a stream of accomplished buildings that it soon established a reputation as one of the finest architectural firms in the long history of Boston."[3]

KMW went on to design many notable buildings in the Boston area and abroad, including the addition to the Boston Five Cents Savings

Bank (1972), Back Bay Station (1987), the American Academy of Arts and Sciences (1981), the U.S. embassy in Bangkok (1996), and the Edward W. Brooke Courthouse (1998). The designs of these buildings vary greatly, revealing the firm's stylistic evolution over the decades. Most significantly, the firm abandoned the Brutalist style of its early commissions (City Hall, the Boston Five, and the Government Center Garage) as public taste for exposed concrete waned quickly in the 1970s. In fact, in its design for a new Back Bay Station, KMW was already upstaging the exposed concrete with polychromatic brickwork and massive wooden trusses. (That said, the station's vaulted central space, with exposed arched trusses, does reference one of the most important early modernist applications of reinforced concrete: the 1920 Ateliers Esders in Paris by the Perret Brothers.)

The most visible turning point in the firm's history came with the design of the headquarters for the American Academy of Arts and Sciences in Cambridge, Massachusetts. The brick and wood structure takes its cues not from Le Corbusier's designs but rather from the work of Greene & Greene and of Frank Lloyd Wright. This change in style was deliberate. As Michael McKinnell explained:

> We had finished City Hall, Five Cents Savings, the gymnasium at Exeter. And we didn't have any work. It was a very lean time when we finally received the commission for the American Academy of Arts and Sciences. I remember Lawrence Anderson fixing us with his very blue eyes and saying: "We want you to do what you want in making a building. We have only one thing to say. There will be not one square inch of concrete exposed in this building." Gerhard very genuinely responded: "Andy, this is the opportunity for us. We're carrying this albatross of concrete and City Hall around with us."[4]

This stylistic change did not go unnoticed. Douglass Shand-Tucci pointed out that "by the 1980s, what Kallmann and McKinnell's work was called mattered to everyone after the success of the American Academy, because it had become the gold standard in architecture in Boston, even for those who thought they were headed in the wrong direction stylistically."⁵ Kallmann and McKinnell had emerged as revolutionaries in 1962, and the architecture world continued to regard them as such long after City Hall was completed.

New York Times architecture critic Paul Goldberger characterized the firm's later work as "a response to the criticism of the City Hall," writing that these projects tended "to be more textured, nuanced."⁶ While Goldberger's comments recognize the firm's aesthetic evolution in the decades following the City Hall competition, they ignore the underlying architectural philosophy, which remained constant. In fact, despite abandoning exposed concrete, Kallmann and McKinnell stayed true to the architectural ideals expressed in Boston City Hall. The reason why City Hall was a mostly concrete building was that at the time this material bucked tradition; it stood in stark opposition to the dogma and ideology of orthodox modernism. Kallmann and McKinnell had sought by this design, as Alex Krieger aptly put it, "to rally architects out of a midcentury malaise."⁷ To that end, Brutalism was an appropriate brickbat, but Kallmann and McKinnell's philosophy was not beholden to one style. By the late 1970s, what McKinnell called the "ideological straightjacket" of modernism, had been "put back in the closet." McKinnell recalled that Kallmann "came to grips with the danger of ideology very early. It is a seducer, but also a tyrant. I was beginning to perhaps understand that."⁸ In other words, Kallmann and McKinnell's philosophy transcended the ideology of any one material or aesthetic.

That said, while KMW's designs responded to changing times and evolving tastes, Kallmann and McKinnell were not architectural chameleons, nor, in the more vulgar expression of Philip Johnson, were they "high-class whores," willing to do whatever a client desired. Rather, the two men explained,

> [our work] is clearly not that of a canonically assertive architecture or ideological crusade but an open-ended patient search, a readiness to expand the formal range of the buildings by the encounter with each new program, site, and client requirements. . . . It is possible however to discern in the designs for a great diversity of buildings a perceptible

preoccupation with themes which are reworked over time and under different circumstances and which give an undercurrent of continuity to the work.[9]

In other words, the architects regarded each building not as an end but as a means. Their designs were not answers but questions. The complexity of each project deliberately intended to incite a reaction in the user and to compel all who encountered it to join the architects in their "patient search."

Several years ago I told a *New York Times* reporter that Boston City Hall was "the purest expression of Kallmann's architectural philosophy." All of the buildings that came afterwards were, I explained, "variations on a theme," which also responded to the imperatives of an established architectural practice that needed to balance an architectural philosophy against practical needs. This statement was never printed, so I suppose there is no cause for a formal retraction. Nevertheless, my subsequent research and thoughts about their architectural oeuvre has led me to reconsider this view. City Hall was not the theme; rather, it was one of the variations on a much larger philosophy. It is thus wrongheaded to measure the firm's subsequent designs against City Hall. Instead, if one is to understand each work individually and the entire output of the firm as a whole, they must be measured against the ideals that Kallmann and McKinnell embraced.

KMW's many achievements have long been recognized by critics, the public, and fellow architects. In 1984, the AIA named KMW the national Firm of the Year. Also, KMW won the Boston Society of Architects' J. Harleston Parker Award six times—more than any other firm to date. This achievement is particularly notable, given the number of internationally renowned firms in the Boston architectural pantheon, including The Architects Collaborative, Hugh Stubbins and Associates, Sert, Jackson and Associates, Graham Gund Architects, Shepley Bulfinch Richardson and Abbott, Benjamin Thompson and Associates, I. M. Pei, and Cram and Ferguson.[10]

During the past fifty years or more, the firm has been featured in architectural and popular periodicals such as *Architectural Forum*,

Architectural Record, Architectural Review, Progressive Architecture, Perspecta, ArchitectureBoston, and a host of newspapers and magazines throughout the world. (The firm's website lists over one hundred feature articles about the architects and their buildings.) KMW also was the subject of a 1988 exhibit at the Harvard University Graduate School of Design, which was accompanied by a 121-page catalogue compiled by Alex Krieger. In 2004, David Dillon wrote a monograph about the firm, which highlighted many of its more recent works.

The pages of architectural history are full of one-hit wonders—architects who designed one magnificent building but afterwards fell into obscurity. This was not the case with Kallmann and McKinnell, who used their success with Boston City Hall as a springboard to other important projects at home and abroad. As Robert Campbell observed, Boston City Hall "proved to be only the beginning of a career in which Kallmann and McKinnell, with their partner Henry Wood, have become in some sense the official civic architects of Boston."[11]

In addition to their remarkable architectural careers, Kallmann and McKinnell also influenced future generations of architects through their teaching. Both men served on the faculty at Harvard University's Graduate School of Design. In this capacity they became as prominent in the academy as they were in the profession. "Students flocked to the studios offered by Gerhard Kallmann and Michael McKinnell," wrote one of their colleagues, "because they were conscious of the integrity and quality of both the instruction and the professional work of these teachers."[12] As in their architecture, Kallmann and McKinnell's teaching was neither sclerotic nor ideological; it evolved over time. Thus the teaching and professional careers of Kallmann and McKinnell were inextricably linked, with the practical and the theoretical constantly informing each other. So it is that the legacy of these men will live on in their many celebrated buildings, as well as in the hundreds of former students who will say of each, "He changed my understanding of architecture."[13]

Boston City Hall was therefore the beginning of an architectural legacy that stretches across the globe. In 2005, Kallmann and McKinnell acknowledged this, saying: "We recognize that [City Hall] was for us a seminal work. Our first and probably most significant building, it defined the major themes that shaped the architecture of the buildings that followed. Though there are obvious differences of style and form in our later work, our preoccupations have essentially remained the same: linkage to the urban fabric and landscape, spatial complexity, the poetics of construction, the language of architecture, and metaphor."[14] When Gerhard Kallmann passed away in June 2012, his obituary in the *New York Times* featured a photograph of him in front of City Hall, and the lead for the article described him as "the architect who, with Michael McKinnell, designed Boston City Hall, a hulking, asymmetrical, Modernist building that has been widely acclaimed by architects for half a century though disparaged by many Bostonians."[15] The first nine paragraphs of the obituary are about Boston City Hall and do not mention a single other building. Similarly, a 2007 petition to the Boston Landmarks Commission made clear the building's professional significance for Kallmann and McKinnell: "Without Boston's national design competition for its new city hall and without the City's commitment to realizing the winning design, this internationally known firm, following in the footsteps of such influential Boston architects as Charles Bulfinch and H. H. Richardson, might never have built a building."[16] Thus, Boston City Hall remained the foundation of Kallmann and McKinnell's long and distinguished careers. It provided them the opportunity to design scores of projects that continue to inspire architects and enrich the global built environment.

Architectural Significance in Boston

Whereas in the decades prior to the 1962 City Hall competition there were remarkably few new buildings of significant architectural merit in Boston, construction—particularly of concrete buildings—boomed in the years that followed. Boston's growing collection of high-quality modern buildings constructed from the late 1960s onward put the city in the vanguard of architectural design. Lawrence Kennedy wrote that the proliferation of modern architecture in the wake of New City Hall "stirred up the city's staid brick and granite character" so that by the mid-1980s, "Bulfinch's Boston boasted some of the most dramatic examples of modern architecture to be found anywhere." This fundamentally changed the character of the city. In Kennedy's words, "The exuberant modern architecture of the 1960s and 1970s fulfilled its purpose by establishing Boston as a forward-looking metropolis that had more going for it than merely a historic past."[17] The rest of the nation and the world observed what was happening in Boston, and many other cities followed in its architectural footsteps. As Ada Louise Huxtable observed, Boston "played a leading role in the practice and dissemination of a movement that changed the face of the twentieth century."[18]

Of course, not all modern buildings in Boston were of the same quality as New City Hall. Lewis Mumford wrote a lengthy essay on the degradation of Copley Square, in which he saw the new City Hall as an anomaly in an epoch of aesthetic disintegration. "As the glass monoliths rise," Mumford wrote, "the one feature of Boston that is irreplaceable, its unmistakably urbane character, becomes more completely obliterated; and it will take more than the new City Hall to recover the civic and esthetic integrity that has been forfeited for the sake of profit, publicity, and technocratic panache."[19] As Mumford's essay makes clear, New City Hall had raised the bar for architectural quality in Boston. Lackluster buildings would seem more conspicuously so next to the KMK design.

Those who have written about Boston architecture over the years have scarcely ignored City Hall's role in paving the way for other avant-garde buildings in the Hub. A guide to Boston's modern architecture, printed by the Boston Preservation Alliance, claimed that Boston City Hall "is widely considered to be the most significant structure built in Boston in the mid-20th century."[20] In a similar vein, Robert A. M. Stern, dean of the Yale School of Architecture, spoke to City Hall's singular position in the city's architectural history when he averred that the building "put Boston back on the architectural map."[21] Likewise, a 2007 petition to the Boston Landmarks Commission claimed that City Hall affected Boston architecture as much as the designs of Charles Bulfinch or H. H. Richardson.[22] Douglass Shand-Tucci, meanwhile, noted that "downtown Boston's first landmark of the radical Modern Movement is at once one of America's foremost landmarks."[23]

One reason for the building's influence was its local prominence. The Boston Society of Architects in 1970 awarded the building its J. Harleston Parker Medal as the best new work of architecture in greater Boston. It is not surprising, then, that local architects were quick to see in the KMK design a new model worthy of emulation. The building compelled local clients to commission, and architects to design, avant-garde structures throughout the city.

This is not to suggest that every concrete building in Boston was a direct descendant of City Hall. Certainly the 1960s were the heyday of concrete architecture globally. From the Trellick Tower in London to the new government complex in Chandigarh, concrete was in the air. But in Boston—a hidebound, stylistically conservative city that was conspicuously slow to embrace modernism—the extent to which concrete buildings proliferated in the 1960s and 1970s can be traced to City Hall. This building showed that it was acceptable to embrace Brutalism— even in the midst of neighborhoods otherwise dominated by Georgian or mansard-style buildings. In other words, New City Hall blazed the path, and other architects—whether influenced by KMK or Louis Kahn or Le Corbusier—were inclined to follow. A city hall is arguably a city's most significant building; its architectural style is inherently an example for others to follow.

Perhaps the most direct architectural consequence of Boston City Hall is the 1972 addition to the Boston Five Cents Savings Bank. Robert Morgan, president of the Boston Five, had served as chairman of the Government Center Commission, and it was on his recommendation that Kallmann and McKinnell were invited, along with two other firms, to submit designs for the addition to the bank's building at the corner of School and Washington Streets. Lawrence Anderson, who had written the competition program for Boston City Hall, also wrote the program for the Boston Five competition. The bank eventually chose the brawny Kallmann and McKinnell scheme, which boasts a five-story concrete colonnade fronting a glass wall enclosing the bank's offices. As in their City Hall, Kallmann and McKinnell exposed the building's structural elements, with the reinforced concrete trusses that support the floors extending through the glass wall to meet the concrete colonnade (fig. 15).

FIGURE 15. Boston Five Cents Savings Bank; Kallmann and McKinnell (1972). The architects used the same brawny concrete in this building that they had earlier used in City Hall. Structure is on display as exposed concrete trusses extend past the glass curtain wall to meet the concrete colonnade. Photograph by the author.

The distinctive modern design—in the midst of some of Boston's most celebrated historic structures (including the Old Corner Bookstore, Old South Meeting House, and Old City Hall)—draws attention to the building and forges a stylistic link between this area and Government Center two blocks away. At the same time, its formal austerity and modesty of scale do not openly challenge its historic neighbors, even as the building contrasts stylistically with them. Donlyn Lyndon, in his guide to Boston architecture, wrote, "Wherever you face the building the profile of the structural system is seen from several different angles, making it seem at once uncommonly active and logically related to its site."[24]

Other architects would soon follow KMK's lead to produce concrete buildings of their own in Boston. These were not obscure parking garages on the outskirts of the city but rather some of the most important architectural commissions of the decade, including Hugh Stubbins's Countway Library at Harvard Medical School (1965); F. A. Stahl Associates' State Street Bank building (1966); I. M. Pei and Araldo Cossutta's Christian Science Church Center (1968–1973); Minoru Yamasaki's Eastern Airlines Terminal (1968); Cambridge Seven Associates' New England Aquarium (1969); Paul Rudolph's Health, Welfare and Education Service Center (1970) and reconstruction of the First and Second Church of Boston (1972); Eduardo Catalano's Charlestown Branch Library (1970); and TAC's Children's Hospital expansion (1972) and Church Park Apartments (1973).

The proliferation of these high-profile concrete structures in a city that recently had none is a testament to City Hall's influence on future Boston architecture. At the same time, very few of these architects were merely aping Boston City Hall; rather, they were expressing their own design philosophies in concrete. Nevertheless, some similarities are striking. Regarding Ashley, Meyer & Associates' design for the Boston Architectural Center, for instance, William J. R. Curtis wrote (in a description that would be equally fitting for Boston City Hall): "The exterior forms arise from a direct expression of the interplay between functional volume and structure. Overhangs and shaded voids provide unity, rhythm and texture."[25] Similarly, Cambridge Seven Associates, in their design for the New England Aquarium, offered a reinterpretation of the neighboring waterfront warehouses. They did so, however, not in brick or granite but rather in concrete deliberately left crude.[26]

Hugh Stubbins's 1965 Francis A. Countway Library of Medicine at Harvard Medical School bears an even more obvious resemblance to New City Hall in terms of material (exposed concrete), tripartite massing, and overhanging top level with repetitive window dividers. These similarities compelled Douglass Shand-Tucci to call Countway "the most notable Boston building influenced by the City Hall."[27]

Some architectural historians, including Curtis and Shand-Tucci, have sought to identify a "Boston School" of architecture in the 1960s. While Shand-Tucci pressed hard for this characterization of the mid-century architecture in New City Hall's orbit, Curtis remained more nuanced in his analysis. "The historian who is determined to define a 'Boston School' of architecture," he wrote, "will have most luck if he looks at the work produced by local firms in the sixties. But the categories stretch very thin and the shared features tend to be superficial." Nevertheless, he recognized that there is in these buildings "a preponderant tendency to employ plain geometrical forms; to adhere to simple rectangular concrete frames and skeletons; to detail buildings in a 'no-nonsense, no frills' manner; and to adopt bare concrete finishes." Among the buildings that Curtis references as evidence of this trend are TAC's John F. Kennedy Federal Building (1966) and Josiah Quincy Community School (1976), Benjamin Thompson & Associates' Design Research Building (1969), and Ashley, Meyer & Associates' Boston Architectural Center (1963–67). "Sobriety and logic" are what Curtis identifies as the obvious affinities among these three schemes.[28]

Both Curtis and Shand-Tucci give most credit for the defining characteristics of this "school" to Le Corbusier and Gropius. "Looking at the matter in a larger perspective," Curtis writes, "one might hazard the guess that Gropius-inspired common sense was being clothed in a rough skin derived from Le Corbusier."[29] KMK, however, deserves more credit than either Gropius or Le Corbusier. New City Hall was far more boldly innovative than anything Gropius was producing in the 1960s (e.g., the widely reviled 1963 Pan Am Building in midtown Manhattan). Charles

Millard, in fact, wrote that considering the Kennedy Federal Building "together with the Pan Am Building in New York and even such earlier works as the Graduate Center at Harvard . . . leaves one with serious reservations about Gropius' ultimate stature as an architect, as opposed to his undoubted talents as a teacher and organizer."[30] City Hall was also far more locally prominent and accessible for Boston architects than all but one of Le Corbusier's buildings—the Carpenter Center at Harvard. But whether other architects were looking for inspiration to Chandigarh and La Tourette or, as is more likely, to Government Center, we can nevertheless credit Kallmann, McKinnell and Knowles as apostles of the Corbusian aesthetic in Boston, paving the way for future concrete buildings in the city.

Not only the building but also the plaza influenced future Boston architecture. Sasaki, Dawson, DeMay Associates' design for Copley Square Plaza, for instance, shares many characteristics with its predecessor at Government Center. The Sasaki group's design was the winner of a 1965 competition to rework the space between two of Boston's most famous architectural landmarks: H. H. Richardson's Trinity Church (1877) and McKim, Mead and White's Boston Public Library (1895).[31] The jury for the Copley Square competition included Pietro Belluschi, who had previously served on the jury for the Boston City Hall competition.

The winning design, as Curtis described it, was "a broad open space with slight level changes, diagonal steps, durable materials, few trees, and a massive fountain intended to complement the masculine forms of Trinity."[32] If we substituted "City Hall" for "Trinity," this would be a remarkably apt description of KMK's plaza. Indeed, the two shared hardscape paving, paired with the softening element of a fountain. Both also were intended to create a suitable setting for monumental buildings. Originally the Sasaki design called for the same materials used at City Hall Plaza—granite steps and walls with brick paving, although subsequent budget constraints resulted in asphalt pavers and concrete walls.[33] Moreover, whereas Kallmann, McKinnell and Knowles incorporated a visually arresting geometry of diagonal steps to respond to preexisting (and unchangeable) topographical gradations, the Sasaki group artificially constructed a similar slope by creating a sunken space for their fountain.

The Copley Square design also shared with City Hall Plaza a profound and protracted controversy. The ten-foot concrete wall between the plaza and busy commercial Boylston Street, intended to produce a sense of enclosure and separation from the bustling city, instead created a forbidding aesthetic and an uncomfortable experience. "The space enclosed is more vacant than eloquent," wrote Donlyn Lyndon.[34] In 1984, Spencer Rice, Trinity's rector, called the area "a sociological nightmare, a place for people to hide and to engage in illicit activities."[35] Somewhat less euphemistically, Robert Trancik wrote, "Hidden from public view, portions of the plaza have become havens for drug dealers, winos, and muggers."[36]

The hardscape itself was also widely panned. Modeled, like City Hall Plaza, after European piazzas and intended as a gathering space, the square never drew the crowds it was intended to attract. Robert Venturi, who also submitted a design for the competition, argued that the buildings surrounding the space did not enclose it enough to create a traditional piazza, and he doubted that Americans would use it as a piazza in any case.[37] These are much the same faults critics have identified in City Hall Plaza. Less than two decades after Copley Square's completion, the city announced a national competition to right the wrongs of the Sasaki plan. The winners, Dean Abbott with Clarke and Rapuano, Inc., did away with the sunken area and minimized the hardscape by including more green space.

Another public space created in the image of City Hall Plaza is the Christian Science world headquarters in the Back Bay. Like the Government Center master plan, this massive project was undertaken by I. M. Pei and Partners, with Araldo Cossutta as the partner in charge. Along with landscape firm Sasaki Associates, the Pei team designed a brick plaza to accentuate the monumentality of the Mother Church and an assortment of new concrete buildings to house various functions of church administration. The project represents not simply a regurgitation of the Government Center forms in a different context, but rather a subtle reworking of them for a different site and purpose. "Here the centerpiece is not a bold new landmark like the City Hall," wrote Douglass Shand-Tucci, "but an old one—the huge domed Mother Church of Christian Science: Chandigarh on Scollay Square has become the Vatican on Huntington Avenue!"[38]

By the 1970s, a reaction against Boston City Hall's broad influence was already emerging. A case in point is the 1972 Capital Bank building near the Government Center garage (Anderson, Notter Associates). Capital Bank's architects used the iconoclastic irony of postmodernism to take a jab at City Hall, as the bank's principal architectural feature is a corner that has been cut away in inverse relation to City Hall's projecting upper floors. It is as if the giant maw to which Ted Landsmark likened City Hall's façade had taken a bite out of the bank. According to Shand-Tucci, the Anderson, Notter building "can be seen as mocking not just the architecture of the 1960s but also Boston's major icon of the previous decade—the City Hall—within sight of which the bank's designers . . . committed lese majesty [sic] in three dimensions by designing a rather top-heavy cut-out corner, surely an architectural pun . . . on Kallmann and McKinnell's nearby masterwork."[39] Nevertheless, that New City Hall was worthy of being the subject of such a "pun" speaks to the strength of its influence on the city's architecture. Had the building not been heroic to begin with, it would hardly have been worth toppling.

Architectural Significance beyond Boston

Given Boston City Hall's success as a headquarters for municipal government and a symbol of progressive midcentury politics, it is not surprising that it had a widespread effect on government architecture throughout the country, at the local, state, and national levels. While not every government building in the 1960s and 1970s would be an exact replica of Boston City Hall, Kallmann, McKinnell and Knowles nevertheless introduced a new paradigm in American civic architecture. Just as the KMK design showed that architects could break free of doctrinaire modernism, it also demonstrated that architects of civic buildings were no longer beholden to outsized domes, columns, and axial symmetry (which, according to Huxtable, "building committees clutch like Linus's blanket").[40] Along those lines, architect Andrea Leers noted that Boston City Hall "meant that there was a way to make an important public building without making it a classical building or a neo-Victorian building."[41] Thus, we can trace back to New City Hall the proliferation of stylistically nontraditional government buildings throughout the United States at the time.

On the local level, as Nathan Silver of the *New Statesman* wrote, during the 1960s and 1970s, "half the towns in America got little Boston City Halls."[42] Several of these were even conceived within grand municipal schemes akin to Boston's Government Center, in whose wake new civic centers emerged across the country, in cities large and small. From Chicago to Dallas, from Fort Worth to Fresno, from Cincinnati to Albany, from Frankfort to Stamford, any city that could afford a new civic center considered it.[43]

One of the most conspicuous "children" of Boston City Hall is Dallas City Hall (fig. 16), designed by I. M. Pei and Partners. Like their counterparts in Boston, Dallas city officials intended to use a boldly avant-garde style to erase painful memories of the recent political past. In the aftermath of John F. Kennedy's assassination in 1963, some Americans scornfully referred to Dallas as the "City of Hate" and the "City That Killed Kennedy." Then-mayor Erik Jonsson sought to remove the stigma of the Kennedy assassination by establishing an official "Goals for Dallas" program, which included building a new city hall.[44]

Construction began in 1972, and the building opened in 1978, replacing the 1914 Beaux-Arts-style Municipal Building. (It was in the basement of the Municipal Building that Jack Ruby killed Lee Harvey Oswald on November 24, 1963, further strengthening that structure's symbolic link to the Kennedy assassination.) Constructed primarily of exposed concrete, the new hall slopes outward at a thirty-four-degree angle as it rises, which provides a welcoming "front porch," offering shelter from the rain and the scorching Dallas sun.[45] On the eve of Dallas City Hall's official opening, Ada Louise Huxtable praised its "monumental, bold, and original design," writing, "This building is not only serious, it is huge . . . , calculatedly symbolic, and overwhelmingly

FIGURE 16. Dallas City Hall; I. M. Pei and Partners (1978). By building a new city hall in the wake of the Kennedy assassination, Dallas adopted the same model for urban revitalization that Boston had used a decade earlier. Library of Congress, Prints & Photographs Division, Historic American Building Survey, HABS TEX, 57-DAL, 1-3.

strong." These descriptors would not seem out of place if they had been applied to Boston City Hall. Indeed, the debt that the Dallas building owed to its predecessor in Boston was not lost on Huxtable, who observed:

> The only other urban group to compare with it is Boston's immensely successful Government Center, which also features a bold and handsome City Hall. One can argue the architectural merits of one or the other indefinitely, but these two sizable public building projects are undeniably among the most interesting urban constructions of the 20th century. This is true for a complex set of reasons having to do with architecture, culture, symbolism and politics, the art of urbanism and the self-perception of cities.[46]

Thus, Dallas adopted the successful model for revitalization that Boston had used, and it also chose the boldness of exposed concrete to provide a distinct visual separation from an unsavory past and a symbol of strength and durability for the future.

Other cities copied not only the style of Boston City Hall but also the competition process used in Boston. For instance, the Fremont, California, City Hall was the result of a competition won by Robert Mittelstadt. Even an untrained eye can identify Boston City Hall as the Fremont building's antecedent: the design in Fremont, as in Boston, features an inverted pyramid of concrete, with its upper stories supported by massive concrete columns. While on the whole far less sculpturally dramatic than its forebear in Boston, the Fremont building does express its internal functions through (albeit more modest) external massing. For instance, in both buildings the council chamber projects dramatically outward from the principal mass of the building. The January–February 1969 issue of *Architectural Forum* noted that features such as this in the Fremont City Hall "are reminiscent of Boston's."[47]

Not all buildings inspired by Boston City Hall have been widely admired. The Kansas City, Kansas, City Hall Annex (Charles E. Mullens, 1971–1973), for instance, has been criticized as a poor imitation of the original. The building, while conforming to the basic massing of Boston City Hall, is more vertically elongated and far less geometrically complex. The middle section is noticeably lacking fenestration, and even the rectangular windows punched into the top section are more vacant than expressive and sculptural. As Alex Krieger pointed out, the Kansas City building, "very much inspired by the Boston original, is a case of 'imitation not always resulting in flattering forms.'"[48]

Like local and state agencies, the federal government also commissioned scores of concrete buildings during the 1960s and 1970s, ranging in purpose and scale from small local departmental branch offices to sprawling administrative campuses in the nation's capital. The impetus for the General Services Administration's brief love affair with concrete was twofold: the KMK design for Boston City Hall and Daniel Patrick Moynihan's 1962 report for the Kennedy administration titled "Guiding Principles of Federal Architecture." The report stated that a federal office building—particularly in Washington, D.C.—should meet two basic requirements: "First, it must provide efficient and economical facilities for the use of Government agencies. Second, it must provide visual testimony to the dignity, enterprise, vigor, and stability of the American Government." The report also referenced a Periclean quotation that John F. Kennedy used in a 1961 speech to the Massachusetts General Court—"We do not imitate—for we are a model to others"—and it stated that "major emphasis should be placed on the choice of designs that embody the finest in contemporary American architectural thought." At the same time, the committee advocated economical and durable buildings, stressing that "designs shall adhere to sound construction practice and utilize materials, methods and equipment of proven dependability. Buildings should be economical to build, operate and maintain."[49]

Boston City Hall, of course, was not built by the federal government and was therefore in no way beholden to Moynihan's report. Nevertheless, it provided a model for federal agencies looking to follow the new guidelines. Brutalism was well suited, for instance, to the report's emphasis on avant-garde, durable, and economical designs. Concrete had first been used by the ancient Romans, and it had thus proved its dependability in a way that recent glass corporate buildings (which were generally a postwar phenomenon) had not.

At the same time, concrete was less expensive than steel throughout the 1960s, which would have made it an attractive material for budget-conscious federal agencies. Although the cost of raw materials for steel had been declining in the 1960s, U.S. Steel and other companies raised prices by six dollars per ton in 1962, in what President John F. Kennedy called "wholly unjustifiable and irresponsible defiance of the public interest."[50] Meanwhile, advancements in reinforced concrete—such as the development in the 1940s and 1950s of plastic insulating concrete forms (ICFs) lowered the cost of concrete construction.

Finally, Moynihan's emphasis on the quality of design, and his stipulation that buildings should be innovative and not imitative, also would have benefited Brutalism—a style that, until Boston City Hall, had not been widely used in government architecture in the United States. One of the first federal buildings constructed after Boston City Hall, and under Moynihan's guidelines, was the Robert C. Weaver Building, which serves as the headquarters for the Department of Housing and

Urban Development. The building, designed by Marcel Breuer and completed in 1968, was the first federal structure to use precast concrete as the primary material for both structure and exterior finish, according to the GSA website. The building was "hailed with optimism as a turning point for public architecture nationwide" when it opened, and other Brutalist federal architecture followed.[51]

While the Weaver Building was widely praised, other concrete federal buildings were met with something less than enthusiasm. One of the most recognizable Brutalist federal buildings is the J. Edgar Hoover Building in Washington, D.C., which houses the Federal Bureau of Investigation. The building was designed by Charles F. Murphy and completed in 1974. By then the country's brief infatuation with Brutalism was ending. The *Chicago Tribune*'s Jerald terHorst derided the building as "fortress-like" and dubbed it "Fort FBI."[52] Similarly, Paul Goldberger criticized the unadorned concrete that covered both the exterior and interior, writing, "It can fairly be said that the color scheme runs the gamut from white to beige."[53]

As was the case with Boston City Hall, criticism of the Hoover Building stemmed not only from changing architectural tastes but also from increasingly negative attitudes toward big government. This was evident in Goldberger's review, which blamed the building's deficiencies on the tortuous process for constructing federal buildings: "How does a fiasco like this occur? The process of creating Federal architecture is so complicated that it is hard to describe at less than book length—but that is itself a large part of the problem." Yet he also recognized that in being a massive, closed-off building, it could be seen as

> an appropriate symbol of the F.B.I. . . . . But, tempting as it is to pass off the F.B.I. building as an amusing reflection of government's banality, such a view remains unconvincing and cynical at bottom. For a building exists to do more than symbolize the uses within. . . . This building turns its back on the city and substitutes for responsible architecture a pompous, empty monumentality that is, in the end, not so much a symbol as a symptom—a symptom of something wrong in Government and just as wrong in architecture.[54]

Goldberger's stinging criticism of the Hoover Building reveals the principal objections to Brutalist government architecture and the extent to which American attitudes about government had shifted by the late 1970s. The toughness and monumentality that are seemingly inherent in the style have long been a principal object of criticism. To many Americans, Brutalism does not seem readily appropriate for American government. Whereas neoclassical architecture reflects the ideals of Athenian democracy and the Roman Republic, the concrete behemoths from the 1960s and 1970s eventually came to symbolize an aloof, unfeeling, and faceless bureaucracy. In the wake of the Kennedy assassination, the Vietnam War, and Watergate, these buildings became associated with such disgraced politicians as Lyndon Johnson, Spiro Agnew, and Richard Nixon. And as with these fallen political figures, the buildings' reputations suffered.

Although Boston City Hall's influence on government architecture in the United States was waning, its effects were still evident in a variety of designs at home and abroad. Even before the building had been completed, there was talk of the widespread impact the design would have throughout the world. Joseph Eldredge, writing in the *Globe* in 1966, predicted: "Long before its completion date, our City Hall will have had a profound effect on other architecture. Already architectural students and not a few firms have been mesmerized by some of its superficial detail. For others, the influence will be subtler, perhaps as much in the organization of spaces as in emancipation from stereotypes."[55] Eldredge's comments were remarkably prescient, as the building spawned scores of stylistic imitators—some of which copied only the superficial details of the KMK design, while others adopted the style, expressiveness, monumentality, or historicism of the building. This is widely recognized and is discussed in a number of publications, including the *AIA Guide to Boston*, which asserts that City Hall "inspired similar buildings across the nation."[56]

In North America, shades of Boston City Hall can be found in the Shapero Hall of Pharmacy at Wayne State University in Detroit (Paulsen & Gardner, 1965), the Minton-Capehart Federal Building in Indianapolis (Woollen Associates, 1975), the Calgary Board of Education

Building (Stevenson Raines Barrett Hutton Seton, 1969), West Palm Beach City Hall (John Marion, 1980), and the Canadian embassy in Washington, D.C. (Arthur Erickson, 1989). In Europe, examples range from the now demolished Birmingham Central Library (John Madin, 1969–1974) to the Palazzo di Giustizia in Macerata, Italy (Alfredo Lambertucci, 1967–1971). Among these buildings can be found top-heavy massing; use of exposed concrete as the dominant material; tripartite arrangement of sections; and small, repetitive fenestration on the upper stories with a largely open ground level. While each architect has his own take on the Boston original, the visual similarities among these diverse and far-flung structures are striking.

Not only the building but also the landscaping around it proved worthy of emulation. Thomas Boylston Adams wrote in 1969: "This plaza that has now come into being is something unique in America. Like Boston's common, it will be copied and repeated in old cities seeking new life and in new cities rising. There is nothing like it in America, nothing half so good."[57] As Adams predicted, similar downtown plazas emerged in several cities in the wake of Boston's City Hall Plaza. For instance, fronting Pei's Dallas City Hall is a massive hardscape area, which, as is the case in Boston, emphasizes the building's monumentality. Pei's plaza also, like Boston City Hall Plaza, conforms to topographical features with steps contoured to the gentle slope of the site. Perhaps the principal difference between these two areas is that the Dallas plaza's fountain is larger and more prominently placed than the Boston one. Given the hotter climate of Dallas, this feature makes sense.

Pei also used an open hardscape plan in his 1969 design, with Zion & Breen, for Cathedral Square in Providence, Rhode Island. Again intended as a monumental approach to an important building (in this case, the Cathedral of Saints Peter and Paul), the same plaza design emerged, with a broad sweep of steps conforming to the site's topography. Also, as in Boston and Dallas, a fountain serves as the only break in the otherwise open, paved space. The Providence plaza is perhaps even more reviled than its counterpart in Boston. According to W. McKenzie Woodward, it is "by far the most problematic of Providence's open spaces," for its neighboring structures fail to generate any activity for the space. Like Boston City Hall Plaza, Cathedral Square was inspired by the great piazzas of Europe, and also like its counterpart in Boston, the Providence square falls far short of its Old World models. "European open spaces rely on activity generators for liveliness," Woodward noted, but the buildings surrounding Cathedral Square (with the exception of the cathedral itself) are "stultifying" structures that attract few regular visitors.[58] Thus, there are several similarities between the Providence and Boston plazas: their European antecedents, their intention to monumentalize important structures, and their failure to attract crowds because they lack "activity generators."

Although bold, monumental concrete buildings like Boston City Hall would fall out of favor in the 1970s, they were regarded as a refreshing cleansing of the air in the 1960s. Even architects who did not subscribe to the particular style of Boston City Hall nevertheless saw in this building evidence that architecture had turned a corner. Andrea Leers, an architect and professor at the Harvard Graduate School of Design, was an MIT graduate student when the Boston City Hall competition took place. In 2005 she recalled: "I must say at the time it was a very exciting building for young architects, for anyone interested in design. It was an actual built example of what we had read about or seen at a distance."[59] Leers's comment reflects the popularity of Brutalism in other parts of the world—particularly the United Kingdom—in the 1950s, but Boston City Hall was the most prominent early Brutalist work in the United States.

Similarly, a *Time* magazine headline proclaimed that Boston City Hall heralded the "End of the Glass Box." As one architect put it, the KMK design signaled a return "to the solid mass." Also, the article noted the building's evocative historicism and its context: "It combines traditional Boston brick with reinforced concrete, but the most striking thing about it is its use of ancient secrets to produce modern magic." The article recounted comments from attendees at the 1962 AIA annual meeting in Dallas, one of whom said: "We're sick of the glass box. For the last 30 years we have abandoned basic architectural precepts, such as light and shadow and depth and beauty." Another observed: "When men lived in caves, they poked holes in them to let air in and smoke out. The holes got bigger. Now the holes have eaten up the box." Others added that glass boxes created "still unsolved problems of glare and temperature control." New City Hall—"as exotically daring as anything Boston has ever seen"—was widely regarded as a much-needed harbinger of change.[60]

So renowned was New City Hall in architectural circles that architects from all over the United States and the rest of the world came to Boston to see it. The American Institute of Architects held its annual convention in Boston in June 1970, in part to showcase the building that had garnered so much acclaim. In fact, the official agenda for the convention included a party at New City Hall.[61] That event attracted five hundred architecture students, meeting concurrently with 3,500 architects, increasing the exposure of the building among current and future American architects.[62] A *Boston Globe* article about the event noted that the architects were "virtually unanimous in their praise of the new City Hall."[63] International architects took notice of the building as well. One said: "I came to Boston from Europe largely *because* of City Hall. I'd heard about the famous competition and traveled here to look at the results. Then I went back to Europe and won a competition, influenced by what I'd seen here. This building influenced a whole generation of international architecture students."[64]

Architects who did not explore Boston City hall *in situ* could hardly have escaped seeing photographs of the building in the hundreds of newspaper, magazine, and journal articles about it. Even negative reviews, when accompanied by photographs, would nevertheless have introduced architects around the world to the building's distinctive design. In addition, Boston City Hall has been featured in architecture textbooks, which speaks to the building's significance within the context of architectural history. This global exposure also served to amplify its influence within the design community.

Even historians and critics who voice aesthetic objections to Boston City Hall cannot help but give (sometimes implicit) credit to the building for its role in shaping the future direction of modern architecture. Vincent Scully, for instance, in one of his many encomiums to the pioneer of postmodernism Robert Venturi, set up Boston City Hall as a straw man to accentuate the virtues of Venturi's architecture. After lambasting the late-modernist architecture that had "laid waste to the urban landscape, flailing about with Neanderthalic roarings," Scully zeroed in on his case in point: "Kallmann, McKinnell and Knowles's Boston City Hall of 1962–69 is a very good example of the late modern, so-called Brutalist buildings that despised, trampled upon, destroyed the scale of the city and, most of all, cut through the complex web of urbanistic adjustments from which a city is made." Having thus vilified the atrocious, Scully turned his attention to the sublime: "Venturi, it seems to me, was the first to begin reversing all of that. He mitigated the abstraction of modern architecture and made it contextual once more. His buildings were prepared to get along with the other buildings in the city, to take up their roles in a gentle comedy of citizenship rather than in a melodrama of pseudoheroic aggression. Venturi's architecture is therefore involved with healing, but it remains a modern architecture."[65]

What Scully and other detractors of City Hall neglect, however, is the role that Brutalism—and Boston City Hall in particular—played in paving the way for Venturi's brand of postmodernism. One might reasonably question whether Brutalism is truly anathema to the ideals expressed in Venturi's *Complexity and Contradiction*. After all, both share a modernist foundation that was reconciled with historicism rather than closed off to it. Both, too, avoid literal references to the past. Indeed, Alex Krieger observed that in a review of the Torre Velasca that served as a "preamble" to City Hall, Gerhard Kallmann seemed to presage Venturi. "Robert Venturi pursued an essentially similar line of reasoning, criticism and language in condemning the reductivist tendencies of contemporary architecture while advocating an architecture of 'complexity and contradiction,'" Krieger wrote.[66]

But whereas Venturi and his ilk chose brazen and ironic historical themes, Kallmann and McKinnell's historicism was more nuanced, subtle, and evocative. One might justifiably argue that this approach is more purely complex and contradictory than Venturi's. Charles Jencks made just this point in his discussion of Boston City Hall, writing of the building that "extreme articulation is obviously an enjoyable exercise with its suspensions and counterpoint, staccato and trills and it shows Late-Modernism moving towards a Baroque *complexity* and nineteenth-century *contradiction*—these two keywords of a poetics not confined to Post-Modernism."[67]

The complex meanings and evocative nature of City Hall's design has, of course, led to profound misinterpretations of the building and its legacy. While Kallmann, McKinnell and Knowles saw their building as open, expressive, representing civic grandeur, Carter Wiseman, in his book *Shaping a Nation,* wrote that it adopted an "otherworldly, defensive posture" that was motivated principally by fear—a fear of downtown areas that in the 1960s and 1970s seemed to be under "assault from social unrest and racial strife." Wiseman claims that New City Hall's "otherworldly defensiveness" eventually influenced the hotel designs of John Portman—buildings intended to "soothe the spirit and reduce anxiety and uncertainty" by giving people not merely convenience and entertainment but also what one promotional brochure on Atlanta called "a gigantic playground, a space where you can live, eat, work and have fun without ever coming 'down to earth.'"[68]

While Wiseman's assessment may in some ways be true of the fortified City Hall today—with armed guards, metal detectors, and x-ray machines at the few entrances that remain open—it does not comport with the architects' original design. Rather than creating a defensive building, disconnected from the city, KMK envisioned a permeable space that was intended to forge links with its surroundings. The pedestrian walkway from the plaza to Congress Street, passing through the building's open courtyard, as well as the massive windows in the ceremonial offices and the south lobby, which conscientiously framed public gathering spaces and neighboring landmarks, hardly suggest an insular, otherworldly space. Rather, the walkway helped to weave New City Hall into the fabric of the downtown area, and the views provided ever-present reminders of the surrounding city to people inside building.

Nevertheless, Wiseman was not alone in reading into the building an aloofness and defensiveness. Nikolaus Pevsner, in his *History of Building Types,* described the building not as an open and accessible celebration of government, but rather as "aggressive and overpowering . . .

aggressively top-heavy and forbidding rather than inviting."[69] Interpretations of the building such as Wiseman's and Pevsner's may well have been motivated by the political and social turmoil of the late 1960s and 1970s. These interpretations reveal more about the social and political context in which they were made than they do about the building itself. Architects striving for an aesthetic of defensiveness, however, would have read these interpretations of City Hall and modeled their designs after it. As Robert Twombly wrote, by the 1970s, Boston City Hall was regarded as "a 1960s icon of the state under siege."[70]

David Monteyne was thus able to use City Hall as the dominant case study in his 2011 book *Fallout Shelter*, finding in the building a perfect model of civil defense architecture during the Cold War. According to Monteyne, Boston City Hall embodied a "bunker aesthetic," which was then featured in the Office of Civil Defense's case study series in 1971, providing a model for other municipalities and governments concerned not only with nuclear war but also with civil unrest. Monteyne acknowledged that the architects "did not design the building with the express purpose of protection from nuclear attack."[71] Nevertheless, the aesthetic of durability embodied in the building merged with the "ethic" of bunker architecture that was prominent in the late 1960s, when the building was completed.

These interpretations reveal a significant and unfortunate dissociation between the building's design intent and its reception. They moreover reveal how the building's meaning changed as the American social and political scene became more tumultuous beginning in the mid-1960s. As other, more deliberately fortress-like structures co-opted some of New City Hall's superficial elements, concrete morphed from signifying durability and fortitude to an image of defense; the overhanging forms evolved from representing an open, transparent government to expressing malevolent state control. Unfortunately, these negative interpretations of Boston City Hall's legacy frequently overshadow other varied (and often positive) aspects of the building's place in the history of architecture.

Local Historical and Political Significance

New City Hall accomplished many of the goals that Mayors Hynes and Collins envisioned for it, and most historians recognize its leading role in the story of Boston's midcentury regeneration. According to Lawrence Kennedy, "numerous critics, visitors, and longtime Bostonians deplore it as an eyesore and periodically propose changes, but its historic significance in the development of Boston transcends its ungainly appearance." Kennedy pointed out that, notwithstanding criticism from its detractors, the building "shocked people into a new view of Boston: the Hub was no longer a provincial backwater, home of historical relics and corrupt politicians; to many, City Hall symbolized the spirit of a new and more confident Boston ready to face the future."[72]

Politically, the symbolism of durability and openness inherent in the design transformed the perception—and, in some ways, the reality—of Boston's municipal government. Whereas Old City Hall had long been an icon of Curley-esque corruption, the new building reflected the honest, capable, dynamic politics of a new generation of city leaders. During the 1970s, as Kevin White had predicted, the progressive design of the building did indeed foster a new era of progressive politics in Boston, leading to greater community involvement in the political process.

As evidence of this sea change in Boston's political history, the tenor of articles about the city in the local, national, and international press changed dramatically between the 1950s and the 1970s. No longer regarded as "a city that is dying on the vine," Boston was instead heralded as a success story in the areas of urban renewal and downtown revitalization. Tales of widespread corruption and graft in municipal politics were replaced by praise for the city's positive approach to renewal. A 1963 article in the Milan-based architecture magazine *Casabella Continuità* praised the favorable effect of New City Hall in an article titled "The Rebirth of a City."[73] Indeed, so dramatic was this reversal of fortunes that in 1969, Ada Louise Huxtable declared from her influential perch at the *New York Times*, "Every mayor and renewal director in every American city, large or small, should be exposed to what is being done in Boston."[74] Two years later, a *Globe* article recounted a conversation between a reporter and the renowned Stockholm city planner Goran Sidenbladh. "You know what Boston is famous for?" Sidenbladh asked. "Your new city hall of course. It's magnificent. It's admired all over the world. It's making Boston famous."[75] Boston's comeback had garnered worldwide attention.

By the mid-1970s, even as many other American cities were still struggling (Cleveland, for instance, declared bankruptcy in 1976), a *New York Times* article proclaimed: "More than ever, Boston is a city of postcard beauty and charm. Tourists are impressed by its architecture and history."[76] In a testament to the political effects of Boston's renewal program, which brought prosperity and stability to municipal government, the article went on to credit "Boston's much-publicized renaissance" for Mayor Kevin White's reelection to an unprecedented fourth consecutive four-year term in 1979.

For White's predecessor, John Collins, the new building seemed, along with his other achievements, to provide the perfect foundation for ascent to higher political office. As early as 1964, on the occasion of his second-term inauguration, Collins appeared poised to run for a four-year term as governor or a six-year term as United States senator. That year, in a tribute to Collins's accomplishments, Harvard University awarded him an honorary doctor of laws degree, making him the first twentieth-century Boston mayor to be so honored. The citation hailed Collins as a "courageous rebuilder of old Boston" and declared that his leadership "had given Boston a new spin."[77]

By 1967, however, as the tenor of national politics turned increasingly rancorous, Collins had grown disenchanted. Thus, his own political career trajectory mirrors that of New City Hall's reputation, for both were scarred by the tumultuous urban uprisings and anti-government demonstrations of the late 1960s. Donlyn Lyndon wrote of Boston City Hall, "Conceived in response to an infatuation with the power and splendor of government and completed just in time to be subjected to the derision of street demonstrators determined to hobble big government, Boston City Hall had the worst of both worlds."[78]

This mirrored the arc of John Collins's mayoral career. When Collins became mayor in 1960, there was still civility in politics. Seven years later, however, this had changed. As Thomas O'Connor wrote: "The idealistic spirit of young John Kennedy—'ask not what your country can do for you, ask what you can do for your country'—had died in a hail of gunfire in Dallas, and Lyndon Johnson's dream of a Great Society was foundering in the rice paddies of Vietnam. The mood of the nation had turned ugly and mean, and the politics of Boston was reflecting much of that same depressing atmosphere." On the morning of June 6, 1967, John Collins held a press conference and announced bluntly, "I am not going to have a political future."[79]

The success of the New Boston that Collins championed, however, far outlasted his own political career. In December 1967, when he had only two weeks left in office, a *Globe* editorial called the unfinished City Hall "a symbol of the Collins legacy," in that it offered the "most impressive evidence" of Collins's skill at modernizing Boston. "It is a powerful and original building," the *Globe* proclaimed, "and Collins will leave it to his successor in the same condition that he will leave Boston itself—with a modern framework and much promise, but still needing a great amount of detail work to finish the job."[80]

By the time Kevin White won his first mayoral election in 1967, the New Boston had already fundamentally changed city politics. White's own political message and tactics in many ways responded to the accomplishments of Hynes and Collins, in that the downtown revitalization compelled White in the campaign of 1967 to shift his focus. "I went into the neighborhoods," White later recalled, "because downtown was already functioning without me. Collins had brought in the money, he had lowered the tax rate, he had brought in the business leaders—those things were *done*. I could draw on that source like an inheritance."[81] During his tenure as mayor, White would continue to maintain the positive relations with the downtown establishment that Hynes and Collins had fostered, but he would focus on the needs of neighborhoods, establishing "Little City Halls" in an effort to make city government more responsive to the needs of the working class, and investing in large capital improvements in the neighborhoods.

The influence of the New Boston—with New City Hall as its centerpiece—was evident from the beginning of White's term. On inauguration day, January 1, 1968, for the first time in fifty years, the mayor was sworn in at Faneuil Hall rather than in Symphony Hall.[82] This conspicuous change of venue gave White the opportunity both to showcase the city's recent accomplishments and to draw more attention to its history. The nearly completed New City Hall stood nearby; this symbol of Boston's renaissance was on display for the one thousand guests who attended the ceremony. The event was a harbinger of things to come under White's administration. With an eye always toward the future, and a deep respect for the city's history, White wanted his administration to be about more than just grandstanding. Whereas Curley's affinity for the limelight was aptly suited to the stage at Symphony Hall, White's abiding concern for the historic city, coupled with his keen vision for the future, was appropriate for Faneuil Hall—with New City Hall providing a hopeful backdrop across the street.

Throughout his tenure in office, White reconciled the recent prosperity of the downtown area with the needs of the neighborhoods, and he balanced new development with preservation of historic structures. City Hall's design—undoubtedly progressive in style, yet conscientiously framing the historic waterfront, Quincy Market, and Faneuil Hall—mirrored White's philosophy, which may explain why he so admired the building.

As time passed, City Hall's historical significance increased by dint of the many events that took place within and around it. To begin with, it signified a new era of inclusion in city government. It was in this building, for example, in 1976 that Louise Day Hicks became the first female president of the Boston City Council. Bruce Bolling became the first black president of the council in 1986, and Felix Arroyo the first Hispanic council member in 2003.[83] Also, in 1993, after nearly a century of Irish American mayors, Thomas Menino became the city's first mayor of Italian descent.

Moreover, since opening, the building and its plaza have hosted hundreds of civic events, including art exhibitions, concerts, community groups, and celebrations that would have been physically impossible to hold at Old City Hall. Although the plaza is decried by many today as a lifeless urban desert, its vast sweep provides a unique venue in Boston for large-scale celebrations, rallies, concerts, and other gatherings—not in some peripheral location, but right in the heart of downtown.

While many of these events were purely for entertainment, some show how the plaza strengthened the democratic political process by providing a gathering place for protests and rallies. Perhaps this was at no other time more obvious than during the busing crisis of the 1970s, when protesters streamed into City Hall Plaza to make their voices heard by government officials. One such protest, on April 5, 1976, led to Stanley Forman's Pulitzer Prize–winning photograph "The Soiling of Old Glory," showing a white demonstrator attacking an African American man, Ted Landsmark (a civil rights attorney who was then the executive director of a trade association), with an American flag as he crossed the plaza on his way to a meeting at City Hall. This incident brought to the immediate attention of city officials (and the nation at large) the severity of social divisions stemming from the mandatory school busing program.

Notwithstanding this momentary descent into violence, political demonstrations on the plaza illustrated the effectiveness of the KMK design in providing a suitable venue for democratic expressions of speech. The small paved area in front of Old City Hall would have been unsuited for rallies of this type and size. The little fenced-in plaza was far easier to police, and thus prevent demonstrations from occurring in the first place. In fact, when Martin Luther King Jr. planned a civil rights protest in Boston in 1965, Mayor Collins expressly forbade demonstrations in front of Old City Hall. "They can march," Collins said, "but there'll be no stopping in front of City Hall."[84]

Moreover, the design of New City Hall, which pulled government officials' offices to the exterior and accentuated their presence overlooking the public spaces, made it impossible for elected officials to ignore these gatherings. In fact, when Landsmark was attacked on City Hall Plaza, Mayor Kevin White and Deputy Mayor Jeep Jones saw the assault from a window.[85] Whereas other government buildings might have insulated elected officials from witnessing such a scene, Boston City Hall's design compelled the mayor to take direct notice of the turmoil manifesting itself throughout the city.

Economic Impact

In early 1963—a year after the Boston City Hall design competition—there was already good news on the economic front. In March, a *Boston Globe* article reported a favorable disposition among investors toward Boston's municipal bonds. "The 'new look' in Boston has done a lot to improve the city's 'image' in the eyes of erstwhile critics of the Hub," the article noted. "Nearly all knowledgeable persons agree that the city will become increasingly stronger, financially and economically, in the years ahead as the 'new Boston' emerges."[86]

Two years later, with New City Hall's construction well under way, financial institutions from around the country, led by the First National Bank of Boston, announced the formation of a national syndicate to bid on Boston's municipal bonds. "The fact that we have formed this new syndicate," said G. Lamar Crittenden, vice president of the First's investment division, "underscores the bank's pride in what Boston has been able to accomplish to date and also our confidence in what is to come."[87] The syndicate acted in spite of Boston's mediocre Baa bond rating from Moody's, which had stripped the city of its A rating in 1959.

In addition to the syndicate led by the First, another local banking behemoth, the National Shawmut Bank, joined in bidding for Boston's $12.4 million bond offering on November 9, 1965. In explaining Shawmut's rationale (given that, for years, Boston's hometown banks had refused to invest in the city), Francis P. Magoun of Shawmut's municipal bond department said that central to the bank's decision was the city's nascent comeback. Magoun considered Moody's Baa rating "an underestimation of the city's potential" and predicted that it would soon be raised.[88] In fact, despite Moody's wary assessment of Boston's debt, the city was able to sell its bonds for A rates. While in December 1964 Baa bonds were yielding 3.52 percent, Boston awarded $13 million in bonds at an average rate of 3.20 percent—a rate almost as low as Moody's Aa-rated yields and well below those rated A.[89] By way of explanation, Guy Garland, vice president of John Nuveen & Co., one of the country's largest dealers in municipal bonds, noted that the positive economic outlook for Boston was a direct result of the

Government Center project: "They [the city] have definitely attracted private capital and more government spending and this is changing the city's creditability."[90]

Boston's reversal of fortunes during this period stemmed from a homegrown impetus rather than any nationwide urban resurgence. Indeed, other cities continued to struggle, even as Boston basked in its dramatic recovery. For instance, at the same time the syndicate led by the First gave a vote of confidence to Boston's municipal bonds, Moody's lowered New York City's bond rating from A to Baa, and Dun & Bradstreet downgraded New York City's debt from "good" to "better medium grade" on the eve of a major ($175 million) bond issue.[91] This was a considerable blow to New York City's bond program, and it occurred at precisely the same time that investors were eyeing Boston's bonds more favorably.

In addition to symbolizing physically the growing confidence in Boston's economy, New City Hall heralded an improvement in Boston's population statistics, as the city was increasingly regarded as a vibrant place to live. In 1979, a decade after City Hall opened, a *New York Times* article highlighted the city's livability, noting that "for many Bostonians, theirs is an exceptionally comfortable city: compact, cosmopolitan and—the word its boosters never tire of—livable. Such qualities are proving to be magnets to affluent young professionals, and after years of decline, the city's population has stabilized."[92] Such laudatory remarks would have been unthinkable only twenty years earlier.

Furthermore, as its proponents had hoped, New City Hall helped to stanch the flow of businesses leaving downtown. In 1966, the Joint Center for Urban Studies of MIT and Harvard published *Boston: The Job Ahead*, which recounted the story of Boston's recent political and economic resurgence. The authors viewed Boston's problems and progress from multiple perspectives, including municipal taxation, transportation, housing, public education, law enforcement, and the relationship between the city and its suburbs.

One chapter dealt with the downtown business district and told of New City Hall's catalytic effect in this area. The authors noted that, notwithstanding continued residential and corporate development in the suburbs, "downtown will continue to be the Boston area's main office center—the place where professional and managerial activities that require frequent face-to-face communication among decision makers are carried on." Similarly, the authors asserted that Boston would remain a key regional headquarters for many national corporations. The city would "hold its own as a wholesale center," they predicted, and the downtown area would "continue to be a cultural and recreational center." They further pointed out that the downtown core in 1966 was already seeing new office development as a result of the Government Center project, and they foresaw this trend continuing.[93]

Among the companies renovating their existing headquarters or constructing new buildings downtown instead of relocating to the suburbs was the Boston Safe Deposit & Trust Company. In 1965 the bank's vice president said, in reference to the New Boston: "Exciting things are going on in Boston. We consider ourselves a part of them. We're good corporate citizens and view our recent renovations of our headquarters as a way of showing it."[94] In a snowball effect, the pace and scale of redevelopment accelerated with each new project. This in turn improved Boston's financial position, which further bolstered corporate confidence in the city and led to still more private development—all of which shows the New Boston's stimulating effect on the city's economy. As a case in point, businessman Harold Hodgkinson noted that the city was collecting more tax revenue from just one new building in the Government Center complex—One Center Plaza—than it had accrued from the entire Scollay Square area before redevelopment.[95]

While there was more to this turnaround than simply New City Hall, the building was widely regarded as the prime mover in the city's recovery. In a speech to the Massachusetts Historical Society, Hodgkinson minced no words when describing the impetus behind Boston's recent "miracle," proclaiming that New City Hall, "which sparked all this construction[,] is the architect's dream of past, present, and future." Hodgkinson also made clear that the rest of Government Center was really peripheral to its centerpiece building, and that, indeed, the entire New Boston revolved around City Hall. In concluding his remarks, Hodgkinson told his audience:

> Truly we saw a miracle in Boston. The years between 1951 and 1972 made history with a new City Hall, the Government Center, and the great surge of buildings built by private capital. The keystone of this period was the rebirth of confidence in this city. The new City Hall is not the highest, loftiest, overpowering "high-rise," but nevertheless it is a pinnacle defying all space and time. It lies, staunchly beating, at the heart of the NEW BOSTON.[96]

For Hodgkinson, as for many others, City Hall was not merely a reflection but rather the taproot of Boston's miraculous midcentury renaissance.

Influence on Future Development

As Hodgkinson's remarks suggest, Boston City Hall not only represented a new political and economic reality but also embodied the city's urban renewal philosophy and approach to development during the 1960s. One picture postcard of the New Boston speaks to City Hall's featured role in Boston's redevelopment program, with the building as the focal point of the sprawling, modernistic Government Center project. Nearby historic structures, such as Faneuil Hall and Old North Church, are conspicuously absent. The image thus represents what Thomas H. O'Connor characterized as a "fairly clear consensus [in the early 1960s], certainly among the movers and the shakers, that the city should be rebuilt."[97] Indeed, throughout the 1960s, tumbledown, neglected areas were replaced with modern buildings, symbolizing the city's newfound prosperity.

Boston became a model for urban development that other cities would emulate. In an article that compared its efforts to the heavy-handed approach to urban renewal used by Robert Moses in New York City, *Time* magazine noted that "Boston evolved a better approach.... It practically reinvented urban renewal in the early 1960s by developing a sound plan to help its decrepit downtown. Then the city's redevelopment agency, which had muscle and was willing to use it, saw that the plan was followed. By having veto power over design schemes, the agency made sure developers used major architects. As a result, planning became a Boston habit."⁹⁸

The effects of urban renewal were evident at once. Upon completion of the new City Hall, as the pace of Boston's economic resurgence quickened, the city continued on what Lawrence Kennedy described as "an unprecedented and explosive building boom" as "developers from all over the world scrambled to invest in America's hottest city."⁹⁹ One area of focus was the long-declining waterfront. "Ten years ago," recounted a 1975 *Globe* article, "decrepit wharves and hazardous building conditions made [the waterfront] an obstacle course for any visitor who wanted to get a glimpse of the water, then blocked by building facades." Perhaps owing to sweeping views of the waterfront from the mayor's office and the BRA suite in New City Hall (which kept the area on the minds of decision makers), the city made a concerted effort to stimulate development. "Today [in 1975], five major 19th century granite structures and several small units have been renovated into luxury apartments, condominiums, offices and restaurants," the *Globe* proclaimed, "and two years ago, a residential enclave emerged for the first time in this former industrial warehouse area of the central city."¹⁰⁰ Moreover, in 1969, Thomas Boylston Adams presciently saw Government Center as a precursor to the Big Dig—still decades in the future—linking Government Center and the waterfront. Adams wrote: "There is plenty yet to do. Not much imagination is needed to see past Faneuil Hall in a clear sweep to the harbor, the elevated highway buried out of sight, and that harbor awakened to a new life, the central living area of the city."¹⁰¹

The 1966 book *Boston: The Job Ahead* spoke to the character of architectural design in Boston's redevelopment program, which also was a result of New City Hall's distinctive aesthetic. As they noted that Boston was entering "a new era of development," the authors warned against wanton construction without regard for architectural distinction. Unlike in other metropolises ("The appalling ugliness of most American cities has long been a subject for comment abroad and embarrassed silence at home," the authors maintained), there was optimism about the quality of development in Boston. The authors singled out the KMK design as evidence of this, writing, "Boston has shown in the case of the new city hall that it knows how to proceed." They particularly praised both the nationwide competition and the city's following through on building the winning design—pointing out (albeit without direct reference to City Hall) that "an architecturally excellent design is very likely to be controversial," while a more conventional design, in "playing it safe," would likely not have architectural merit. They furthermore extolled the psychological and sociological virtues of City Hall by likening great architecture and great civic design to the moralizing and uplifting effect of great art: "It may well be that more people will get more pleasure from looking at Boston's new city hall than from looking at Rembrandt's painting of Aristotle Contemplating the Bust of Homer."[102]

Other influential observers echoed this viewpoint. In 1976, for instance, Walter Muir Whitehill wrote that the Boston City Hall design "did much more than house the obscure and neglected processes of government in a visible, productive environment. It sparked an urban renewal process unequaled anywhere for the quality of its architecture."[103] Two years later, John Morris Dixon, editor of *Progressive Architecture,* proclaimed Boston "a better place now than in the early '50s." He gave the most credit for this change to Government Center, which he called "the most visible area of planned public intervention—the showcase of the Boston Redevelopment Authority." Dixon asserted that subsequent downtown development would not have been possible had this project not paved the way.[104]

Despite his enthusiasm for Government Center, Dixon pointed out an unforeseen consequence. "[Government Center's] very success," he wrote, "has attracted private office towers to the edge of the redeveloped zone, which violate the historical scale prevalent inside it."[105] Other observers were less troubled by this prospect. Thomas O'Connor wrote, "Soaring structures of reflecting glass and shining steel supplanted time-worn buildings of outmoded design; the irregular silhouette of a new skyline replaced the familiar monotony of the old low-lying waterfront; banks, insurance companies, brokerage houses, real-estate firms, and advertising agencies took up residence in the downtown canyons of State Street."[106]

Without a change in its approach to development, the entire historic city might well have fallen victim to unbridled new construction. Indeed, by the late 1960s, while the pace of development in Boston remained high, its nature was already changing. Development during Kevin White's tenure would not follow the raze-and-build model that had given rise to the new West End and Government Center. While that tonic had proved effective during the 1960s, White wisely understood the risk of overdose. His development philosophy focused mostly on adaptive reuse of historic buildings. With the passage of the National Historic Preservation Act in 1966, and the continued availability of private capital from Boston's business community, historic buildings that a decade earlier might have been demolished were instead protected and repurposed.[107] In this way, development during the White years followed the same path that the mayor had set through his inauguration at Faneuil Hall. By seeking not only revitalization and renewal through new construction but also the preservation of the historic city, throughout his sixteen years in office, White proved that the "New Boston" could peacefully coexist with "Good Old Boston."

Granted, it was not only Kevin White's personal philosophy that led to a new kind of development in the 1970s but also a change in public sentiment about urban renewal. Here again was a shift in the national mood reflected in Boston. The factors leading to the demise of top-down urban renewal in the late 1960s were legion, and I will mention only three here. First, the publication of Jane Jacobs's seminal work *The Death and Life of Great American Cities* in 1961—a strident critique of urban renewal—discredited the policies of urban planners and would cause Americans to reconsider their cities. Second, the destruction of McKim, Mead & White's Pennsylvania Station in New York City in 1963 was immediately and almost universally regarded as a mistake. Even champions of modernism such as Philip Johnson protested its demolition. Ada Louise Huxtable, who had been appointed full-time architecture critic at the *New York Times* that same year, used her not inconsiderable influence to decry the demolition of Penn Station and champion historic preservation. This led to the third factor:

the passage of the National Historic Preservation Act in 1966, which made federal funds available for rehabilitating existing structures.

At the end of Collins's tenure as mayor, the *Boston Globe* praised the "bridge of confidence" that he had built between the financial community and municipal government, which had led to a broad consensus about the city's urban renewal program. Some, however, came to see this as a bridge too far. When Collins and Edward Logue attempted to bring urban renewal into the city's ethnic neighborhoods, the consensus evaporated. In Scollay Square, in the financial district, and along the waterfront, there were few residents who would be relocated, so the principal stakeholders—businesses and local government—had been able to reform the landscape in a way that boosted real estate values, increased tax revenues, and (in the words of the BRA) brought a "new, slick, and shiny image" to the city. In the neighborhoods, however, there were still bitter memories of the wholesale destruction of the West End, which had marked Boston's initial, stumbling foray into urban renewal. The coalition of developers, bankers, politicians, and academics that had effected such profound changes downtown came to be regarded as the common enemy by working-class neighborhood residents.[108]

For these reasons, urban renewal techniques would change significantly during the New Boston's second decade. New constituencies were brought into the decision-making process: preservationists, neighborhood groups, religious leaders, and community residents. This meant that it would be difficult—if not impossible—for the city to embark on another large renewal project on the same scale, and with the same speed, as Government Center. Much of Boston's future redevelopment would be more democratic, but also more piecemeal and modest, further emphasizing the singular importance of Government Center and City Hall in the city's history.

Faneuil Hall Marketplace

The venture that best showcases Kevin White's approach to renewal, as well as City Hall's lasting influence, is the redevelopment of Faneuil Hall and Quincy Market. Today, the area known as Faneuil Hall Marketplace is a thriving shopping, dining, and entertainment destination and historical site. In 2011, *Travel + Leisure* magazine ranked it seventh on its list of "World's Most-Visited Tourist Attractions." According to the magazine, the marketplace draws over 18 million visitors annually.[109] Across the street, meanwhile, City Hall stands in a state of abject neglect and is widely regarded as an eyesore. To many, Faneuil Hall Marketplace represents the quintessence of Boston: dignified, historical, bustling—the product of two of the greatest architects in the early history of the city (Charles Bulfinch and Alexander Parris), while City Hall is seen as forbidding and un-Bostonian.

Fifty years ago, however, the situation was reversed: New City Hall was the pride of the city, while Faneuil Hall was neglected and Quincy Market stood in shabby disrepair—one foot and four toes through the door to demolition. Conceived by Mayor Josiah Quincy and designed by Alexander Parris in the 1820s as one of Boston's earliest urban renewal projects, the market remained a vibrant, prosperous mercantile center for decades. By the turn of the century, though, the swelling immigrant population was overcrowding the central city, congesting the narrow streets and compelling merchants to decamp for newer buildings in more accessible locations.[110]

By the end of World War II, according to Thomas O'Connor, "the market buildings and the surrounding warehouses had become so dingy and dilapidated that in 1956 the city planning board gave up all hope of renovation and designated the area for wholesale clearance to make way for office buildings." It was not until 1963—the same year that construction began on New City Hall across the street—that the city changed its policy and decided to restore the buildings. The change in policy came after a group of historians and preservationists convinced Logue that the buildings were worth saving because of their historical significance. Logue in turn secured federal funds to undertake a renewal study of the entire marketplace area and waterfront. This set in motion the renewal project that would come to fruition in the years after New City Hall was built.[111]

Several scholars and critics have credited New City Hall's proximity and relationship to Faneuil Hall–Quincy Market for the latter's

FIGURE 17. Boston City Hall, mayor's office, looking toward Faneuil Hall. By deliberately framing the "Cradle of Liberty" with this window, KMK ensured that Boston's mayors would remember the city's rich history. The view of a dilapidated Quincy Market also led Kevin White to redevelop the area. Library of Congress, Prints & Photographs Division, Historic American Building Survey, HABS MASS, 13-BOST, 71-11.

renovation. Even before City Hall had been completed, a *Globe* editorial predicted: "Perhaps the most inspiring aspect of the new City Hall is the effect it seems bound to have on the attitude of those who will work there serving Boston.... And this effect can only be increased by the breathtaking views the new City Hall affords." The editorial mentioned, in particular, the view from the mayor's office (fig. 17) as being "especially reassuring and inspiring, looking out as it does on Faneuil Hall where our civic traditions had their origin."[112]

Similarly, in 1969, Ada Louise Huxtable pointed out in a *New York Times* column titled "The View from the Mayor's Windows" that Faneuil Hall "stands directly behind City Hall, its delicate scale and Georgian propriety acknowledged and framed by the massive modernity of the new structure.... The superb but shabby old gray granite market complex and the waterfront beyond—are the view from the Mayor's windows."[113] The architects were deliberate in creating this powerful visual effect. Charles Millard maintained that the mayor's office overlooks Faneuil Hall and the waterfront "to remind him of Boston's past, its people, and its maritime tradition.... [The] conscious intention of the architects was to relate their building to the city around it, and they are particularly fond of pointing out how the office projecting from the east side of the building seems to hold a dialogue with Faneuil Hall."[114]

This dialogue was not lost on Kevin White. Thomas O'Connor wrote that White's most immediate concern when he assumed office was "the unsightly Faneuil Hall market area, its narrow streets congested with delivery trucks, broken-down pushcarts, and piles of debris, which lay in all its embarrassing ugliness directly beneath the windows of [White's] shiny office in the new City Hall." White said of the run-down marketplace: "It was an eyesore, right in front of me. If you can visualize the expanse of window in my office as a mural, it was a mural of disrepair."[115]

While the deliberate placement of the mayor's suite across from this historic site kept it in view (and on the mind) of the man occupying that office, the marketplace still might have been razed had it not been for White's preservationist instincts. In fact, new development in the area surrounding Faneuil Hall and Quincy Market picked up as Government Center neared completion. Huxtable noted in 1969 that "the new banks and skyscrapers sparked by the Government Center construction, of which City Hall is a part, are closing in, pushing history."[116] In other words, the historic buildings might well have become victims of Government Center's success, had the city not renewed its commitment to preservation—a commitment, not coincidentally, that was part of the original Government Center plan and City Hall competition program.

After entertaining a variety of proposals for redeveloping the site, the city eventually backed an architectural plan by Benjamin Thompson & Associates. The developer was James Rouse, an urban enthusiast and shopping mall pioneer. The innovative "festival marketplace" emphasized a pedestrian-friendly retail and tourist environment, preserving the original buildings while adding sympathetic additions to make them suitable for modern retail establishments and for shoppers used to enclosed suburban malls. Rouse paired restaurants, stores, and pushcart vendors with intensive entertainment programming to make the area not simply a museum of historic buildings but rather a vibrant and thriving urban destination that would complement the surrounding financial and government districts, harmoniously juxtaposing the old with the new.

In the end, Faneuil Hall Marketplace was a remarkable success. In 1977, the first year of operation, it attracted 10 million visitors (a figure equal to the gate count that year at Disneyland), and increased to 12 million the following year.[117] With a stunning sales revenue of $233 per square foot in its first year—which climbed to $500 per square foot within a decade—Faneuil Hall Marketplace became the first successful downtown historic rebuilding project in the nation. It would inspire similar projects in other cities across the country, from Baltimore's Inner Harbor to New York City's South Street Seaport—projects also developed by Rouse in the same mold as the Faneuil Hall project. It also moved Boston closer to achieving the goals of Hynes, Collins, Logue, and White, in that, as Thomas O'Connor wrote, it "brought middle-class residents back to town, attracted visitors from all over the world, brought bright lights and open spaces to a part of the city that had always been dark and deserted, and turned the downtown area into a major resource for a thriving metropolis."[118]

The project's success along those lines is widely recognized. What often gets lost, however, in the prosperity of the marketplace today is that it was largely made possible by the design of City Hall in the 1960s. Rather than turning its back on a dilapidated area, New City Hall deliberately framed the old market buildings for the most powerful man in the city, ultimately compelling him to act. Kallmann, McKinnell and Knowles did not see their project as a discrete building, removed from the larger redevelopment plans of the city; rather they heeded the overall vision of Hynes, Collins, and Logue, and incorporated the dreams of these men into their design by not letting the mayor lose sight of the city's rich history.

The architects could have situated the mayor's office over the plaza, with a view of Government Center's modern architecture, perhaps limiting the mayor's focus solely to the future. Instead, KMK recognized the value and potential of the historic area across Congress Street, and their design responded appropriately. Thus, Huxtable wrote, Boston "found a way to keep the past and the present in one of the happiest architectural, historical, and urban triumphs of any modern city."[119] More important, KMK showed that the Government Center project was holding true to the promise of preserving the city's important historic legacy rather than sweeping it away in wholesale demolition.

CONCLUSION

Boston City Hall at Fifty

In the new millennium, Boston City Hall is facing a midlife crisis. As is the case with any fifty-year-old building, there are crucial yet costly upgrades required to keep the building both functional and meaningful in the twenty-first century. The situation is exacerbated by decades of deferred maintenance, and complicated by the general distaste for the building.

It also is at risk of becoming a victim of its own success. The goals of architects, politicians, and planners in the 1960s—to redeem and revitalize an ailing city—have largely been realized. Today, Boston is thriving economically, socially, culturally, and politically. Accordingly, some Bostonians crave a city hall that represents the city in the new millennium, rather than a relic from the mid-twentieth century. The architectural symbolism of a beleaguered city struggling to reinvent itself seems incompatible with a modern metropolis that would just as soon forget an unsavory chapter in its history.

Plans and Proposals

In recent decades Boston City Hall's reputational crisis has come to a head, as the city government has on multiple occasions proposed selling or tearing down the building. Nevertheless, there are ongoing efforts among prominent architects, scholars, and preservationists to save it. Moreover, plans to renovate or modify City Hall and the plaza continue to emerge. These proposed solutions are useful both for identifying perceived problems and for determining what the future may hold.

Perhaps the most widely criticized aspect of the KMK design today is the plaza, and it has inspired several plans for alterations. In the 1980s, the city considered restoring the fountain (which had stopped working early in the decade) and adding a winter solstice steam-and-sound fountain designed by Joan Brigham and Chris Janney.[1] In 1994, one year after becoming mayor, Thomas Menino launched an "Ideas Competition" that invited everyone—from architects to schoolchildren—to submit suggestions for improving the plaza.[2] The 190 submissions were not taken seriously, however, because the city lacked funding to follow through on the often fanciful designs (turning the plaza, for example, into a "Tomb of the Bambino" in which to inter the fabled curse that had long beset the Red Sox).

The following year, Menino and developer Norman Leventhal established the Trust for City Hall Plaza, an independent body charged with devising new public-private uses for the area. The trust proposed building a 350-room hotel with parking garage on the plaza. This would generate revenue to finance other improvements, such as new planting, paving, street furniture, and public art. At one time, the trust also proposed extending Hanover Street through the plaza to connect the North End with Cambridge Street.[3] These plans died when the General Services Administration objected on account of the proximity of the proposed alterations to the Kennedy Federal Building. Many citizens also balked at converting public space for private use.[4] Another proposal by Mayor Menino himself, to complete the pedestrian bridge from City Hall Plaza to Faneuil Hall Marketplace (which had been proposed in the original design but then abandoned), was also shot down.⁵

Working independently from the trust, cellist Yo-Yo Ma in 1996 teamed up with landscape architect Julie Moir Messervy to design a garden at City Hall Plaza inspired by J. S. Bach's Cello Suite no. 1 in G Major. Ma's efforts were filmed and made into a documentary titled *Music Garden*. Initially, civic leaders seemed to back the effort, with Mayor Menino publicly declaring his support and thanking Ma for his vision. The city eventually canceled the project, however, deeming it "too complex."⁶ After being rejected in Boston, Ma took his idea to Toronto, which enthusiastically embraced the project and constructed the music garden along the city's waterfront.

In 1998, the BRA appointed a Citizens' Advisory Committee, led by Suffolk Law School dean John Fenton, to hold public meetings about the trust's proposals. Fenton's efforts were undercut, though, when Menino proposed that the city consider selling City Hall.⁷ In December 1999, the trust released a new proposal without a hotel, but including a new rapid transit station and a trellis-lined walkway, dubbed the "Community Arcade." This walkway along Cambridge Street—the only tangible (and woefully modest) product of five years of effort—finally opened in 2001.

Other abortive plans also aimed to bring life to the plaza. In 2004, KMW principal Henry Wood proposed planting a "green bracelet" of trees around the central plaza, while retaining the hardscape area directly in front of City Hall for events and rallies.⁸ Another proposal emerged from Albert, Righter & Tittmann, calling for kiosks, booths, and small stores to populate the plaza every summer. Henry Lee called this "a moveable feast, literally. It was a wonderful design. If they could have raised the funds, they would have brought a lot of life to what is certainly on weekends and evenings a completely dead area."⁹ Architect Gretchen Schneider also suggested that the plaza be enlivened with private attractions, such as restaurants, hotels, and shops.¹⁰

One significant change to the plaza came in May 2006, when the city finally paved over the fountain, which had not been functioning for more than a decade.¹¹ Other ideas have been proposed off and on

FIGURE 18. Government Center MBTA station; HDR (2016). The new station brought several functional improvements (such as natural light and handicap accessibility), but the oversized headhouse blocked views of historic buildings and signified the revenge of the glass box. Photograph by the author.

since then, but none garnered an enthusiastic response until February 2011, when Boston received funding from the Environmental Protection Agency's Greening America's Capitals program.[12] This grant led to two proposals for introducing more trees and grass to the area and, in one of the proposals, removing the plinth alongside the Kennedy Federal Building.[13]

In 2016, a new Government Center MBTA station opened, replacing the modest brick structure designed by KMK. The new station (fig. 18), designed by HDR, improved handicap accessibility and circulation, allowed natural light onto the station platform, and provided more space for fare-vending machines. The $113 million restoration has been deemed a success by many. The *Globe* referred to the old station as "a lump of brick that rose like a boil amid the wider expanse of brick known as City Hall Plaza."[14]

Yet the massive superstructure—a forty-foot-high glass box— destroyed important vistas that the modest 1960s headhouse preserved. Previously, one could see the steeple of Old North Church from Tremont Street when approaching Government Center from the direction of Park Street. Also, the Sears Block and Sears Crescent were visible from Cambridge Street to those coming from Bowdoin Square. Both views are now blocked by the station. Whereas *Time* magazine in 1962 hailed City Hall as symbolizing the "End of the Glass Box," today the glass box has exacted revenge through the new subway station.

In addition to the many ideas for the plaza, there have been intermittent suggestions for altering City Hall as well. Only one year after the building officially opened, a BRA official complained, "I think City Hall is an inhuman building." The official, Jan Wampler, head of the Planning Design Group at BRA, proposed adding features that would attract both local residents and tourists. These included roof gardens, outdoor parks and coffeehouses, theaters, food markets, rooftop tennis courts, shops, nightclubs, and a cafeteria. "We'd like to see it become a peoples' [sic] hall instead of an administrators' hall," Wampler explained. "We want to find out what can be done to make it more responsive to the people, to make it a meeting place for the city as well as a place of employment." Among those who agreed with Wampler's plans was Michael McKinnell. He and Gerhard Kallmann were "definitely enthusiastic about making City Hall more human," he said. "The building was designed to inspire this type of activity within its fabric, and we think it's susceptible to it. . . . The building is supposed to be flexible."[15]

Similar abortive proposals occasionally cropped up throughout the following decades. In 1997, architect Henry MacLean proposed a rooftop restaurant for City Hall, as well as a retail arcade along Congress Street.[16] In 2005, the city contracted Schwartz/Silver Architects to redesign the main entry to accommodate maintenance and security requirements, as well as to simplify and lighten what some felt was a dark and confusing entrance. The architects proposed a glass canopy projecting from under the City Council chamber with new entry steps and expanded lobby, which would have accommodated larger public events and exhibits.[17] The plan eventually proved too complex and costly and was abandoned.

Other proposals emerged from City Hall enthusiasts such as Robertson Ward, who suggested glazing over the central courtyard and increasing the amount of natural sunlight in the space.[18] Architect Robert Neiley, meanwhile, proposed creating a winter garden at the front of the building and establishing a café inside.[19] In 2007, Alex Krieger called for moving many offices out of City Hall (while retaining the mayor's suite, City Council offices, and bureaucratic spaces in the upper levels) and replacing them with more public functions, such as a Museum of the City of Boston in the lower level.[20] Gretchen Schneider contended that City Hall would benefit from windows being cut into the mound at Congress Street, noting that the area surrounding the building had improved considerably since the 1960s. "Let's modify our most important civic structure for the city of today," she urged.[21]

In addition to these independent proposals, two design contests have called on young architects and students to devise changes to the building. In 2007, *ArchitectureBoston* invited six teams of young architects to resolve the building's perceived deficiencies. It listed these problems: City Hall is too opaque (i.e., entrances are fortified and the interior is screened from passersby), too big, too mute (i.e., confusing to navigate), too ugly, too dark, too empty, too costly to operate, and too aloof.

The contest was by nature hypothetical, and the theoretical solutions ranged from the imaginative to the fantastical. For instance, Höweler + Yoon Architecture proposed wrapping the building in complex glass sheathing (fig. 19). While effectively softening with glass the concrete that many Bostonians find off-putting, the proposal would obscure (for better or worse) many of the KMK building's expressive details. This proposal, and many other entries, imaginatively sought to create a modernist statement (by today's standards) that would update the once daring 1960s building by making it cutting-edge once again. But this design exercise—calling for drastic interventions to keep the building relevant—begs the question. First we must consider whether such dramatic changes are appropriate or necessary.

Many would say yes. Not long after the *ArchitectureBoston* contest, the 2010 Rotch Design Competition, sponsored by the Boston Society of Architects, challenged young architects to transform City Hall for the twenty-first century.[22] The competition stipulated that the

FIGURE 19. Proposal for alterations to Boston City Hall; Höweler + Yoon Architects (2007). Boston City Hall has been the subject of several theoretical design contests which have invited architects to reimagine the building for the twenty-first century. Courtesy of Höweler + Yoon Architects.

contestants must incorporate a Museum of Massachusetts History into their final designs. The entries called for adding new wings of glass-enclosed shops, creating a rooftop garden, and even replacing City Hall with a new building altogether. The winning proposal, by Christopher Shusta, built the museum into the Congress Street side of the mound, adding outdoor terraces above. Shusta connected the terraces to the existing central courtyard to create a dynamic interplay of interior and exterior spaces that both penetrate the building and allow it to relate more effectively to its surroundings.[23]

The building is seemingly receptive to these changes. Gerhard Kallmann and Michael McKinnell said that when they designed City Hall, they intended for it to be an armature—a framework—that future

234 Conclusion

generations could embellish and adorn. In 2005, they expressed their dismay that this had not happened. Likewise, Kallmann and McKinnell's partner, Henry Wood, who oversaw much of City Hall's construction, remarked in 2007 that he hoped a skylight might cover the courtyard to make it a more useful place for Bostonians to gather and interact with their neighbors and city officials.[24]

The lack of substantive modifications to the KMK design during the past half century speaks to the difficulty of the task. Gary Wolf noted that any eventual changes to the design—particularly to the plaza—that are "dependent on the cooperation of federal, state and municipal government are going to be difficult to implement. Nevertheless, that concerted effort is exactly what it took to create the New Boston, and City Hall, in the first place."[25] Douglass Shand-Tucci pointed out that there are likely no solutions that will satisfy everyone. "The dissatisfaction," he wrote,

> is as much an affair of taste as of style, the core issues being part and parcel of a perennial conflict in all styles between elite culture, so often concerned with refinement and taste and very comfortable with spare elegance and formal space, and mass culture—with its pop taste, distinctly uncomfortable with spare, formal settings, and so apt to want to "warm things up" in a way some would call "homey," others "schlock." When the space in question surrounds public buildings, the politics of such a situation is obvious.[26]

During the Menino administration, with the mayor openly antagonistic toward City Hall, it was unlikely that substantial investment in the building would be forthcoming. Menino's successor, Martin Walsh, went so far as to state during the 2013 mayoral campaign that if elected, he would abandon the building: a front-page photo in the *Boston Herald* showed Walsh standing in front of City Hall with a headline reading "Marty Walsh's Grand Plan for City Hall: BULLDOZE IT!"[27] Since assuming office in 2014, though, Walsh has seemingly reversed course and made modest investments in the building, such as updating lighting fixtures and installing lounge chairs on the plaza. In July

2017, Walsh unveiled lobby renovations that were initiated to "make City services more accessible, welcoming and efficient," according to a statement from Walsh's office.[28] The $2.1 million project included a variety of features intended to enliven the building: security equipment was repositioned to improve flow, a coffee bar and new seating were added to attract visitors, and touchscreen kiosks were installed to provide self-service access to city services.

As he faced reelection in 2017, it remained to be seen what Walsh's long-term plans for the building would be. Certainly without John Collins's unflagging support, City Hall would likely not have been built in the first place, and absent Kevin White's enthusiasm, it would not have enjoyed such widespread acclaim during the first two decades of its existence. As Herb Gleason argued, "City Hall just needs to have a believer again, in order to bring it back to the style to which it should be accustomed."[29]

Preservation

Some have argued that it is hypocritical to talk of preserving Boston City Hall, which was the impetus for the destruction of Scollay Square. David Kruh, author of two books on Scollay Square, wrote that Thomas Menino's proposal to sell or demolish City Hall was as timely as Collins's Government Center plan in the 1960s.[30] Many others, however, have made forceful arguments in favor of preserving the building. Henry Moss, a principal at Bruner/Cott & Associates, compared Boston City Hall to Fenway Park, which in the late 1990s also "was written off as an unusable, irredeemable artifact." Yet, Moss pointed out, the ballpark was saved and is now once again beloved.[31] Similarly, Jane Holtz Kay, in 1988, when some of the first murmurs about demolishing City Hall emerged, wrote, "City Hall is a period piece that deserves some forbearance—not to mention admiration—as a work of architecture and art that few today could equal in terms of the boldness and purpose of its civic posture."[32]

In response to Menino's 2007 proposal to sell City Hall, a group of architects and citizens petitioned the Boston Landmarks Commission to grant landmark status to the building. Gary Wolf wrote a twelve-page essay explaining the building's architectural and historical significance. The commission received dozens of letters supporting the petition. Among the supporters were several politicians, including Maureen Feeney, president of the Boston City Council. "There is little debate that its 200 million pounds of concrete and steel is a great physical and defining presence in Government Center," Feeney wrote. "In history and architecture, its national awards stand as credentials to its significance as a masterpiece, albeit a rather less than aesthetically pleasing one to many an untrained eye."[33] Tufts University professor Daniel Abramson noted in his letter that "City Hall is in danger of becoming Boston's Penn Station."[34] And David Eisen, architect and architecture critic for the *Boston Herald,* asked:

> Should we tear down the last generation's answer to the questions we still struggle with today because their proposal was something short of perfect—with the arrogant assumption that we, unlike them, can finally create the perfect image of a modern American metropolis? I suggest that we shouldn't. Another new City Hall will offer its own imperfect solutions, and another round of adulation followed by condemnation, because buildings represent the realities of flawed societies as well as the dreams of their ambitious builders. . . . [Boston City Hall] was hailed upon its completion for accomplishing exactly what Mayor Menino asks the city hall of his dreams to do. How can memories be so short?[35]

The Landmarks Commission considered the petition at a public meeting, at which forty concerned citizens spoke. After nearly an hour and a half, the commission voted eight-to-one to accept the petition.[36] This put Boston City Hall on a list of buildings that would be given further study for landmark status; if the commission were to recommend such status, however, it would require the approval of the City Council and the mayor.[37]

This is more than merely a local issue. Since the turn of the twenty-first century, Boston City Hall has become a bellwether in a global debate about historic preservation. In his book *Preservation of Modern*

Architecture, Theodore H. M. Prudon cast the building, along with Paul Rudolph's embattled Orange County Government Center in Goshen, New York, as examples "of government buildings that received considerable public and professional acclaim at the time of their completion but were never fully embraced by their respective localities and have been regularly threatened with severe alterations or demolition." Prudon maintained that City Hall "must be considered a modern landmark that deserves thoughtful preservation."[38]

Prudon also discussed the link between preservation and perception, pointing out that all architectural styles go through a reputational slump before eventually gaining heritage value. In a similar vein, William J. Mitchell, former dean of architecture at MIT, observed of the present distaste for Boston City Hall:

> These things are cyclical. And the big danger with cultural heritage is that the moment when things are at the bottom of their cycle in the popular imagination is precisely when you can lose them.... Responsible cultural stewardship isn't a matter of personal taste. When a building is culturally significant, architects and political leaders have a duty to preserve it, whether they personally like it or not. The mayor is entitled to his obvious dislike of City Hall, but this simply shouldn't be a factor in determining its future.

David Fixler, in this same roundtable discussion, added: "These cycles seem to be getting shorter—especially in the way people view Modern architecture. I'm intrigued that people of my son's generation seem to have an appreciation for Modern architecture that was lost in the '80s and '90s. They think City Hall is cool."[39]

In addition to succumbing to these vicissitudes of fashion, midcentury concrete buildings are now in that phase of life when they require considerable investment. This is true of most buildings, regardless of style, when they have been around for half a century. Over time, systems become outdated, functional needs change, unsympathetic accretions cling like barnacles to the original structure, and materials age and succumb to the ravages of time. Add to this mix the fact that Brutalist buildings—many of which were controversial from the start—have fallen stylistically out of favor, and we have a multidimensional problem that renders these buildings both out of shape and out of fashion.

The question of preserving modern architecture—particularly Brutalist buildings—presents a peculiar set of challenges. First, there is a touch of irony in preserving modern buildings. Many of these structures, after all, were built as part of urban renewal programs that were, at the time they were constructed, anathema to preservationists. They stand not only as products but also as symbols of top-down large-scale urban renewal, which has since been vilified. As such, some of them still stick in the craw of the preservation community because they caused wholesale destruction of neighborhoods and historic structures. Moreover, as Thomas Jester and David Fixler have noted, modernism was predicated on a philosophy that endorsed perpetual architectural change, which is seemingly inimical to historic preservation.[40]

Because of these issues, preservation of Brutalist buildings continues to incite controversy worldwide. On one side is a bloc of detractors ready to see the wrecking ball swing. Among them is George Ferguson, who as president of the Royal Institute of British Architects (RIBA) in 2004 proposed establishing a "Grade X" listing of the "most vile" buildings in the UK, with Brutalist structures (such as Owen Luder's Trinity Square Gateshead and John Madin's Birmingham Central Library) in the crosshairs.[41] While the idea received some popular support after a British reality show invited the public to choose an ugly building to be demolished on national television, others balked. An article in *Apollo* magazine called Ferguson's suggestion "philistine" and "knee-jerk prejudice" while pointing out that "the history of taste—of changing perceptions of vileness and ugliness—is rather less straightforward than the President of the RIBA would have us believe."[42]

As high-profile unpopularity contests seek to tear them down, there is also a growing movement to preserve these spurned buildings. Organizations such as Docomomo (the International Committee for Documentation and Conservation of Buildings, Sites and Neighbourhoods of the Modern Movement), Britain's Twentieth Century Society, and local preservation groups have come to see in Brutalism, the reviled architecture of today, an analogue to the unfairly hated buildings of the past—from Penn Station to the Chicago Stock Exchange. And while critics, particularly in the United States, are quick to counter that preservation of unwanted buildings is often cost-prohibitive and infringes on private property rights, many Brutalist buildings have made their way onto landmarks registers, effectively staving off the bulldozers.

There are certainly no easy answers to the complex questions of preservation, and it would be wrongheaded to generalize about thousands of specific cases, each with its unique circumstances. But the pages of architectural history are rife with cautionary tales, and many a regret has grown out of the rubble of a too hastily demolished building. At the very least, we would do well to avoid any rash decisions and to foster a deliberate, informed critical dialogue that moves beyond promulgating fleeting biases and derogatory hype.

Into the Future

As Bostonians come to reevaluate the architecture and politics of the 1960s, they are likely to develop more respect for this concrete symbol of that era. After all, the passage of time often brings a new appreciation of both political epochs and architectural styles. As the John Huston character, Noah Cross, in the 1974 movie *Chinatown* observes, "Politicians, ugly buildings, and whores—they all get respectable if they last long enough."[43]

One example of this Crossian paradigm is Boston's Old City Hall, which, in the early twentieth century, drew many of the same aspersions now cast on the 1960s building. It was considered ugly, dirty, and old-fashioned. It also symbolized a period in Boston's history that many would just as soon forget. As Lawrence Kennedy wrote: "Those who wanted to demolish the building saw this as a way of sweeping out the old in order to bring in the new."[44] Fortunately, Old City Hall was spared the wrecking ball when, at the behest of Walter Muir Whitehill, Mayor Kevin White held a national competition for designs to repurpose the building for private use. The winning design, submitted by Roger Webb, head of the nonprofit Architectural Heritage, preserved the exterior while gutting and rebuilding the interior to serve a variety of uses, from offices to a restaurant. The building eventually won an award for adaptive reuse.

Today, Old City Hall is widely regarded as a magnificent landmark of Boston's political and architectural past. Likewise, the reputation of its most infamous and longest-serving mayoral occupant, James Michael Curley, has improved over time. The man who once brought shame to the city has now been elevated to the status of local folk hero. Unlike John Hynes and John Collins, politicians today do not seek to distance themselves from Curley, and some even gain political capital by forging associations with his memory. For example, in 2011, former Massachusetts Senate president William Bulger published an adulatory biography of Curley, peppered with personal reminiscences.[45]

This cycle of admiration and contempt is a recurring theme in both architecture and politics. Just as people now wax nostalgic about Old City Hall and the Curley-esque wiles it represented and for which it was once reviled, they will likely in the future appreciate New City Hall as a still relevant symbol of the city in the twenty-first century. Indeed, the innate characteristics of Boston embodied in the KMK design—chief among them fortitude and innovation—are as much a part of the city's spirit today as they were in the 1960s, or even the 1770s. When terrorists detonated two homemade bombs at the finish line of the Boston Marathon in 2013, the city rallied with the slogan "Boston Strong." Such a sentiment would not have seemed out of place in Boston during the mid-twentieth-century economic crisis, or the British blockade of Boston Harbor two hundred years earlier. What better expression of "Boston Strong"—the city's unbreakable resolve in the face of adversity—than the brawny concrete form of City Hall?

Boston also has long regarded itself as an innovative city. From the Puritan settlers, who sought to establish a novel, exemplary society in the New World, to the Sons of Liberty, who fought for the revolutionary idea of creating a nation founded on democratic and egalitarian principles, Boston has a storied history of fearless trailblazing. This progressive zeal has not diminished over the centuries. In his first State of the City address in January 2015, Mayor Martin Walsh laid out his vision for the city's future, which centered on fostering innovation and creativity.[46] As the building that revolutionized the city's architecture, City Hall compellingly represents these ideals. Those critical of the building on the grounds that it fails to reflect the city and its history would do well to think about Boston's true identity. Neither timidity, nor imitation, nor a slavish obeisance to the past, but rather boldness, strength, and innovation: these are the timeless and enduring traits that have for centuries defined Boston, and these are the qualities so conspicuously and appropriately embodied in its City Hall.

In a 1630 sermon, John Winthrop, first governor of the Massachusetts Bay Colony, proclaimed, "We shall be as a City upon a Hill, the eyes of all people are upon us."[47] Boston remains a model city today (economically thriving, politically stable, culturally vibrant, and eminently livable), to which municipalities the world over can look for inspiration. Nothing better represents Boston's success than New City Hall, which catalyzed an improbable political, architectural, and economic resurgence. In this way, the building has meaning and purpose beyond the city limits. While such an embattled building might seem an unlikely model to emulate, it nevertheless provides a compelling case study. As an inherently symbolic building, with a cutting-edge, high-quality design, Boston City Hall demonstrated both the monumental and the practical effects of new architecture in a city striving to reinvent itself. While it is admittedly doubtful that Detroit, Ferguson, or other troubled cities would stake their futures on a Brutalist design today, Boston City Hall nevertheless provides lessons on the transformative potential of architecture.

Chief among these lessons is the importance of quality design. New development, regardless of artistic merit, has the potential to bring about some degree of salutary change, but only architecture of quality can spark the kind of renaissance that Boston needed in the 1960s and that many cities continue to seek. While great architecture costs more than the merely prosaic, there is a much higher return on investment. Boston could have hired a cut-rate architect to design its new City Hall, which likely would have been an anonymous structure that garnered scant attention from locals and even less from outside the city limits. It would have done little to inspire confidence in the city's future, much less to communicate a message of innovation and durability. Likewise, as construction costs escalated, the city might have demanded the architects scale back their design, making it cheaper to build but also rendering it less prestigious and keeping it out of the architecture textbooks and design magazines. But Bostonians in the 1960s understood the value of quality architecture, and they found additional funds to construct the building as designed.

Today this phenomenon is often called the "Bilbao effect," in reference to Frank Gehry's iconic 1997 Guggenheim Museum in Bilbao, which transformed a dying industrial center into a cultural mecca. A 2013 article in *The Economist* explained how "an imaginatively designed museum commissioned by an energetic mayor can turn a city around."[48] Thirty years before Bilbao, Boston City Hall achieved the same result, symbolizing a more stable, effective, and honest municipal government; instilling a new sense of pride in a beleaguered city; and drawing visitors from around the world to what had been a run-down backwater.

A second lesson is the effectiveness of symbolism. Architectural symbols can communicate in a glance what might take thousands of words to explain. Anyone who, in the 1960s, might otherwise have written off Boston as a historic relic without a future would have gotten a different impression from the avant-garde KMK design. City Hall extinguished the popular conception of Boston politics as a corrupt backroom enterprise through its forceful expression of the majesty of government, which revealed rather than obscured the governmental process, invited citizen participation, and celebrated the public as the foundation of municipal government. These symbols were appropriate for Boston in the 1960s, and other cities in different eras would require their own unique symbols. Nevertheless, the lesson of architecture as a potent reflection of local values remains a universal constant.

While these symbolic associations are essential, practicality cannot be sacrificed on the altar of monumentality. This is the third lesson of Boston City Hall. Much of the building's success derives from its not only containing civic-ceremonial spaces but also serving sometimes prosaic functions. The modular design of the upper stories allows for easy alteration of office configurations as needs change over time. Moreover, by creating a building that invites citizens to enter and interact with their government, rather than an untouchable monument cordoned off from the public, Boston invited greater civic engagement. The numerous public demonstrations that have taken place on City Hall Plaza during the past half century—on issues ranging from civil rights to gay marriage to bicycle safety—have demonstrated the belief of Bostonians that their elected officials would listen to them, and that citizens could bring about change in a democracy. Whereas Bostonians during the Curley administration had largely regarded civic corruption with indifference or apathy if not tolerance, later generations have been empowered by their City Hall—a fertile space for civilian heroism.

Of course, the controversy surrounding Boston City Hall's design may give some cities pause. What mayor would want his or her city hall to be labeled the "ugliest building in the world?" But in some ways Boston's midcentury renaissance took place precisely because its City Hall elicited strong opinions. The debate surrounding the building is a function of its conspicuousness. A mundane design would likely have avoided controversy, but it also would have failed to bring the New Boston to the attention of the world. If the building were easy to ignore, it would have been similarly easy to overlook the political, economic, architectural, and social phenomena that it represented. Absent risk, there is little likelihood of gain. Boston took a risk in constructing an unorthodox building, and it succeeded in reversing the city's fortunes. So too should other cities in similar circumstances not shy away from exploiting the redemptive potential of bold—even controversial—architecture.

While the controversy surrounding Boston City Hall has occasionally overshadowed its achievements, appreciation for the building continues to increase. For example, it has been featured in a book about Boston's midcentury concrete architecture titled *Heroic: Concrete Architecture and the New Boston*.[49] Meanwhile, Mayor Walsh came to adopt a softer attitude toward the building than his predecessor. During his first year in office, Walsh put out a call for proposals on improving City Hall Plaza.[50] The project brought a great deal of positive media attention to the plaza and the building, and in the summer of 2015, the city devoted a section of the plaza to lounge chairs and lawn games; while impermanent, this demonstrated how even a simple and inexpensive experiment can bring new energy to the space.[51] While it remained to be seen whether Walsh would succeed in restoring public respect for the building, these actions suggested that he was serious about putting in the effort.

The positive attention that scholars, architects, and, increasingly, local politicians have been bringing to Boston City Hall are likely to compel other Bostonians to reevaluate the building. As they do so, they will discover that the structure's illustrious history reveals wide-ranging social, cultural, economic, and, indeed, political effects of architecture. New City Hall showed that the New Boston was not simply the far-fetched dream of a few idealists or the empty promise of an ambitious politician. The building catalyzed a declining city's resurgence. At the same time, it was the product of a specific moment in political and architectural history, synthesizing both the ideals of the Kennedy years and the philosophy of "Action Architecture" in its imaginative and captivating form. Notwithstanding its checkered reputation, the building simultaneously triggered a dying city's political, economic, and physical regeneration, and changed the future of architecture in the United States and abroad.

Notes

Introduction: The Building That Changed Boston

1. Throughout this book, I use the terms "New City Hall," "Boston City Hall," and just "City Hall" interchangeably to refer to the 1960s building. I use "Old City Hall" when referring to the 1860s building.
2. Ian Menzies, "Architects Give Boston a 'Bronze,'" *Boston Globe*, August 11, 1976.
3. Paul Heyer, *Architects on Architecture: New Directions in America* (New York: Walker, 1978), 257.
4. Gerhard Kallmann, "The Action Architecture of a New Generation," *Architectural Forum* 111 (October 1959): 135.

Chapter 1: Dying on the Vine

1. David Kruh, "Because Boston Still Matters," *Boston Herald*, December 27, 2006.
2. John Powers, "In 1960, Timing Was Right to Begin: Collins, Planner Logue Awakened a Dying City," *Boston Globe*, September 22, 1985.
3. City of Boston Office of Budget Management, Operating Budget, Fiscal Year 2012, "Boston's People and Economy," 207.
4. Gerald H. Gamm, *The Making of New Deal Democrats: Voting Behavior and Realignment in Boston, 1920–1940* (Chicago: University of Chicago Press, 1989), 112.
5. Powers, "Timing Was Right to Begin."
6. Boston Redevelopment Authority, "History of Boston's Economy: Growth and Transition, 1970–1998," (November 1999), 3.
7. Martin Meyerson and Edward C. Banfield, *Boston: The Job Ahead* (Cambridge: Harvard University Press, 1966), 11.
8. National Planning Association Committee of New England, *The Economic State of New England* (New Haven: Yale University Press, 1954), 666.
9. Ibid.
10. Jane Jacobs, *The Death and Life of Great American Cities* (1961; New York: Vintage Books, 1992), 4.
11. Hilary Ballon and Kenneth T. Jackson, *Robert Moses and the Modern City: The Transformation of New York* (New York: Norton, 2007), 66.

12. Meyerson and Banfield, *Boston*, 55.
13. Thomas H. O'Connor, *Building a New Boston: Politics and Urban Renewal, 1950 to 1970* (Boston: Northeastern University Press, 1995), 42.
14. Meyerson and Banfield, *Boston*, 11.
15. Thomas H. O'Connor, *The Boston Irish: A Political History* (Boston: Northeastern University Press, 1995), 176–78.
16. Ibid., 177–78.
17. Jack Beatty, *The Rascal King: The Life and Times of James Michael Curley, 1874–1958* (Reading, Mass.: Addison-Wesley, 1992), 219.
18. O'Connor, *Boston Irish*, 20.
19. M. E. Hennessy, "Curley Would Sell the Public Garden," *Boston Daily Globe*, January 15, 1914.
20. O'Connor, *Building a New Boston*, 12.
21. Ibid., 12, 42.
22. Ibid., 43.
23. Ibid., 10.
24. Thomas H. O'Connor, *Bibles, Brahmins, and Bosses: A Short History of Boston*, 3rd ed. (Boston: Trustees of the Public Library of the City of Boston, 1991), 204.
25. O'Connor, *Building a New Boston*, 25.
26. John Harris, "Hynes In; Pledges New Era," *Boston Globe*, January 3, 1950.
27. "B.C. Opens Seminars on Boston Problems," *Boston Globe*, October 24, 1954. See also O'Connor, *Bibles, Brahmins, and Bosses*, 205.
28. O'Connor, *Building a New Boston*, 44.
29. Ibid., 45.
30. Ibid., 47.
31. O'Connor, *Bibles, Brahmins, and Bosses*, 205.
32. "Hynes Will Ask $5 Million for Municipal Auditorium," *Boston Globe*, December 6, 1950.
33. Christopher Marstall, "Boston's Vanished New York Streets," *Boston Globe*, August 19, 2012.
34. Mel King, *Chain of Change: Struggles for Black Community Development* (Cambridge: South End Press, 1981), 29. See also Harry Stanton, "Slum Clearance Benefits Evictees," *Boston Globe*, January 11, 1957.
35. O'Connor, *Building a New Boston*, 83.
36. Harry Stanton, "Just Wait a While: Great Central Artery Better Than It Looks," *Boston Globe*, August 23, 1953.
37. Joseph Keblinsky, "Hynes Envisions Brighter Future," *Boston Globe*, January 3, 1956. See also O'Connor, *Building a New Boston*, 116.
38. Lawrence W. Kennedy, *Planning the City Upon a Hill: Boston since 1630* (Amherst: University of Massachusetts Press, 1992), 161. See also Joseph Keblinsky, "Boston's Own Renewal Unit Pleases All," *Boston Globe*, March 10, 1957.
39. Robert Hanron, "West End Project Could Be Spark to Revitalize Boston," *Boston Globe*, December 20, 1959. See also "Capraro Labels West End Plan a 'Land Grab,'" *Boston Globe*, October 8, 1957.
40. Herbert Gans, "The Urban Village Revisited: The Worst of the West End Just before Its Destruction," in *The Last Tenement: Confronting Community and Urban Renewal in Boston's West End*, ed. Sean M. Fisher and Carolyn Hughes (Boston: Bostonian Society, 1992), 14.
41. Hanron, "West End Project."

42. O'Connor, *Bibles, Brahmins, and Bosses*, 206.
43. Thomas H. O'Connor, "The Urban Renewal Chronicle: The Politics of Urban Renewal in Boston," in Fisher and Hughes, *The Last Tenement*, 64.
44. O'Connor, *Building a New Boston*, 135.
45. O'Connor, *The Boston Irish*, 228.
46. For a comprehensive account of the Prudential Center project, see Elihu Rubin, *Insuring the City: The Prudential Center and the Postwar Urban Landscape* (New Haven: Yale University Press, 2012).
47. John H. Fenton, "Boston Hopeful on Civic Center," *New York Times*, May 1, 1960.
48. O'Connor, *Building a New Boston*, 175.
49. Ibid.
50. Ibid., 180.
51. "McCormack to Demand Garage Books," *Boston Globe*, March 26, 1962.
52. Robert B. Hanron, "The Common Draws Tourists—Because of Garage Case," *Boston Sunday Globe*, July 14, 1963.
53. Kennedy, *Planning the City Upon a Hill*, 162.
54. O'Connor, *Building a New Boston*, 145.
55. Jacobs, *Death and Life of Great American Cities*, 271–87.
56. O'Connor, *Bibles, Brahmins, and Bosses*, 207.
57. John H. Fenton, "Collins Wins in Boston Upset," *New York Times*, November 4, 1959.
58. Kennedy, *Planning the City Upon a Hill*, 168.
59. Ibid. See also Frederick McCarthy, "Hub Bonds Sell Easily Despite Drop in Credit," *Boston Globe*, November 18, 1959.
60. O'Connor, *Building a New Boston*, 170.
61. Carol Liston, "The Vault: Boston's Elite Committee of 14 Keeps a Canny Eye on the City," *Boston Globe*, September 13, 1967.
62. O'Connor, *Building a New Boston*, 147.
63. Liston, "The Vault."
64. O'Connor, *Building a New Boston*, 168.
65. Kennedy, *Planning the City Upon a Hill*, 170.
66. Ibid.
67. O'Connor, *Building a New Boston*, 173.
68. Ibid.
69. Kennedy, *Planning the City Upon a Hill*, 174.
70. Ibid.
71. "Bold Architecture Changes Scollay Sq.," *Boston Sunday Globe*, February 24, 1963.
72. O'Connor, *Building a New Boston*, 141.
73. Ibid.
74. Walter Muir Whitehill and Lawrence W. Kennedy, *Boston: A Topographical History*, 3rd ed. (Cambridge: Belknap Press of Harvard University Press, 2000), 200.
75. O'Connor, *Building a New Boston*, 141.
76. Ibid., 142.
77. David Ellis, "With Grace and a Touch of Boldness," *Boston Globe*, February 9, 1969.
78. O'Connor, *Building a New Boston*, 143.
79. Ibid., 184.
80. Lizabeth Cohen, "Ed Logue and the Struggle to Save America's Cities," *Real Estate Academic Initiative at Harvard University Research Notes* (March 2010): 4.

81. Whitehill and Kennedy, *Boston*, 204.
82. Ibid., 204–5.
83. James Doyle, "City Council Rejects Gov't Center Plans: Objects to Tower," *Boston Globe*, July 19, 1963.
84. Whitehill and Kennedy, *Boston*, 215.
85. Lawrence Anderson, "A Competition to Select an Architect for the New City Hall in the Government Center of the City of Boston," competition brief (Boston: Government Center Commission, 1961), 15.
86. "Address of the Mayor, Frederic W. Lincoln Jr.," in *Proceedings at the Dedication of the City Hall, September 18, 1865* (Boston: Boston City Council, 1865), 29.
87. Douglass Shand-Tucci, *Built in Boston: City and Suburb, 1800–2000*, rev. and expanded ed. (Amherst: University of Massachusetts Press, 1999), 35.
88. Donlyn Lyndon and Alice Wingwall, *The City Observed: Boston—A Guide to the Architecture of the Hub* (New York: Random House, 1982), 10.
89. "Address of the Mayor, Frederic W. Lincoln Jr.," 31.
90. Martin Nolan, "City Hall Debate Has Been Raging 300 Years," *Boston Globe*, May 6, 1962.
91. City of Boston Office of Budget Management, "Boston's People and Economy," 207.
92. "Proposed Extension to City Hall," *Boston Daily Globe*, December 18, 1890.
93. "City's Condition: Mayor Hart Reviews It in His Inaugural Address," *Boston Daily Globe*, January 2, 1900.
94. "New City Hall," *Boston Globe*, January 11, 1902.
95. "Where Boston Could Build a Noble City Hall," *Boston Globe*, September 6, 1903.
96. Lyndon and Wingwall, *The City Observed*, 17.
97. "New City Hall Again Agitated," *Boston Globe*, April 16, 1922.
98. Nolan, "City Hall Debate Has Been Raging 300 Years."
99. "New City Hall Seems Certain," *Boston Globe*, November 21, 1936.
100. David McCord, *About Boston: Sight, Sound, Flavor & Inflection* (Boston: Little, Brown, 1973), 123.
101. Whitehill and Kennedy, *Boston*, 267.
102. Edwin O'Connor, *The Last Hurrah* (Boston: Little, Brown, 1956), 40.
103. Joseph Dinneen, "New City Hall a Dazzling Gem," *Boston Globe*, August 20, 1967.
104. O'Connor, *Building a New Boston*, 164–65.
105. Anderson, "Competition to Select an Architect," 15.
106. Ada Louise Huxtable, "An Architectural Shot Heard 'round the World," *New York Times*, September 28, 1980.
107. Robert Campbell et al., "Tracings of the Future," panel discussion, BSA Space, Boston, October 22, 2013.
108. Huxtable, "Architectural Shot Hear 'round the World."
109. O'Connor, *Building a New Boston*, 19.
110. N. Michael McKinnell, interview by the author, Boston, June 7, 2011, digital recording.
111. Paul Venable Turner, *Campus: An American Planning Tradition* (New York: Architectural History Foundation; Cambridge: MIT Press, 1987), 249.
112. Ibid., 260.
113. Shand-Tucci, *Built in Boston*, 232.
114. Rubin, *Insuring the City*, 201–2.

115. "Travelers Skyscraper Upgraded Neighborhood," *Boston Globe,* May 28, 1961.
116. "A High Street Enhancement," *Boston Globe,* December 7, 1986.

Chapter 2: Competition and Construction

1. N. Michael McKinnell, interview by the author, Boston, June 7, 2011, digital recording. Also Thomas H. O'Connor, *Building a New Boston: Politics and Urban Renewal, 1950 to 1970* (Boston: Northeastern University Press, 1995), 185.
2. G. E. Kidder Smith, *Source Book of American Architecture: 500 Notable Buildings from the 10th Century to the Present* (New York: Princeton Architectural Press, 1996), 494.
3. "The Way We Were: Boston in the 60s," *ArchitectureBoston* 8, no. 3 (May–June 2005): 20.
4. Harold D. Hodgkinson, "Miracle in Boston," *Proceedings of the Massachusetts Historical Society* 3, no. 84 (1972): 77.
5. Edward J. Logue, "Boston 1960–1967: Seven Years of Plenty," *Proceedings of the Massachusetts Historical Society* 3, no. 84 (1972): 95.
6. Nelson Aldrich, interview, Terra Foundation Center for Digital Collections, Washington, D.C., January 22, 1982–April 4, 1985, transcript.
7. Logue, "Boston 1960–1967," 95–96.
8. Anthony Yudis, "And Here's New City Hall: Apt to Stir Controversy," *Boston Globe,* May 4, 1962.
9. Hélène Lipstadt, ed., *The Experimental Tradition: Essays on Competitions in Architecture* (New York: Princeton Architectural Press, 1989), 160.
10. "Conferama on Municipal Administration," *City Record,* February 25, 1961, 130. The quotation is from the transcript of the Conferama on Municipal Administration held at the Boston Public Library on November 17–18, 1960.
11. Gary Wolf, "Designing the Great Building of 20th-Century Boston: Kallmann, McKinnell & Knowles' Drawings for Boston City Hall," exhibition catalogue, Historic New England (May 15–31, 2008), 5.
12. Ibid.
13. "Competition for San Francisco's City Hall," *Architect and Engineer of California* 27, no. 3 (January 1912): 49.
14. Lawrence Anderson, "A Competition to Select an Architect for the New City Hall in the Government Center of the City of Boston," competition brief (Boston: Government Center Commission, 1961), appendix, ii.
15. "2003 Jury Citation: Jørn Utzon," Pritzker Architecture Prize, http://www.pritzker prize.com/2003/jury (accessed June 12, 2012).
16. Antonio Román, *Eero Saarinen: An Architecture of Multiplicity,* 1st ed. (New York: Princeton Architectural Press, 2003), 186.
17. "A Step Forward in Time: Toronto's New City Hall," http://www.toronto.ca/archives/city_hall_competition.htm (accessed November 15, 2012).
18. Mark Osbaldeston, *Unbuilt Toronto: A History of the City That Might Have Been* (Toronto: Dundurn Press, 2008), 94.
19. "A Step Forward in Time."
20. Christopher Hume, "New City Hall," in *Concrete Toronto: A Guidebook to Concrete Architecture from the Fifties to the Seventies,* ed. Michael McClelland and Graeme Stewart (Toronto: Coach House Books, 2007), 70.

21. Sarah Bradford Landau, "Coming to Terms: Architecture Competitions in America and the Emerging Profession, 1789–1922," in Lipstadt, *The Experimental Tradition*, 63–72.
22. Eric Larrabee, "Boston Chooses the Future," *Horizon* 5, no. 3 (January 1963): 12.
23. David Kirby, "St. John the Unfinished," *New York Times*, January 10, 1999.
24. Hélène Lipstadt, "In the Shadow of the Tribune Tower," in Lipstadt, *The Experimental Tradition*, 80.
25. Ibid., 97–98.
26. Ibid., 99.
27. Anderson, "A Competition," foreword.
28. "Mayor's Committee for New City Hall Has First Meeting," *Boston Globe*, November 27, 1958.
29. Anderson, "A Competition," foreword.
30. Ibid., 7.
31. Ibid., 15.
32. Ibid., 8, 16.
33. Ibid., 9, 15.
34. Ibid., 16.
35. Ibid..
36. Ibid., 18.
37. Logue, "Boston 1960–1967," 96.
38. Anderson, "A Competition," appendix, i.
39. Smith, *Source Book of American Architecture*, 397.
40. Meredith L. Clausen, *Pietro Belluschi: Modern American Architect* (Cambridge: MIT Press, 1994), 200.
41. For more about Netsch, see Walter A. Netsch, *FAIA: A Critical Appreciation and Sourcebook* (Evanston: Northwestern University Press, 2008).
42. Dave Parker and Antony Wood, *The Tall Buildings Reference Book* (London: Routledge, 2013), 97.
43. For an account of Rapson's career, see Jane King Hession, Rip Rapson, and Bruce N. Wright, *Ralph Rapson: Sixty Years of Modern Design* (Afton, Minn.: Afton Historical Society Press, 1999).
44. Linda Mack, "The Guthrie's First Drama Was about How the Theater Was to Be Designed," *Minneapolis–St. Paul Star Tribune*, June 2, 1993.
45. Marc Treib and David Gebhard, *An Everyday Modernism: The Houses of William Wurster* (Berkeley: University of California Press, 1999), 98.
46. "Merchandising: Bargains beneath Boston," *Time*, September 27, 1963, 78.
47. Hodgkinson, "Miracle in Boston," 77.
48. Ibid.
49. Robert Hanron, "Model Wins Praise with Qualification," *Boston Globe*, May 4, 1962.
50. "Sidney R. Rabb," Babson College, Academy of Distinguished Entrepreneurs, http://www.babson.edu/Academics/centers/blank-center/academy-of-distinguished-entrepreneurs/Pages/rabb-sidney.aspx (accessed March 17, 2012).
51. Anderson, "A Competition," appendix, ii.
52. David Halberstam, *The Fifties* (New York: Villard Books, 1993), x.
53. Anderson, "A Competition," appendix, iii.
54. Ibid., iv.
55. Anthony J. Yudis, "What Will New City Hall Look Like?" *Boston Globe*, April 29, 1962.

56. Anderson, "A Competition," appendix, xi.
57. Lipstadt, "In the Shadow of the Tribune Tower," 99.
58. Wolf, "Designing the Great Building of 20th-Century Boston," 10.
59. Larrabee, "Boston Chooses the Future," 15.
60. Lipstadt, "In the Shadow of the Tribune Tower," 99.
61. Yudis, "And Here's New City Hall."
62. Ibid.
63. Hodgkinson, "Miracle in Boston," 78.
64. Ibid.
65. Yudis, "And Here's New City Hall."
66. Hodgkinson, "Miracle in Boston," 78.
67. Yudis, "And Here's New City Hall."
68. Logue, "Boston 1960–1967," 96.
69. Larrabee, "Boston Chooses the Future," 10.
70. "The Way We Were," 22.
71. Ibid.
72. Yudis, "And Here's New City Hall."
73. Citizens' Committee for a Bostonian City Hall, scrapbook 4, Kallmann, McKinnell & Knowles Collection, Historic New England.
74. Hodgkinson, "Miracle in Boston," 78.
75. Ibid., 77.
76. Logue, "Seven Years of Plenty," 96.
77. Edward F. Knowles, interview by the author, New York, May 25, 2011, digital recording.
78. "2 Noted Architects . . . 2 Views," *Boston Globe*, May 6, 1962.
79. Ada Louise Huxtable, "Boston's New City Hall: A Public Building of Quality," *New York Times*, February 8, 1969.
80. Lipstadt, "In the Shadow of the Tribune Tower," 99.
81. Larrabee, "Boston Chooses the Future," 15.
82. Lipstadt, "In the Shadow of the Tribune Tower," 109.
83. "Historic Netsch Campus at UIC," guidebook (Chicago: University of Illinois, Chicago, 2008), 8.
84. Blair Kamin, "Chicago Architect Walter A. Netsch Dies at 88; Designed UIC Campus and Air Force Academy Chapel," *Chicago Tribune*, June 15, 2008.
85. Quoted in Donald Freeman, *Boston Architecture* (Cambridge: MIT Press, 1971), 57.
86. Larrabee, "Boston Chooses the Future," 11–15.
87. "The Way We Were," 21.
88. Ibid.
89. Anthony J. Yudis, "New Hub City Hall Given Tender, Loving Care," *Boston Globe*, November 11, 1962.
90. Anderson, "A Competition," appendix, v.
91. Charles E. Claffey, "O.K. Design for City Hall," *Boston Globe*, June 28, 1962.
92. "2 Noted Architects."
93. Aldrich interview, Terra Foundation.
94. Gerhard Kallmann and Michael McKinnell, "Original Thinking: Reflections on the Genesis of Boston City Hall," *ArchitectureBoston* 8, no. 3 (May–June 2005): 34.
95. Yudis, "New Hub City Hall Given Tender, Loving Care."
96. Claffey, "O.K. Design for City Hall."

97. Yudis, "New Hub City Hall Given Tender, Loving Care."
98. James Doyle, "Collins to Press U.S. on City Hall," *Boston Globe,* August 6, 1963.
99. Anthony Yudis, "New City Hall Begun with High Hopes," *Boston Globe,* September 19, 1963.
100. "Remarks of the Honorable John F. Collins, Mayor, City of Boston, on the Occasion of the Public Ground-Breaking for the New City Hall, September 18, 1963," transcript, Boston Redevelopment Authority resource library.
101. Yudis, "New City Hall Begun with High Hopes."
102. Ibid.
103. Anthony Yudis, "High Bids Stall City Hall," *Boston Globe,* May 15, 1964.
104. "$1 Million to Equip Hub City Hall Asked," *Boston Globe,* August 23, 1967.
105. Yudis, "High Bids Stall City Hall."
106. "City Acts to Fill Big Hole in Ground," *Boston Globe,* May 22, 1964.
107. Robert B. Kenney, "Extra $5 Million Gets Council City Hall OK," *Boston Globe,* June 16, 1964.
108. Anthony Yudis, "Plaza, Chapel, Rink OK'd at Govt Center," *Boston Globe,* May 14, 1965.
109. "Government Center Construction Forges Ahead," *Boston Globe,* May 16, 1965.
110. Ibid.
111. Joseph Eldredge, "City Hall—At Midpoint It Begins to Show Its Style," *Boston Globe,* February 20, 1966.
112. Ibid.
113. Edward Logue to Gerhard Kallmann, December 9, 1966, Kallmann, McKinnell & Knowles Collection, Historic New England.
114. Mark Kelley, "Visiting Officials Heap Praise on Boston's New City Hall," *Boston Globe,* July 31, 1967.
115. "Collins in His New Home," *Boston Globe,* December 19, 1967.
116. William A. Davis, "Mayor's Boston Tea Party Shows Off New City Hall," *Boston Globe,* December 18, 1967.
117. Ibid.
118. Logue, "Seven Years of Plenty," 96.
119. "$1 Million to Equip Hub City Hall Asked."
120. Ibid.
121. "Facts, Figures on Boston's New City Hall," *Boston Globe,* December 18, 1967.
122. "Bright New Symbol," *Boston Globe,* October 13, 1968.
123. David Ellis, "Mayor Shows Off New City Hall," *Boston Globe,* November 14, 1968.
124. Marjorie Sherman, "City Hall of the Century," *Boston Globe,* November 14, 1968.
125. "$1 Million to Equip Hub City Hall Asked."
126. Robert Taylor, "A Plain Man's Guide to City Hall," *Boston Globe,* February 9, 1969.
127. Robert A. Jordan, "Week-Long Party for New Boston's New City Hall," *Boston Globe,* February 8, 1969.
128. Kallmann and McKinnell, "Original Thinking," 34.
129. Press release from Nancy Huntington, Boston Director of Public Celebrations, in "America's City Halls: New City Hall, Boston, Massachusetts," pamphlet, Boston Redevelopment Authority resource library.
130. "City Hall Is 'Fun Hall' for Dedication Week," *Boston Globe,* February 9, 1969.
131. John Robinson, "City Hall Week Gets Champagne Finale," *Boston Globe,* February 17, 1969.

132. Ibid.
133. David Ellis, "New City Hall a Natural as a Civic Center," *Boston Globe*, February 16, 1969.
134. James Wehler to Michael McKinnell, February 19, 1969, Kallmann, McKinnell & Knowles Collection, Historic New England.
135. Walter Netsch to Gerhard Kallmann and Michael McKinnell, February 18, 1969, ibid.
136. Edward J. Logue to Gerhard Kallmann and Michael McKinnell, February 20, 1969, ibid.
137. Robinson, "City Hall Week Gets Champagne Finale."

Chapter 3: The New City Hall Design

1. N. Michael McKinnell, interview by the author, Boston, June 7, 2011, digital recording.
2. Ada Louise Huxtable, "Boston's New City Hall: A Public Building of Quality," *New York Times*, February 8, 1969.
3. John Silber, "Architecture of the Absurd," lecture at Barnes & Noble, Boston University, December 4, 2007.
4. "Keiner hat der SS den Namen gegeben," Humboldt-Universität zu Berlin, http://www.hu-berlin.de/ueberblick/geschichte/juedische-studierende/biographien/gerhard-kallmann (accessed December 13, 2013). See also Kathryn Lasky, *Ashes* (London: Penguin, 2010), acknowledgments.
5. Architects' biographies, Kallmann, McKinnell & Knowles Collection, Historic New England, Boston.
6. Gerhard Kallmann and Michael McKinnell, "Original Thinking: Reflections on the Genesis of Boston City Hall," *ArchitectureBoston* 8, no. 3 (May–June 2005): 33.
7. N. Michael McKinnell, interview by the author, Boston, June 11, 2011, digital recording.
8. Edward F. Knowles, interview by the author, New York, May 25, 2011, digital recording.
9. Ibid.
10. Ibid.
11. Alfred H. Barr Jr., "What Is Happening to Modern Architecture," *Bulletin of the Museum of Modern Art* 15, no. 3 (Spring 1948): 17.
12. Gerhard Kallmann, "The Action Architecture of a New Generation," *Architectural Forum* 111 (October 1959): 133.
13. Ibid.
14. Gerhard M. Kallmann, "Lessons of the Bauhaus for the Second Machine Age," in *Four Great Makers of Modern Architecture* (New York: Columbia University School of Architecture, 1961), 271.
15. Gerhard M. Kallmann, "New Perspectives for the Second Machine Age," ibid., 279.
16. Kallmann, "Action Architecture," 134.
17. Ibid.
18. Reyner Banham, *The New Brutalism: Ethic or Aesthetic?* (London: Architectural Press, 1966).
19. Ibid., 89.
20. Noah Chasin, "Ethics and Aesthetics: New Brutalism, Team 10, and Architectural Change in the 1950s" (PhD diss., City University of New York, 2002), 2.
21. William J. R. Curtis, *Modern Architecture since 1900* (Englewood Cliffs, N.J.: Prentice-Hall, 1983), 319.
22. Kallmann, "Action Architecture," 135.

23. Curtis, *Modern Architecture*, 289.
24. Barbara Bradley Hagerty, "Future of Brutalist-Designed Church Not Concrete," National Public Radio, http://www.npr.org/templates/story/story.php?storyId=93844919 (accessed July 23, 2013).
25. Kallmann, "Action Architecture," 137, 244.
26. N. Michael McKinnell, interview by Mark Pasnik, September 2009, http://www.overcommaunder.com/heroic/essays/an-interview-with-michael-mckinnell/ (accessed January 9, 2013).
27. Ibid.
28. Gerhard M. Kallmann, "Modern Tower in Old Milan," *Architectural Forum* 108, no. 2 (February 1958): 109–11.
29. Lewis Mumford, "The Death of the Monument," in *Circle: International Survey of Constructive Art* (London: Faber and Faber, 1937), 264.
30. Paul Heyer, *Architects on Architecture: New Directions in America* (New York: Walker, 1978), 260.
31. Kallmann and McKinnell, "Original Thinking," 33.
32. Heyer, *Architects on Architecture*, 260–61.
33. Joseph Eldredge, "City Hall—At Midpoint It Begins to Show Its Style," *Boston Globe*, February 20, 1966.
34. Gary Wolf, "Inventing a City Hall," *Historic New England* 9, no. 3 (Winter–Spring 2009): 3.
35. Lawrence Anderson, "A Competition to Select an Architect for the New City Hall in the Government Center of the City of Boston," competition brief (Boston: Government Center Commission, 1961), 14.
36. Charles Millard, "The New Boston: City Hall," *Hudson Review* 23, no. 1 (Spring 1970): 112.
37. Sibyl Moholy-Nagy, "Boston's New City Hall," *Architectural Forum* 130, no. 1 (January–February 1969): 47.
38. Millard, "The New Boston," 112.
39. Gary Wolf, "Designing the Great Building of 20th-Century Boston: Kallmann, McKinnell & Knowles' Drawings for Boston City Hall," exhibition catalogue, Historic New England (May 15–31, 2008), 10.
40. Millard, "The New Boston," 111.
41. Wolf, "Designing the Great Building," 10.
42. Robert Taylor, "A Plain Man's Guide to City Hall," *Boston Globe*, February 9, 1969.
43. Millard, "The New Boston," 113.
44. Ibid., 115.
45. Heyer, *Architects on Architecture*, 261.
46. Kallmann and McKinnell, "Original Thinking," 33.
47. Millard, "The New Boston," 112.
48. Kallmann and McKinnell, "Original Thinking," 34.
49. Taylor, "A Plain Man's Guide."
50. Millard, "The New Boston," 111.
51. Kallmann and McKinnell, "Original Thinking," 33–34.
52. Millard, "The New Boston," 111.
53. Heyer, *Architects on Architecture*, 262.
54. Kallmann and McKinnell, "Original Thinking," 35.

55. Taylor, "A Plain Man's Guide to City Hall."
56. Joseph Dinneen, "New City Hall a Dazzling Gem," *Boston Globe*, August 20, 1967.
57. Harold D. Hodgkinson, "Miracle in Boston," *Proceedings of the Massachusetts Historical Society* 3, no. 84 (1972): 80.
58. Millard, "The New Boston," 114.
59. Heyer, *Architects on Architecture*, 262.
60. Antoine Picon, "Architecture and Technology," in *Liquid Stone: New Architecture in Concrete*, ed. Jean-Louis Cohen and Gerard Martin Moeller (New York: Princeton Architectural Press, 2006), 8.
61. Adrian Forty, "The Material without a History," ibid., 38.
62. McKinnell, interview by Mark Pasnik.
63. Ibid.
64. Ibid.
65. Eldredge, "City Hall—At Midpoint It Begins to Show Its Style."
66. Heyer, *Architects on Architecture*, 263.
67. Taylor, "A Plain Man's Guide to City Hall."
68. "Site," in "America's City Halls: New City Hall, Boston, Massachusetts," pamphlet, Boston Redevelopment Authority resource library.
69. Wolf Von Eckardt, "Boston's New City Hall: It Has Vigor," *Boston Sunday Globe*, April 2, 1967.
70. Taylor, "A Plain Man's Guide to City Hall."
71. Quoted in Von Eckardt, "Boston's New City Hall."
72. Taylor, "A Plain Man's Guide to City Hall."
73. Ibid.
74. Kallmann and McKinnell, "Original Thinking," 35.
75. Taylor, "A Plain Man's Guide to City Hall."
76. McKinnell, interview by the author.
77. Taylor, "A Plain Man's Guide to City Hall."
78. Wolf, "Designing the Great Building," 16.
79. Kallmann and McKinnell, "Original Thinking," 35.
80. Moholy-Nagy, "Boston's New City Hall," 45.
81. "Bright New Symbol," *Boston Globe*, October 13, 1968.
82. Wolf, "Designing the Great Building," 7.
83. Heyer, *Architects on Architecture*, 262.
84. Charles Jencks, *Late-Modern Architecture and Other Essays* (New York: Rizzoli, 1980), 42.
85. Kallmann and McKinnell, "Original Thinking," 34.
86. McKinnell, interview by the author.
87. McKinnell, interview by Mark Pasnik.
88. Kallmann, "Action Architecture," 135.
89. McKinnell, interview by Mark Pasnik.
90. Millard, "The New Boston," 115.
91. Moholy-Nagy, "Boston's New City Hall," 44.
92. Renato De Fusco, *Storia dell'Architettura Contemporanea* (Roma: Laterza, 1974), 414.
93. Knowles, interview by the author.
94. Millard, "The New Boston," 115.
95. Heyer, *Architects on Architecture*, 263.

96. Kallmann, "Modern Tower in Old Milan," 109.
97. David Dillon, *The Architecture of Kallmann McKinnell & Wood* (New York: Edizioni Press, 2004), 7.
98. Kallmann, "Modern Tower in Old Milan," 108.
99. Huxtable, "Boston's New City Hall," 33.
100. Moholy-Nagy, "Boston's New City Hall," 44.
101. Kallmann and McKinnell, "Original Thinking," 34.
102. Gerhard M. Kallmann, interview by the author, Boston, June 7, 2011, digital recording.
103. Peter Collins, "Action Architecture," *The Guardian*, September 13, 1962.
104. Kallmann and McKinnell, "Original Thinking," 33.
105. McKinnell, interview by the author.
106. Charles Jencks, *Modern Movements in Architecture* (New York: Doubleday, 1973), 228.
107. Knowles, interview by the author.
108. Moholy-Nagy, "Boston's New City Hall," 44.
109. Alex Krieger, *The Architecture of Kallmann McKinnell & Wood* (New York: Rizzoli, 1988), 16–17.
110. Knowles, interview by the author.
111. McKinnell, interview by Mark Pasnik.
112. Ibid.
113. Knowles, interview by the author.
114. Millard, "The New Boston," 115.
115. "Landmark Petition Form: Boston City Hall," Boston Landmarks Commission (April 2007), 4.
116. Wolf, "Designing the Great Building," 10.
117. David Ellis, "With Grace and a Touch of Boldness," *Boston Globe*, February 9, 1969.
118. Heyer, *Architects on Architecture*, 263.
119. Wolf, "Designing the Great Building."
120. "Landmark Petition Form," 4.
121. Ibid.
122. McKinnell, interview with Mark Pasnik.
123. Susan Southworth and Michael Southworth, *AIA Guide to Boston*, 3rd ed. (Guilford, Conn.: Globe Pequot, 2008), 52.
124. McKinnell, interview by the author.
125. McKinnell, interview by Mark Pasnik.
126. Jack Thomas, "Boston City Hall: A Beautiful Disaster," *Boston Globe*, February 27, 1991.
127. Gerhard Kallmann et al., "Architects' Statement," in "America's City Halls," 2.
128. "Bright New Symbol."
129. Heyer, *Architects on Architecture*, 261.
130. Taylor, "A Plain Man's Guide to City Hall."
131. Millard, "The New Boston," 110.
132. McKinnell, interview by the author.

Chapter 4: An Evolving Reputation

1. Charles Dickens, *A Tale of Two Cities* (London: Chapman & Hall, 1859), 1.
2. Anthony Yudis, "And Here's New City Hall, Apt to Stir Controversy," *Boston Globe*, May 4, 1962.

3. Ibid.
4. Eric Larrabee, "Boston Chooses the Future," *Horizon* (January 1963): 14–15.
5. "Is Winning City Hall Design (and Others) All It Should Be?" letter to the editor, *Boston Globe*, May 21, 1962.
6. "City Hall Plans Not for Boston, Graham Says," *Boston Globe*, May 13, 1962.
7. Robert Taylor, "A Plain Man's Guide to City Hall," *Boston Globe*, February 9, 1969.
8. Hélène Lipstadt, "Transforming the Tradition: American Architecture Competitions, 1960 to the Present," in *The Experimental Tradition: Essays on Competitions in Architecture*, ed. Hélène Lipstadt (New York: Princeton Architectural Press, 1989), 99.
9. Robert A. M. Stern, ed., *Perspecta: The Yale Architectural Journal* 9–10 (1965): 6.
10. Anthony Yudis, "Federal Building, City Hall Go Together," *Boston Globe*, May 13, 1962.
11. N. Michael McKinnell, interview by Mark Pasnik, September 2009, transcript, http://www.overcommaunder.com/heroic/essays/an-interview-with-michael-mckinnell/ (accessed February 9, 2013).
12. Robert S. Sturgis, "An Also-Ran Sings the Praises of Winning City Hall Design," *Boston Globe*, May 8, 1962.
13. "Right Choice, Collins Says of City Hall," *Boston Globe*, May 7, 1962.
14. "Horrors of War in Perpetuity," letter to the editor, *Boston Globe*, May 14, 1962.
15. "City Hall Design Bold, Exciting," letter to the editor, *Boston Globe*, May 11, 1962.
16. "What Is It?" letter to the editor, *Boston Globe*, May 19, 1962.
17. "It Will Grow on You, 3 Architects Predict," *Boston Globe*, May 10, 1962.
18. "Jewel of the New Boston," *Boston Globe*, February 10, 1969.
19. "An Airy Fortress," *Time*, February 21, 1969, 62.
20. Wolf Von Eckardt, "Boston's New City Hall: It Has Vigor," *Boston Sunday Globe*, April 2, 1967.
21. Ada Louise Huxtable, "Boston's New City Hall: A Public Building of Quality," *New York Times*, February 8, 1969.
22. Ibid.
23. "Spirit, Energy," letter to the editor, *Boston Globe*, March 28, 1969.
24. "City Hall, New Skyline Praised by Architects," *Boston Globe*, June 25, 1970.
25. James Marston Fitch, "City Hall Boston," *Architectural Review* 147, no. 880 (June 1970): 400.
26. Nikolaus Pevsner, *A History of Building Types* (Princeton: Princeton University Press, 1976), 62.
27. Anne Ford, "Architects Can Make Mistakes," *Boston Globe*, March 16, 1970.
28. "Right Choice, Collins Says of City Hall," *Boston Globe*, May 7, 1962.
29. Anthony Yudis, "Federal Building, City Hall Go Together," *Boston Globe*, May 13, 1962.
30. William J. Lewis, "Eloquent Ted Echoes JFK in City Hall Plea," *Boston Globe*, February 16, 1969.
31. Edward Logue to Gerhard Kallmann and Michael McKinnell, June 27, 1967, Kallmann, McKinnell & Knowles Collection, Historic New England, Boston.
32. "You Can Fight City Hall," *Newsweek*, July 7, 1969, 93.
33. David Ellis, "With Grace and a Touch of Boldness," *Boston Globe*, February 9, 1969.
34. Ibid.
35. "Inside," *ArchitectureBoston* 8, no. 3 (May–June 2005): 46.
36. Ibid., 48.
37. Ibid., 47–48.

38. "Historic City Hall," *Boston Globe*, January 21, 2004.
39. "A Great City Hall," *Boston Globe*, January 30, 1996.
40. Ada Louise Huxtable, "The Beauty in Brutalism, Restored and Updated," *Wall Street Journal*, February 25, 2009.
41. Peter Collins, "Action Architecture," *The Guardian*, September 13, 1962.
42. Sibyl Moholy-Nagy, "Boston's New City Hall," *Architectural Forum* 130, no. 1 (January–February 1969): 47.
43. "Winning City Hall Design."
44. Nelson Aldrich, interview, Terra Foundation Center for Digital Collections, Washington, D.C., January 22, 1982–April 4, 1985, transcript.
45. Citizens' Committee for a Bostonian City Hall, scrapbook 4, Kallmann, McKinnell & Knowles Collection, Historic New England.
46. Albert Bush-Brown, "Critic Hails Prizewinner: No Copy Cat of Hub Styles," *Boston Globe*, May 4, 1962.
47. Anthony Yudis, ". . . with Respect for Past, Eye to Future," *Boston Globe*, February 24, 1965.
48. Ibid.
49. Yudis, "Federal Building, City Hall Go Together."
50. Ibid.
51. "What Is It?"
52. "When the Novelty Wears Off Will City Hall Be a Joke," letter to the editor, *Boston Globe*, May 22, 1962.
53. "To Every Age Its Own Style," letter to the editor, *Boston Globe*, May 31, 1962.
54. Taylor, "A Plain Man's Guide to City Hall."
55. Ian Menzies, "Boston's City Hall Is Still a Beacon of Modernity," *Quincy Patriot Ledger*, April 15, 1998.
56. Ellis, "With Grace and a Touch of Boldness."
57. Anthony Yudis, "Ten Years from Now . . . ," *Boston Globe*, February 9, 1969.
58. Bud Collins, "City Hall . . . Cold, Maybe, but Exciting," *Boston Globe*, December 14, 1968.
59. Jack Thomas, "Boston City Hall: A Beautiful Disaster," *Boston Globe*, February 27, 1991.
60. Larrabee, "Boston Chooses the Future," 13.
61. Collins, "Action Architecture."
62. Henry Millon, "MIT Expert Looks at City Hall Plan," *Boston Globe*, May 13, 1962.
63. Moholy-Nagy, "Boston's New City Hall," 44.
64. "An Airy Fortress," *Time*, February 21, 1969, 62.
65. David Monteyne, "Boston City Hall and a History of Reception," *Journal of Architectural Education* 65, no. 1 (October 2011): 59.
66. Sturgis, "An Also-Ran Sings the Praises."
67. Ellis, "With Grace and a Touch of Boldness."
68. Huxtable, "Boston's New City Hall."
69. "If You Can't Fight City Hall, Here's a Different Idea: Sell It," *Boston Globe*, January 10, 1988.
70. Thomas, "Boston City Hall."
71. Robert Campbell, "It's Time We Started Treating Boston City Hall with Pride," *Boston Globe*, January 19, 1988.
72. "A Great City Hall."
73. Thomas, "Boston City Hall."

74. Joseph A. Keblinsky, "They Don't Make City Halls Like They Used To," *Boston Globe*, February 9, 1969.
75. "The Way We Were: Boston in the 60s," *ArchitectureBoston* 8, no. 3 (May–June 2005): 23.
76. Ibid., 22.
77. Ellis, "With Grace and a Touch of Boldness."
78. Jack Thomas, "'I Wanted Something That Would Last,'" *Boston Globe*, October 13, 2004.
79. Thomas, "Boston City Hall."
80. Thomas, "'I Wanted Something That Would Last.'"
81. Nikolaus Pevsner, *An Outline of European Architecture*, 4th ed. (Harmondsworth, Middlesex: Penguin Books, 1954), 22.
82. Yudis, "Ten Years from Now."
83. Huxtable, "Boston's New City Hall."
84. Von Eckardt, "Boston's New City Hall."
85. Charles Millard, "The New Boston: City Hall," *Hudson Review* 23, no. 1 (Spring 1970): 110.
86. "City Hall—a Dissent," letter to the editor, *Boston Globe*, November 5, 1968.
87. "When the Unstoppable Meets the Immovable," *ArchitectureBoston* 10, no. 5 (September–October 2007): 18.
88. Ibid.
89. Ibid.
90. Gay-Diane Baratta, "Boston City Hall: Architecture for a Democratic Era" (term paper, University of Vermont, 1972), Kallmann, McKinnell & Knowles collection, Historic New England.
91. Taylor, "A Plain Man's Guide to City Hall."
92. Moholy-Nagy, "Boston's New City Hall," 44.
93. "The Way We Were," 24.
94. Edward Logue, "What's Wrong with City Hall?" *Boston Globe*, May 1, 1998.
95. David Eisen, "Fix City Hall, Don't Leave It," *Boston Herald*, April 13, 1998.
96. Ian Menzies, "Boston's City Hall Is Still a Beacon of Modernity," *Quincy Patriot Ledger*, April 15, 1998.
97. "A Great City Hall," 14.
98. "Don't Slight City Hall," *Boston Globe*, April 9, 1998.
99. William Landay, "Our City Hall," *ArchitectureBoston* 10, no. 5 (September–October 2007): 56. Landay refers to the notorious 1976 incident in which Landsmark, an African American attorney, was assaulted by an anti-busing demonstrator wielding an American flag.
100. Yudis, "Ten Years from Now."
101. Albert Bush-Brown, "Critic Hails Prizewinner: No Copy Cat of Hub Styles," *Boston Globe*, May 4, 1962.
102. John Morris Dixon, "Boston's Open Center," *Architectural Forum* 132, no. 5 (June 1970): 25.
103. "Project for Public Spaces: Boston City Hall," http://www.pps.org/great_public_spaces/one?public_place_id=148 (accessed September 10, 2012).
104. Thomas Boylston Adams, "Boston Achieves a Triumph in Architecture," *Boston Globe*, December 21, 1969.
105. Dixon, "Boston's Open Center," 25.

106. Von Eckardt, "Boston's New City Hall."
107. Fitch, "City Hall Boston," 400.
108. "Project for Public Spaces."
109. Campbell, "It's Time."
110. Robert Campbell, "For Pedestrian Boston," *Boston Globe*, November 3, 1974.
111. Menzies, "Boston's City Hall Is Still a Beacon of Modernity."
112. Thomas, "Boston City Hall."
113. Gary Wolf, "Boston City Hall Plaza: A Modern Space for the City upon a Hill," *DOCOMOMO US* (Winter 2008): 4.
114. Adams, "Boston Achieves a Triumph in Architecture."
115. "Boston City Hall," *Interiors* 128, no. 9 (April 1969): 97.
116. Walt Lockley, "Brutalized in Boston," http://www.american-architecture.info/USA/USA-Boston/BO-011.htm (accessed January 17, 2013).
117. Taylor, "A Plain Man's Guide to City Hall."
118. "Boston's New City Hall," letter to the editor, *Boston Globe*, July 28, 1969.
119. David Ellis, "New City Hall a Natural as a Civic Center," *Boston Globe*, February 16, 1969.
120. Edgar J. Driscoll, "Art Project for New City Hall," *Boston Globe*, May 13, 1969.
121. "Apollo Exhibit Seems at Home in Boston's New City Hall," *Boston Globe*, July 16, 1969.
122. Marjorie Sherman, "First Party at New City Hall Poshest in Years," *Boston Globe*, November 22, 1969.
123. Harold D. Hodgkinson, "Miracle in Boston," *Proceedings of the Massachusetts Historical Society* 3, no. 84 (1972): 72.
124. "Landmark Petition Form: Boston City Hall" (Boston: Boston Landmarks Commission, April 2007), 8.
125. Thomas, "Boston City Hall."
126. "The Way We Were," 22.
127. Ibid., 24.
128. Ibid.
129. Campbell, "It's Time."
130. Huxtable, "The Beauty in Brutalism."
131. Gary Wolf, "Designing the Great Building of 20th-Century Boston: Kallmann, McKinnell & Knowles' Drawings for Boston City Hall," exhibition catalogue, Historic New England (May 15–31, 2008), 16.
132. "When the Unstoppable Meets the Immovable," 18.
133. "The Way We Were," 23.
134. "Boston City Hall Employee Guide" (Boston: City of Boston, December 1968), 5.
135. "The Way We Were," 22.
136. Thomas, "Boston City Hall."
137. "The Way We Were," 22.
138. "When the Unstoppable Meets the Immovable," 18.
139. "Don't Slight City Hall."
140. "Is City Hall Out of Date?" *Boston Herald*, April 9, 1998.
141. Logue, "What's Wrong with City Hall?"
142. Robert Campbell, "Memo on City Hall: Fix It, Don't Forsake It," *Boston Globe*, April 10, 1998.
143. Eisen, "Fix City Hall."

144. Menzies, "Boston's City Hall Is Still a Beacon of Modernity."
145. "Saving a Modern Masterpiece," *Boston Globe*, April 16, 2007.
146. Donlyn Lyndon, "Why City Hall Is Worth Saving," *Boston Globe*, March 18, 2007.
147. Adam Reilly, "City Hall Smackdown," *Boston Phoenix*, August 3–9, 2007.
148. Thomas H. O'Connor, "City Hall Represents Heart of Boston," *Boston Globe*, December 19, 2006.
149. David Kruh, "Because Boston Still Matters," *Boston Herald*, December 27, 2006.
150. Paul Restuccia, "Debating the Over-Hall," *Boston Herald*, December 17, 2006.
151. "Landmark Petition Form," 8.
152. Reilly, "City Hall Smackdown."
153. "Logue Still Defends Destroying True Boston," letter to the editor, *Boston Globe*, June 18, 1998.
154. Thomas Boylston Adams, "Boston Achieves a Triumph in Architecture," *Boston Globe*, December 21, 1969.
155. Ellis, "With Grace and a Touch of Boldness."
156. Thomas, "'I Wanted Something That Would Last.'"
157. Ibid.
158. Thomas, "Boston City Hall."
159. Ibid.
160. Wolf, "Designing the Great Building," 16.
161. Sigmund Freud, *Group Psychology and the Analysis of the Ego* (New York: Liveright, 1959), 17.
162. Michael J. Crosbie, "The Role of Editors as Critics," in *Architecture Beyond Criticism*, ed. Wolfgang F. E. Preiser et al. (New York: Routledge, 2015), 37.
163. Allison Arieff, "Why Don't We Read about Architecture?" Opinionator, *New York Times*, March 2, 2012, http://opinionator.blogs.nytimes.com/2012/03/02/why-dont-we-read-about-architecture/?_r=0.
164. Mario Vargas Llosa, *Notes on the Death of Culture: Essays on Spectacle and Society* (New York: Farrar, Straus and Giroux, 2015), 27.
165. Huxtable, "The Beauty in Brutalism."
166. Thomas, "'I Wanted Something That Would Last.'"

Chapter 5: Legacy and Significance

1. Wolf Von Eckardt, "Boston's New City Hall: It Has Vigor," *Boston Sunday Globe*, April 2, 1967; "Bright New Symbol," *Boston Globe*, October 13, 1968.
2. "Remarks of the Honorable John F. Collins, Mayor of the City of Boston, on the Occasion of the Public Ground-Breaking for the New City Hall, September 18, 1963," Boston Redevelopment Authority resource library.
3. Gary Wolf, "Designing the Great Building of 20th-Century Boston: Kallmann, McKinnell & Knowles' Drawings for Boston City Hall," exhibition catalogue, Historic New England (May 15–31, 2008), 14.
4. N. Michael McKinnell, interview by Mark Pasnik, September 2009, http://www.overcommaunder.com/heroic/essays/an-interview-with-michael-mckinnell/ (accessed January 9, 2013).
5. Douglass Shand-Tucci, *Built in Boston: City and Suburb, 1800–2000* (Amherst: University of Massachusetts Press, 1999), 324.

6. Dennis Hevesi, "Gerhard Kallmann, Architect, Is Dead at 97," *New York Times*, June 25, 2012.
7. Alex Krieger, ed., *The Architecture of Kallmann McKinnell & Wood* (New York: Rizzoli, 1988), 14.
8. McKinnell, interview by Mark Pasnik.
9. David Dillon, *The Architecture of Kallmann McKinnell & Wood* (New York: Edizioni Press, 2004), 10–11.
10. Wolf, "Designing the Great Building," 13.
11. Robert Campbell, "Kallmann McKinnell & Wood: Architects of the Metaphorical, the Narrative and the Evocative," in Krieger, *The Architecture of Kallmann McKinnell & Wood*, 101.
12. Eduard Sekler, "Gerhard Kallmann and Michael McKinnell as Educators," ibid., 98.
13. Ibid., 100.
14. Gerhard Kallmann and Michael McKinnell, "Original Thinking: Reflections on the Genesis of Boston City Hall," *ArchitectureBoston* 8, no. 3 (May–June 2005): 33.
15. Hevesi, "Gerhard Kallmann, Architect, Dead at 97."
16. "Landmark Petition Form: Boston City Hall," Boston Landmarks Commission (April 2007), 9.
17. Walter Muir Whitehill and Lawrence W. Kennedy, *Boston: A Topographical History*, 3rd ed. (Cambridge: Belknap Press of Harvard University Press, 2000), 241.
18. Ada Louise Huxtable, *Architecture Anyone?* (New York: Random House, 1986), 21.
19. Lewis Mumford, "The Back Bay as a Work of Art," *Boston Globe*, November 2, 1969.
20. "Mid-Century Modern Buildings in Downtown Boston: Map and Guide," pamphlet, Boston Preservation Alliance, n.d.
21. "Saving a Modern Masterpiece," *Boston Globe*, April 16, 2007.
22. "Landmark Petition Form," 2.
23. Shand-Tucci, *Built in Boston*, 282.
24. Donlyn Lyndon and Alice Wingwall, *The City Observed: Boston; A Guide to the Architecture of the Hub* (New York: Random House, 1982), 20.
25. William J. R. Curtis, *Boston: Forty Years of Modern Architecture* (Boston: Institute of Contemporary Art, 1980), 34.
26. Lyndon and Wingwall, *The City Observed*, 56.
27. Shand-Tucci, *Built in Boston*, 324.
28. Curtis, *Boston*, 10.
29. Ibid.
30. Charles W. Millard, "The New Boston: Government Center," *Hudson Review* 21, no. 4 (Winter 1968–69): 692.
31. "Boston Architectural Competitions: 1960–1983," exhibition catalogue, Boston Architectural Center, (February 21–March 30, 1984), 7.
32. Curtis, *Boston*, 37.
33. Yvonne V. Chabrier, "Back to the Drawing Board," *Boston Phoenix*, October 2, 1984.
34. Lyndon and Wingwall, *The City Observed*, 172.
35. Chabrier, "Back to the Drawing Board."
36. Robert Trancik, *Finding Lost Space: Theories of Urban Design* (New York: Wiley & Sons, 1986), 79.
37. Ibid., 80.

38. Shand-Tucci, *Built in Boston*, 283–84.
39. Ibid., 303.
40. Ada Louise Huxtable, "Boston's New City Hall: A Public Building of Quality," *New York Times*, February 8, 1969.
41. "The Way We Were: Boston in the 60s," *ArchitectureBoston* 8, no. 3 (May–June 2005): 23.
42. Quoted in Shand-Tucci, *Built in Boston*, 282.
43. Gretchen Schneider, "We Don't Need Another Hero: The Problem of Heroic Modernism," *ArchitectureBoston* 8, no. 3 (May–June 2005): 42–43.
44. Jeffrey Weiss, "Echoes of Dallas' Reaction Resonate Nearly 50 Years after JFK Assassination," *Dallas Morning News*, January 5, 2013.
45. Pei Cobb Freed and Partners, "Dallas City Hall," http://www.pcfandp.com/a/p/6602/s.html (accessed June 14, 2013).
46. Ada Louise Huxtable, "One of Our Most Important Buildings," *New York Times*, November 28, 1976.
47. "Noncity Hall," *Architectural Forum* 130, no. 1 (January–February 1969): 65.
48. Quoted in Shand-Tucci, *Built in Boston*, 324.
49. U.S. General Services Administration, "Report to the President by the Ad Hoc Committee on Federal Office Space" (June 1, 1962).
50. John F. Kennedy, "Statement on the Steel Crisis," April 11, 1962, http://www.networker.www3.50megs.com/jfk14.html (accessed October 5, 2013).
51. General Services Administration, http://www.gsa.gov/portal/ext/html/site/hb/category/25431/actionParameter/exploreByBuilding/buildingId/1225 (accessed May 10, 2013).
52. Jerald terHorst, "FBI Fortress Casts a Shadow," *Chicago Tribune*, October 5, 1975.
53. Paul Goldberger, "$126-Million F.B.I. Building, Named for Hoover," *New York Times*, October 1, 1975.
54. Ibid.
55. Joseph Eldredge, "City Hall: At Midpoint It Begins to Show Its Style," *Boston Globe*, February 20, 1966.
56. Susan Southworth and Michael Southworth, *AIA Guide to Boston*, 3rd ed. (Guilford, Conn.: Globe Pequot Press, 2008), 52.
57. Thomas Boylston Adams, "Boston Achieves a Triumph in Architecture," *Boston Globe*, December 21, 1969.
58. W. McKenzie Woodward, *PPS/AIAri Guide to Providence Architecture* (Providence: Providence Preservation Society, 2003), 292–93.
59. "The Way We Were," 23.
60. "End of the Glass Box," *Time*, May 25, 1962, 87.
61. Jane Holtz Kay, "3500 Architects Gather," *Boston Globe*, June 21, 1970.
62. Robert Sales, "Architects, Students to Meet in Hub," *Boston Globe*, June 7, 1970.
63. Gloria Negri, "City Hall, New Skyline Praised by Architects," *Boston Globe*, June 25, 1970.
64. Joan Wickstrom, "How to Reprieve a Building in 83 Minutes," *ArchitectureBoston* 10, no. 5 (September–October 2007): 13.
65. Vincent Scully, "Robert Venturi's Gentle Architecture," in *Modern Architecture and Other Essays*, ed. Neil Levine (Princeton: Princeton University Press, 2003), 261–62.
66. Krieger, *The Architecture of Kallmann McKinnell & Wood*, 15.
67. Charles Jencks, *Late-Modern Architecture and Other Essays* (New York: Rizzoli, 1980), 42.

68. Carter Wiseman, *Shaping a Nation* (New York: Norton, 1998), 359–60.
69. Nikolaus Pevsner, *A History of Building Types* (Princeton: Princeton University Press, 1976), 24.
70. Quoted in Shand-Tucci, *Built in Boston*, 302.
71. David Monteyne, *Fallout Shelter* (Minneapolis: University of Minnesota Press, 2011), 268, 256.
72. Lawrence Kennedy, *Planning the City upon a Hill* (Amherst: University of Massachusetts Press, 1992), 179–80.
73. Francesco Tentori, ed., "Boston Government Center: Rinascita di una città," *Casabella Continuità* 271 (January 1963): 4–16.
74. Ada Louise Huxtable, "The View from the Mayor's Windows," *New York Times*, April 20, 1969.
75. Ian Menzies, "Bare Bricks at City Hall," *Boston Globe*, June 17, 1971.
76. Howard Husock, "Boston: The Problem That Won't Go Away," *New York Times*, November 25, 1979.
77. Thomas H. O'Connor, *Building a New Boston: Politics and Urban Renewal, 1950–1970* (Boston: Northeastern University Press, 1993), 211–12.
78. Lyndon and Wingwall, *The City Observed*, 34.
79. O'Connor, *Building a New Boston*, 255–56.
80. "Collins in His New Home," *Boston Globe*, December 19, 1967.
81. O'Connor, *Building a New Boston*, 257.
82. Ibid., 266.
83. "Landmark Petition," 1.
84. Richard J. Connolly, "Mrs. Hicks Bids Dr. King Address School Board," *Boston Globe*, April 18, 1965.
85. J. Anthony Lukas, *Common Ground* (New York: Vintage Books, 1986), 325.
86. Frederick McCarthy, "Boston Municipal Bonds Rated Tops by Buyers," *Boston Globe*, March 6, 1963.
87. Bruce Davidson, "The First Heads Hub Bond Syndicate," *Boston Globe*, May 3, 1965.
88. Bruce Davidson, "A Big Boost for Hub," *Boston Globe*, October 28, 1965.
89. Davidson, "The First Heads Hub Bond Syndicate."
90. Bruce Davidson, "How Does Hub Fare Now in Bond Market?" *Boston Globe*, July 22, 1965.
91. Charles Bennett, "One Agency Gives 'A' Credit Rating to City's Bonds," *New York Times*, July 20, 1965.
92. "Boston: The Problem That Won't Go Away," *New York Times*, November 25, 1979.
93. Martin Meyerson and Edward C. Banfield, *Boston: The Job Ahead* (Cambridge: Harvard University Press, 1966), 63–65.
94. Davidson, "The First Heads Hub Bond Syndicate."
95. Harold D. Hodgkinson, "Miracle in Boston," *Proceedings of the Massachusetts Historical Society* 3, no. 84 (1972): 79.
96. Ibid. 81.
97. O'Connor, *Building a New Boston*, 255.
98. "Downtown Is Looking Up," *Time*, July 5, 1976, 58.
99. Kennedy, *Planning the City upon a Hill*, 214.
100. Anthony Yudis, "Boston's Pieces Coming Together," *Boston Globe*, November 23, 1975.

101. Thomas Boylston Adams, "Boston Achieves a Triumph in Architecture," *Boston Globe*, December 21, 1969.
102. Meyerson and Banfield, *Boston*, 109–11.
103. Walter Muir Whitehill, introduction to *Architecture Boston* (Boston: Boston Society of Architects, 1976).
104. John Morris Dixon, "A Better Place Now Than in the Early '50s," *Boston Globe*, October 31, 1978.
105. Ibid.
106. Thomas H. O'Connor, *The Boston Irish: A Political History* (Boston: Back Bay Books, 1995), 244.
107. Naomi Miller and Keith Morgan, *Boston Architecture, 1975–1990* (Munich: Prestel-Verlag, 1990), 61.
108. O'Connor, *The Boston Irish*, 245–46.
109. Kate Appleton et al., "World's Most-Visited Tourist Attractions," *Travel + Leisure*, October 2011, 26.
110. O'Connor, *Building a New Boston*, 271.
111. Ibid.
112. "Bright New Symbol."
113. Huxtable, "The View from the Mayor's Windows."
114. Charles W. Millard, "The New Boston City Hall," *Hudson Review* 23, no. 1 (Spring 1970): 112.
115. O'Connor, *Building a New Boston*, 271.
116. Huxtable, "The View from the Mayor's Windows."
117. O'Connor, *Building a New Boston*, 271.
118. Ibid., 279.
119. Huxtable, "The View from the Mayor's Windows."

Conclusion: Boston City Hall at Fifty

1. Jane Holtz Kay, "Saving a Modern Monument," *Progressive Architecture* 69, no. 4 (April 1988): 25.
2. Thomas M. Keane, "Between a Rock and a Hard Place," *ArchitectureBoston* 8, no. 3 (May–June 2005): 37.
3. Gary Wolf, "Designing the Great Building of 20th-Century Boston: Kallmann, McKinnell & Knowles' Drawings for Boston City Hall," exhibition catalogue, Historic New England (May 15–31, 2008), 17.
4. Richard Kindleberger, "Plan for Hotel at City Hall Plaza May Have Hit a Snag," *Boston Globe*, January 23, 1997.
5. Keane, "Between a Rock and a Hard Place," 39.
6. Jim Whiting, *Yo-Yo Ma: A Biography* (Westport, Conn.: Greenwood Press, 2008), 111.
7. Keane, "Between a Rock and a Hard Place," 38.
8. "Past Futures: Proposals to Fix City Hall and Its Plaza," *ArchitectureBoston* 10, no. 5 (September–October 2007): 24.
9. "The Way We Were: Boston in the 60s," *ArchitectureBoston* (May–June 2005): 24.
10. Gretchen Schneider, "We Don't Need Another Hero: The Problem of Heroic Modernism" *ArchitectureBoston* 8, no. 3 (May–June 2005): 44.

11. "Boston City Hall," Docomomo US, http://www.docomomo-us.org/register/fiche/boston_city_hall_0 (accessed June 10, 2013).
12. Jeremy Fox, "Designers Hope to Grow a Greener City Hall Plaza," *Boston Globe*, February 11, 2011.
13. Utile Design, Greening America's Capitals, http://www.utiledesign.com/projects/greening-americas-capitals-bostons-city-hall-plaza/ (accessed June 10, 2013).
14. Eric Moskowitz, "Government Center Shines as It Opens Again," *Boston Globe*, March 21, 2016.
15. Nathan Cobb, "Humanizing City Hall," *Boston Globe*, July 26, 1970.
16. Keane, "Between a Rock and a Hard Place," 39. Also "Past Futures," *ArchitectureBoston* 10, no. 5 (September–October 2007): 24.
17. "Past Futures," 24.
18. Wolf, "Designing the Great Building," 17.
19. "Landmark Petition Form: Boston City Hall," Boston Landmarks Commission (April 2007), 10.
20. "When the Unstoppable Meets the Immovable," *ArchitectureBoston* 10, no. 5 (September–October 2007): 20.
21. Schneider, "We Don't Need Another Hero," 44.
22. "A Softer City Hall," *Boston Globe*, April 4, 2010.
23. A complete overview of the winning solution is available at the BSA's website, http://www.rotch.org/scholarship/2010/winning-solution/index.html.
24. Henry Wood, "Doing More with What We Have," *Boston Globe*, March 18, 2007.
25. Wolf, "Designing the Great Building," 17.
26. Douglass Shand-Tucci, *Built in Boston: City and Suburb, 1800–2000*, rev. and expanded ed. (Amherst: University of Massachusetts Press, 1999), 283.
27. Chris Cassidy, "Marty Walsh: Bulldoze Government Center, Privatize City Hall," *Boston Herald*, September 15, 2013.
28. Ben Thompson, "Mayor Walsh Unveils Renovated 'Welcoming' City Hall Lobby," *Boston Globe*, July 26, 2017.
29. "The Way We Were: Boston in the 60s," *ArchitectureBoston* 8, no. 3 (May–June 2005): 24.
30. David Kruh, "Because Boston Still Matters," *Boston Herald*, December 27, 2006.
31. "When the Unstoppable Meets the Immovable," 19.
32. Kay, "Saving a Modern Monument," 25.
33. Matt Viser, "It's Unique, but Is It a Landmark?" *Boston Globe*, April 25, 2007.
34. "The Rabble, Roused: Excerpts from Letters to the Boston Landmarks Commission," *ArchitectureBoston* 10, no. 5 (September–October 2007): 21.
35. Ibid.
36. Joan Wickstrom, "How to Reprieve a Building in 83 Minutes," *ArchitectureBoston* 10, no. 5 (September–October 2007): 13–15.
37. Viser, "It's Unique, but Is It a Landmark?"
38. Theodore H. M. Prudon, *Preservation of Modern Architecture*, (Hoboken, N.J.: John Wiley & Sons, 2008), 26–27.
39. "When the Unstoppable Meets the Immovable," 21.
40. Thomas Jester and David Fixler, "Modern Heritage: Progress, Priorities, and Prognosis," *APT Bulletin* 42, no. 2–3 (2011): 4.
41. Jim Packard, "Vision That Will See Eyesores Tumbling," *Financial Times*, August 7, 2004.

42. Gavin Stamp, "Anti-Ugly," *Apollo* 161, no. 515 (January 2005): 89.
43. Roman Polanski, dir., *Chinatown* (New York: Paramount Pictures, 1974).
44. Walter Muir Whitehill and Lawrence W. Kennedy, *Boston: A Topographical History*, 3rd ed. (Cambridge: Belknap Press of Harvard University Press, 2000), 267.
45. William M. Bulger, *James Michael Curley: A Short Biography with Personal Reminiscences* (Boston: Commonwealth Editions, 2011).
46. "Mayor Walsh Lays Out Plans to Build a Thriving, Healthy, Innovative City in State of the City Address," City of Boston press release, January 13, 2015.
47. John Winthrop, "Model of Christian Charity," reprinted in Matthew S. Holland, *Bonds of Affection: Civic Charity and the Making of America—Winthrop, Jefferson, and Lincoln* (Washington, D.C.: Georgetown University Press, 2007), 274.
48. "If You Build It, Will They Come?" *The Economist*, December 21, 2013.
49. Mark Pasnik, Chris Grimley, and Michael Kubo, eds., *Heroic: Concrete Architecture and the New Boston* (New York: Monacelli, 2015).
50. Andrew Ryan, "City Seeking Ideas to Repurpose Brick-Bound City Hall Plaza," *Boston Globe*, March 9, 2015.
51. Jon Kamp, "Boston's Maligned Plaza Gets a Makeover," *Wall Street Journal*, July 31, 2015.

Index

Page numbers in *italics* refer to figures.

Abramson, Daniel, 236
Action Architecture, 3, 97–98, 123, 181, 244
Adams, Howard, and Greeley, 29
Adams, Thomas Boylston, 167, 177, 203, 218
Aldrich, Nelson, 31, 51, 78, 82, 148
American Institute of Architects (AIA), 60, 80, 84, 143, 168–69, 186, 204–5
Anderson, Lawrence B., 31, 42, 55, 59–60, 70, 184, 190
Anderson, O. Kelley, 18, 67–68, 169
Art Brut, 100

Banham, Reyner, 100
Barnes, Edward Larrabee, 42, 96
Belluschi, Pietro, 31, 42, 46, 65, 68, 98, 194
Bilbao effect, 242
bond rating, 24, 214–15
Boston City Council, 13, 36, 39, 63, 76, 77, 84, 85–88, 91, 154, 175, 178, 212, 236
Boston City Hall (old), 33–41, *35*, 130–31, 138, 154, 156, 173, 192, 209, 212–13, 239–40, 245n1
Boston City Hall Annex, 33, 37–40, *38*, 139, 156
Boston City Planning Board, 19, 27–29, 59, 222
Boston Common, 39, 162, 164, 166, 203; underground garage, 22, 145

Boston Coordinating Committee (The Vault), 25–26
Boston Five Cents Savings Bank, 18, 60, 183–84, 190, *191*
Boston Housing Authority (BHA), 20
Boston Landmarks Commission, 175–76, 188–89, 235
Boston Pops, 92
Boston Public Garden, 14, 36–37, 39, 166, 173
Boston Redevelopment Authority (BRA), 11, 17, 20–22, 27–29, 31, 37, 48, 59, 63, 84, 88, 90, 113, 218, 219, 221, 229
Boston Safe Deposit and Trust Company, 18, 26, 216
Boston Society of Architects, 59, 175, 186, 190, 232
Boston Town House, 33
Boston University, 44–45, 94
Bourne, Philip W., 50
Breuer, Marcel, 42, 58, 98, 201
Brutalism, 42, 80–81, 97–101, 179, 185, 190, 200–206, 238
Bulfinch, Charles, 41, 61, 76, 116, 135, 152, 188–89, 222
Bush-Brown, Albert, 149, 152, 163
busing crisis, 213, 259n99

Cabot, Cabot & Forbes, 43, 84, 88
Campbell, Aldrich & Nulty, 82

Campbell, Robert, 43, 122, 154, 165, 170, 174, 179–80, 187
Catlin, Ephron, 15, 17
Central Artery (John F. Fitzgerald Expressway), 19, 60, 62
Christian Science Church Center, 192, 195–96
Citizens' Committee for a Bostonian City Hall, 78, 148
Collins, Bud, 151
Collins, John F., 2, 8, 12, 16, 40–41, 48–49, 78–79, 83–87, *87*, 90, 132, 136, 138, 145, 172, 182, 210–13, 221, 225, 235; 1959 election, 23–24; Boston City Hall competition and, 50–52, 59–60, 76, 82, 94; Boston Coordinating Committee and, 25–26; Edward Logue and, 26–33
Collins, Peter, 96, 115, 147, 152
Copley Square, 30, 37, 189; redevelopment of plaza, 80, 194–95
Cram, Ralph Adams, 41, 45, 57, 186
Curley, James Michael, 13–18, 39–40, 48, 79, 112, 173, 209, 240, 243
Cushing, Richard Cardinal, *87*, 92

Dallas City Hall, 197, *198*, 203
displacement of residents, 22, 23
Dock Square, 63, 76, 84, 105, 117, 126

Eisen, David, 161, 174, 236
Eldredge, Joseph, 89, 115, 202
Elizabeth II (queen), 172

Faneuil Hall, 32–34, 61, 63, 73, 76, 84–85, 88, 104, *106*, 109, 113, 121, 130–31, 162, 165, 212, 217–20; Faneuil Hall Marketplace, 170, 221–25
Feeney, Maureen, 236
Finance Commission (FinCom), 12–13
First Church of Christ, Scientist. *See* Christian Science Church Center
First National Bank of Boston, 15, 214
Fitch, James Marston, 144, 165
Fitzgerald, John F., 13, 139
Fixler, David, 237–38
Floete, Franklin G., 30–31

Flynn, Raymond, 151, 155, 173
Franklin Delano Roosevelt Memorial, 58, 64, 72, 96
Freud, Sigmund, 179

Gans, Herbert, 20
Gehry, Frank, 81, 242
General Court of Massachusetts, 9, 12–13, 21, 28, 36, 59, 86–88, 200
General Services Administration, 30, 199, 201, 228
Gleason, Herb, 77, 156, 161, 171–72, 235
Goldberger, Paul, 185, 201–2
Good Government Association (GGA), 13
Government Center Garage, 184
Government Center station (MBTA), 109, 166, *230*
Graham, Edward T. P., 38, 139, 148
Gropius, Walter, 41–43, 57, 98, 127, 140, 149, 193–94

Hart, Thomas N., 36
Harvard University, 42–44, 45, 67–68, 210, 215; Graduate School of Design, 42, 72, 187; Medical School, Countway Library, 192–93
Haymarket Square, 32
Hodgkinson, Harold, 67–68, 76, 78, 112, 168–69, 216–17
Hudnut, Joseph, 42, 44–45
Huxtable, Ada Louise, 42–43, 46, 79, 94, 125, 142–43, 147, 154, 158, 170, 179–81, 189, 197–98, 209, 220, 223–26
Hynes, John B., 2, 16–25, 28–31, 33, 40, 60, 68, 79, 158, 209, 211, 225, 240

Irish American community, 11–18, 20, 49

Jacobs, Jane, 9, 23, 220
J. Edgar Hoover Building (Federal Bureau of Investigation Headquarters), 201–2
John F. Kennedy Federal Building, 30, 32, 62–63, 84, 88, 117, 149, 193–94, 228, 230
John Hancock Building (1947), 45–46

Johnson, Philip, 42, 96, 101, 128, 140–41, 185, 220

Kahn, Louis, 3, 121, 127, 190
Kallmann, Gerhard, 3, 83, 90–91, 95–97, 125–26, 128, 130, 132, 157, 166, 177, 181, 184, 187–88, 206, 231, 233
Kallmann McKinnell & Wood (KMW), 183–87
Kane, Katherine D., 174
Kay, Jane Holtz, 235
Keane, Thomas, 160, 173
Kennedy, Edward, 92, 145
Kennedy, John F., 4, 132–34, 197, 200, 211
Kennedy, Lawrence, 5, 27, 40, 188–89, 209, 218, 239
King, Mel, 22
Knowles, Edward F., 2, 78, 82, 95–97, 124, 127–29, 183
Kruh, David, 175, 235

Lally, Francis J., 21
Landay, William, 162–63
Landsmark, Theodore, 145–46, 162, 196, 213, 259n99
Larrabee, Eric, 74, 138
Last Hurrah, The (Curley), 40
Le Corbusier, 3, 99, 121–25, 127, 184, 190, 193; Carpenter Center, 45, 194; Chandigarh government complex, 94, 99, 123, 190, 194, 196; monastery of Sainte Marie de La Tourette, 99, 123–24, 194
Leers, Andrea, 197, 204
Leventhal, Norman, 228
Lever Brothers, 11
Lincoln, Frederic, 34
Lipsey, Ellen, 146
Logue, Edward, 22, 26–28, 31, 48, 50–51, 76, 78, 79, 84, 88–90, 93, 132, 145, 161, 174, 222
Lyndon, Donlyn, 34, 37, 175, 192, 195, 210

McCord, David, 39
McKinnell, N. Michael, 79, 82, 91, 95–97, 101–3, 107, 110–11, 114, 120, 142, 161, 183–84, 187, 233

Ma, Yo-Yo, 229
Massachusetts General Court. *See* General Court of Massachusetts
Massachusetts Institute of Technology (MIT), 17, 41–44, 65, 68
megastructure, 109
Menino, Thomas M., 146, 151, 173–76, 212, 228–29, 234–36
Menzies, Ian, 150, 162, 166
Millard, Charles W., 110, 113, 124, 129, 134, 159, 194, 224
Minoan palace at Knossos, 94, 122, 126, 152
Mitchell, William J., 159, 237
Moholy-Nagy, Sibyl, 105, 121, 124–25, 127, 147–48, 153, 161
Moody's Investors Service, 24, 26, 214–15
Morgan, Robert, 18, 50, 52, 60, 75, 78–79, 87, 91, 190
Moses, Robert, 10–11, 217
Moss, Henry, 171, 235
Moynihan, Daniel Patrick, 199–200
Mumford, Lewis, 67, 102, 189

National Shawmut Bank, 214
Netsch, Walter, 42, 65–68, 80–81, 93
New York Streets initiative, 19–20, 22–23
Nixon, Richard M., 161, 202
North End, 14, 23, 116, 228

O'Connor, Thomas H., 5, 15, 21, 175, 211, 217, 219, 222, 224–25
Old City Hall (Boston). *See* Boston City Hall (old)
Old Howard, 29, 176–77
Old State House, 32, 34, 61, 73, 106, 116, 130, 148, 151
One Center Plaza, 85, 88, 216
O'Neill, Thomas P., 18
Oud, J. J. P., 137, 139

Parcel 8, 32–33, 84–85, 88
Parker, William Stanley, 78, 139, 148
Pasnik, Mark, 5
Peabody, Endicott, 25, 85, *87*

Pei, I. M., 42, 149, 186, 192, 195; Cathedral Square, Providence, 203; Government Center master plan, 31–33, 54, 62, 64, 71, 104, 130
Pevsner, Nikolaus, 144, 158, 207–8
Portman, John, 207
Powers, John E., 18, 24, 25
Project for Public Spaces, 164–65
Prudential Center, 21–22, 33, 46–47, 49
Public Garden. *See* Boston Public Garden

Rabb, Sidney R., 67–68
Rapson, Ralph, 65–66, 68
Richardson, Henry Hobson, 41, 61, 130, 148, 152, 188–89; Trinity Church, 162, 169, 194
Rotch Design Competition, 232
Roth, Emery, 3, 98, 115, 128–29
Rouse, James, 170, 224–25
Rubin, Elihu, 46
Rudolph, Paul, 42, 192, 237
Rushing, Byron, 170

Saarinen, Eero, 43, 56–57, 74, 115
San Francisco City Hall, 53–55, *54*, 58, 69, 80
Sargent, Francis, 92
Scollay Square, 8, 28–32, *30*, 126, 131, 151, 175–77, 196, 216, 221, 235
Scully, Vincent, 205–6
Sears Crescent, 32, 63, 130, *177*, 231
Sert, José Luis, 31, 42, 45, 98, 186
Shand-Tucci, Douglass, 34, 36, 184, 189, 193, 196, 234
Shepley Bulfinch Richardson & Abbott, 41, 44, 186
Sidenbladh, Goran, 210
Silber, John R., 94
Simonian, Kane, 17, 20
Skidmore, Owings & Merrill (SOM), 66
Stahl, F. A., 50, 81, 192
Stern, Robert A. M., 140, 189
Stockton, Philip, 15

Stone, Edward Durell, 3, 42, 129, 137, 139
Stubbins, Hugh, 31, 42, 46, 149, 152, 186; Countway Library, 192–93
Sturgis, Robert, 141, 143
Sydney Opera House, 55–56, 58, 65, 69

The Architects Collaborative (TAC), 41, 43, 45, 46, 149, 192
The Vault. *See* Boston Coordinating Committee
Thompson, Benjamin, 186, 193, 224
Thompson, John F., 25
Torre Velasca, 102, 125, 206
Toronto City Hall, 55–56, 58, 65, 69, 72
Travelers Insurance Building, 46–47, 49
Trust for City Hall Plaza, 228–29

Venturi, Robert, 102–3, 121, 195, 206
Vietnam War, 4, 202, 211
Volpe, John A., 25, 90, 145
Von Eckardt, Wolf, 46, 142, 159, 164–65, 179, 182

Walsh, Martin, 234–35, 240, 243–44
waterfront area, 8, 89, 94, 175, 218, 222
West End, 20–23, 27, 29, 220–21
White, Kevin H., 77, 90–93, 137, 145, 151–52, 155, 168, 171–74, 209–13, 220–21, 224–25, 235, 239
Whitehill, Walter Muir, 32, 81, 137, 219, 239
Wilkie, Carter, 146
Winthrop, John, 241
Wiseman, Carter, 207–8
Wolf, Gary, 74, 120–21, 129, 131, 160, 166, 171, 176, 178, 183, 234, 236
Wood, Henry, 146, 183, 187, 229, 234
Wood, Joan, 156, 170
Wright, Frank Lloyd, 67, 127–28, 184
Wurster, William, 42, 65, 67–68, 76

Yale Art and Architecture Building, 170–71, 175
Yudis, Anthony, 151–52, 158, 163

Architectural historian Brian M. Sirman studies the relationship between architecture, politics, and culture. Having earned a PhD from Boston University's American and New England Studies Program, he has held teaching positions at Boston University, Lesley University, Massachusetts College of Pharmacy and Health Sciences, Trinity Washington University, and Wentworth Institute of Technology. He is frequently called upon to give lectures and walking tours about architecture in Boston and has presented at scholarly conferences throughout North America and Europe. Originally from Westminster, Maryland, he lives with his spouse, Thiago, in Brookline, Massachusetts.